Implementing SAP™ R/3™
Using Microsoft®

Implementing SAP™ R/3™ Using Microsoft® Cluster Server

DAVID WATTS ■ MAURO GATTI ■ RALF SCHMIDT-DANNERT
MATTHEW CALI ■ EDWARD CHARLES
DAVID DARIOUCH ■ OLIVIER DE LAMPUGNANI

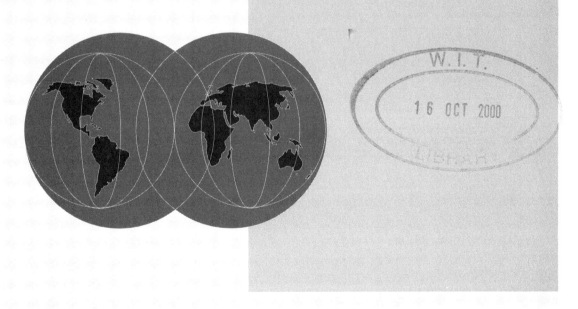

PRENTICE HALL PTR, UPPER SADDLE RIVER, NEW JERSEY 07458
www.phptr.com

For information about redbooks:
`http://www.redbooks.ibm.com`

Send comments to:
`redbooks@us.ibm.com`

Published by Prentice Hall PTR
Prentice-Hall, Inc.
Upper Saddle River, NJ 07458

Prentice Hall books are widely used by corporations and government agencies for training, marketing, and resale. The publisher offers discounts on this book when ordered in bulk quantities. For more information, contact

        Corporate Sales Department,
        Phone: 800-382-3419; Fax: 201-236-7141
        E-mail (Internet): corpsales@prenhall.com

Or write: Prentice Hall PTR
        Corporate Sales Department
        One Lake Street
        Upper Saddle River, NJ 07458

Take Note! Before using this information and the product it supports, be sure to read the general information in Appendix A, "Special Notices," on page 277.

Printed in the United States of America
10 9 8 7 6 5 4 3 2 1

ISBN   0-13-019847-1

Prentice-Hall International (UK) Limited, *London*
Prentice-Hall of Australia Pty. Limited, *Sydney*
Prentice-Hall Canada Inc., *Toronto*
Prentice-Hall Hispanoamericana, S.A., *Mexico*
Prentice-Hall of India Private Limited, *New Delhi*
Prentice-Hall of Japan, Inc., *Tokyo*
Pearson Education Asia Pte. Ltd.
Editora Prentice-Hall do Brasil, Ltda., *Rio de Janeiro*

Contents

Preface

Many of today's corporations run their businesses on the SAP R/3 application suite. High availability of these applications to the user community is essential. Downtime means lost sales, profits and worse. The combination of SAP R/3 and Microsoft Cluster Server is an important element in providing the required access to key business applications.

This book will help you plan and install SAP R/3 4.5B in a Microsoft Cluster Server environment running Microsoft Windows NT 4.0 and Windows 2000. Installation procedures complement the existing SAP documentation and cover the integration of the three major database management systems: Oracle, DB2 and SQL Server.

The first three chapters introduce high availability and clustering and how these concepts apply to SAP R/3 environments. Chapter 4 describes planning needed before implementing a clustered SAP R/3 configuration. Discussions include certification of hardware and software components, server sizing, disk layout, and network configurations. SAP R/3 and Windows 2000 are also discussed. The installation part of the book is a step-by-step set of instructions to lead the reader through the process of installing SAP R/3, Microsoft Cluster Server and the particular database you choose to install, Oracle, DB2 or SQL Server. How to configure an SAP backbone network is also described. The remaining two chapters describe how to tune your SAP R/3 configuration, how to verify your installation is working correctly and where to look if you have problems.

This book should be especially helpful to people who are involved with planning or installing SAP R/3 in a Microsoft Cluster Server environment. Such people will often be technical planners and IT managers in user organizations who need to understand the requirements of such an installation, IT professionals or consultants who need to install SAP R/3 in an MSCS environment, and experienced SAP R/3 professionals who need to understand the ramifications of clustering on SAP R/3 and how to implement such a solution.

The team that wrote this redbook

This redbook was produced by a team of specialists from around the world working at the International Technical Support Organization, Raleigh Center.

David Watts is an Advisory Specialist for Netfinity Servers at IBM's ITSO Center in Raleigh. He manages residencies and produces redbooks on hardware and software topics related to IBM Netfinity Servers. He has authored over a dozen publications; his most recent include *Netfinity Performance Tuning with Windows NT 4.0*, *Implementing Netfinity Disk Subsystems* and *Netfinity Server Management*. He has a Bachelor of Engineering degree from the University of Queensland (Australia) and has worked for IBM for over 10 years. He is an IBM Professional Server Specialist. He can be contacted via e-mail at dwwatts@us.ibm.com.

Mauro Gatti is an Advisory IT Specialist in IBM's Netfinity Presales Technical Support in Italy. He is a Microsoft Certified System Engineer. He is responsible for supporting the main SAP installations on Netfinity servers in Italy. He is part of the IBM SAP Technical Focus Group and the BI Focus Group in EMEA. Before joining IBM a year ago, Mauro was a trainer and consultant for Microsoft, Hewlett Packard, IBM and other companies. Mauro holds a degree in Physics and a PhD in Theoretical Physics.

Ralf Schmidt-Dannert is a Senior IT consultant working in IBM's Advanced Technical Support ERP organization. He has seven years of experience in different UNIX flavors as a system programmer and kernel driver developer. The last four years he worked on Windows NT-based ERP solutions with DB2 UDB at IBM Germany, at SAP Walldorf and at IBM US. He was responsible for the port of SAP R/3 with DB2 from AIX to Windows NT and for the technical design of SAP R/3 with DB2 in a Microsoft Cluster Server environment. His areas of expertise include SAP R/3, MSCS, performance analysis in Windows NT and SAP Ready-To-Run R/3 with DB2 UDB. He holds a degree in Computer Science.

Matthew Cali is the Technical Alliance Manager for SAP in the Netfinity Partners in Development organization within IBM. He has 12 years of experience in IBM including eight years with the T.J. Watson Research Laboratory as a development engineer involved in semiconductor and microelectronics design, prototyping and process formulation. He was also the IBM Global Services project manager for the IBM fixed assets SAP implementation used throughout the company. He currently holds five patents, four of which are associated with mainframe electronic circuit repair and the other is with a prototype of the IBM TrackPoint strain gauge design. He has a master's degree in Mechanical Engineering from Manhattan College, New York.

Edward Charles is a Senior IT Specialist in IBM Global Services, Network Integration in Fort Lauderdale, Florida. He has over 10 years of experience designing enterprise networks. He holds a BA in Management Information Systems and an MBA. He is a certified SAP R/3 consultant on UNIX/Oracle Release 4.x. Edward is also a certified Cisco Network Associate, CNE and MCP. For the past five years he has been consulting and teaching networking for IBM.

Olivier De Lampugnani is an IT Specialist working for IBM Global Services in the Service Delivery EMEA West group, located in La Gaude, France, where he is responsible for Windows NT administration outsourcing. He has worked for IBM for four years. His areas of expertise include all Microsoft Windows NT products and Netfinity hardware. Olivier is a Microsoft Certified Systems Engineer.

David Dariouch is a Systems Engineer in IBM France, where his is an Advisory IT specialist supporting Netfinity technologies and network operating systems implementation on the Netfinity Presales Technical Support team. His area of expertise includes Windows NT-based ERP solutions, Netfinity hardware and software engineering. He is part of the IBM SAP Technical Focus Group in EMEA. David holds an Engineering Degree in Computer Science from the Ecole Speciale de Mecanique et d'Electricite school of engineering in Paris.

This Prentice Hall publication is based on two IBM Redbooks, *Implementing SAP R/3 4.5B Using Microsoft Cluster Server on IBM Netfinity Servers*, SG24-5170-01 and *High Availability for SAP R/3 on IBM Netfinity Servers*, SG24-5170-00. Thanks to the additional authors of these books:

Bill Sadek
Peter Dejaegere
Guy Hendrickx
Fabiano Matassa
Torsten Rothenwaldt

Thanks to the following people from the ITSO Center in Raleigh for their assistance and contributions:

Jakob Carstensen
Gail Christensen
Rufus Credle
Tate Renner
Linda Robinson
Steve Russell
Shawn Walsh

Thanks to the following people from IBM for their invaluable contributions to the project:

Steve Britner, PC Institute, Raleigh
Andrew Castillo, North America ERP Solution Sales, San Jose
Peter Dejaegere, IBM SAP International Competency Center, Walldorf
Rainer Goetzmann, IBM SAP International Competency Center, Walldorf
Andreas Groth, Second Level EMEA Technical Support, Greenock
Thomas Knueppel, Netfinity SAP Sales, Stuttgart
Gregg McKnight, Netfinity Development Performance, Raleigh
Salvatore Morsello, Netfinity Presales Technical Support, Milan
Kiron Rakkar, MQSeries Early Programs, Raleigh
Torsten Rothenwaldt, Netfinity Technical Support, Frankfurt
Siegfried Wurst, Data Management Solutions, Germany

Thanks to the following people from SAP AG for their invaluable contributions to the project:

Frank Heine
Reiner Hille-Doering

Comments welcome

Your comments are important to us!

We want our redbooks to be as helpful as possible. Please send us your comments about this or other redbooks in one of the following ways:

- Fax the evaluation form found in "IBM Redbooks evaluation" on page 311 to the fax number shown on the form.
- Use the online evaluation form found at http://www.redbooks.ibm.com/
- Send your comments in an Internet note to redbook@us.ibm.com

Chapter 1. Introduction

High availability in computing is defined as making a business application set available to the users as high a percentage of the time as possible.

This simple statement covers a lot of ground. It can be as simple as planning for the loss of electrical power for a piece of equipment, or as disastrous as a fire and earthquake, which can cause the loss of the entire computing site.

Murphy's Law says anything that can go wrong will. The space shuttle is built on this premise. All critical systems have one or more redundant backup systems. In case of a failure, the backup system automatically takes over the function of the failed primary system. Fault tolerance is the concept that a system can survive any failure in a hardware or software component and continue to function. This obviously will help to maintain the high availability we are looking for in our business applications.

This same idea is used in designing high availability into computer systems supporting business-critical applications. For example, a mail order business comes to a screeching halt if the order entry application becomes unavailable to the users for any reason.

1.1 Clustering — a means to an end

Clustering is the use of two or more computers or nodes for a common set of tasks. If one computer fails, the others will take up the slack. This design supports the idea of fault tolerance. A second computer can be used as the redundant backup for the first computer.

Clustering can be used to increase the computing power of the entire computer installation. This also allows a system to be scalable. Adding more computers increases the power and hence the design can support more users. In our case, we use clustering for application availability with increasing processing power as a fortunate side effect.

1.2 What clustering provides

The current range of clustering solutions allows for a level of fault tolerance. The degree to which failures can be tolerated depends largely on two things:

1. The location of the failure

   If the failure is within the cluster (for example, failed hardware in a node or a trapped operating system), then the high availability software will probably be able to recover and continue servicing its users. If the failure is outside the cluster, it is less likely that the high availability software will be able to maintain service. Failures such as power distribution failures, complete network outages, and data corruption due to user error are examples of faults that cannot be contained by products such as Microsoft Cluster Server.

2. The ability of applications to cope with the failure

   Microsoft Cluster Server, for example, allows applications and resources that were running on a failed system to be *restarted* on the surviving server. For "generic" applications, this is simply a matter of restarting the program. For more complicated applications (for example, SAP R/3 servers), there must be a certain sequence to the restart. Certain resources, such as shared disks and TCP/IP addresses, must be transferred and started on the surviving server before the application can be restarted. Beyond that, other applications (for example database servers) must have clustering awareness built into them so that transactions can be rolled back and logs can be parsed to ensure that data integrity is maintained.

Microsoft Cluster Server provides high availability only. The Microsoft solution does not as yet address scalability, load balancing of processes nor near-100% up time. These can currently be achieved only through more mature clustering, such as that which is implemented in RS/6000 SPs.

Microsoft also offers its Windows Load Balancing Service, part of Windows NT 4.0 Enterprise Edition. It installs as a standard Windows NT networking driver and runs on an existing LAN. Under normal operations, Windows Load Balancing Service automatically balances the networking traffic between the clustered computers.

1.3 Business data — to replicate or not?

Adding computers, networks and even cloning entire computer centers for fault tolerance purposes does not solve all the problems. If the business is relatively unchanging, the databases can be replicated along with the rest of the system. Any updates can be accomplished for all the replicated copies on a scheduled basis. An example of this is a Web server offering product information to customers. If one Web server is down the other servers can serve the customer. In this example the cluster is used for both performance and availability.

On-line Transaction Processing (OLTP) applications have different data requirements. As the name implies the data is always changing based on business transactions. A customer places an order for a product. Inventory is allocated to the order and is then shipped from the warehouse to the customer. If this data is replicated, there would be the possibility of promising the same item to two different customers. Somebody would be unhappy.

1.4 Disk sharing

Shared disks is one of the cluster architectures in the industry today. It may be used for scalability as well as for high availability purposes. In a typical two-node high availability cluster, both nodes can access the same storage devices, but only one server at a time controls the storage devices shared by both servers. If one server fails, the remaining server automatically assumes control of the resources that the failed server was using, while still controlling its own resources at the same time. The failed server can then be repaired offline without the loss of time or work efficiency, because access to that server's data and applications is still available.

The key point is that only one server has control of the storage devices at any point in time. There is only one copy of the data, so data accuracy is maintained.

For an overview of cluster architectures, see *In Search of Clusters*, by Gregory F. Pfister.

1.5 MSCS-based solutions

As part of the early adopter's agreement with Microsoft, IBM has announced validated solutions of hardware and software to enable customers to run Microsoft Cluster Server (MSCS) in a shared disk environment.

For managing Microsoft Cluster Server configurations, IBM has developed IBM Cluster Systems Management (ICSM). It provides portable, generic cluster systems management services that integrate into existing systems management tools such as IBM Netfinity Manager, Intel LANDesk, and Microsoft SMS.

ICSM offers enhancements to the manageability of MSCS in three distinct categories:

1. Ease-of-use
2. Productivity
3. Event/Problem notification

1.5.1 Shared-disk configurations

Shared-disk configurations, such as those implemented with Microsoft Cluster Server, use an external disk enclosure to house drives containing data, as shown in Figure 1. The external disks can be connected to both servers using SCSI RAID (for example, IBM's ServeRAID), SSA, or Netfinity Fibre Channel hardware.

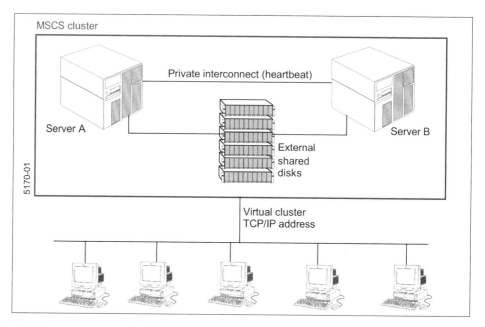

Figure 1. Typical MSCS cluster configuration

The external resources (that is, the drives and the data on the drives) are controlled (or *owned*) by one of the two servers. Should that server fail, the ownership is transferred to the other server. The external resources can be divided into groups so that each server can own and control a subset of them. The shared-disk configuration is also known as a *swing-disk* configuration.

This configuration offers the advantages of lower cost and quick recovery. Only one set of disks is required to hold the data used by both servers. The external disk enclosure should be configured for RAID to ensure data redundancy. When a failure does occur, since there is only one copy of the data, the time to recover and bring the failed system back online is minimal.

1.6 What the user sees

The clustering solution offers high availability to a certain degree but does not offer 100% error-free non-stop system availability.

Each configuration offers certain benefits over the others but in each there are trade-offs to be made: cost versus redundancy, capacity, bandwidth and the degree to which systems are isolated are some examples.

Within the specified service level and the specified level of fault tolerance, users should expect little or no interruption to service. The level of interruption depends largely on the applications running on the servers at the time of failure. For applications such as word processors where the server does not maintain status information about clients (*stateless connections*), the interruption is quite short.

For transaction-based applications such as databases or SAP R/3, there may be a relogin requirement once the application has been restarted. All uncommitted transactions are rolled back during restart and may have to be reentered.

Typically, the failover and restart process involves three steps:

- Failure detection
- Resource relocation
- Application restart

The restarting of applications typically takes the longest time. For a simple application, the failover process can take as little as 30 seconds, but large applications such as databases may take several minutes to recover from such failures.

1.7 SAP R/3 support for Microsoft clustering

In Windows NT 4.0, Microsoft has chosen the shared storage approach to its two-node clustering solution. SAP R/3 supports this natively in its kernel. Although other solutions may work, SAP only supports the Microsoft clustering solution. More information can be obtained at the SAP Web site:

http://www.sap.com

1.8 IBM Netfinity clustering solutions

For the latest information on Netfinity cluster solutions check the following Web sites:

- IBM Netfinity cluster solutions:
  http://www.pc.ibm.com/us/netfinity/clustering.html

- IBM/SAP Alliance Home: http://www.ibm.com/erp/sap/

Chapter 2. Introduction to high availability

Mission-critical applications such as ERP and e-mail, are quickly moving from RISC to Intel-based servers. Driving factors are lower prices and satisfactory scalability. While some environments such as Data Warehousing are still out of range for Intel-based servers, many others can be hosted on lower-priced Intel-based servers. Actually, only a few applications needing very large amounts of memory are out of range for the Intel platform, and this is even less with Windows 2000 Datacenter Server and the 64-bit IA-64 architecture.

As a consequence of this trend, Intel-based servers hosting mission-critical applications must be as reliable as possible. Reliability (that is, minimal interruption of the service) produces availability (that is, able to achieve the service). High levels of availability can be obtained only by setting up a complete strategy to address all the weak points, both on the hardware and the software. In order to provide a clear and consistent description of how to get high availability, we take as our starting point the following mathematical formula often used to measure the availability of a system (for an example, see section 9.2 of *Scalable Parallel Computing* by Hwang-Xu):

$$Availability = \frac{MTBF}{MTBF + MTTR}$$

where:

- *MTBF* stands for *mean time between failures* and is defined as the average time between two failures, and
- *MTTR* stands for *mean time to repair* and is the average time it takes to repair the system.

The target is to have this availability ratio as high as possible. Obviously the ratio can be increased either by increasing the MTBF or by decreasing the MTTR. A multifaceted strategy should be planned out in order to achieve optimal availability. The next two sections will separately examine how to get a high MTBF and a low MTTR.

2.1 High MTBF

Figure 2 provides a description of the most relevant factors allowing to increase the MTBF factor.

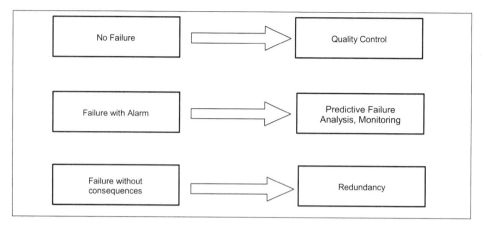

Figure 2. High MTBF

2.1.1 Quality control

The only way to avoid failure is to control the quality of the product before shipment. That may be a daunting task in the SAP R/3 environment discussed in this book. Indeed the following main components must be checked:

- **Hardware**

  A typical Intel processor-based server contains components from many manufacturers: microprocessors from Intel, memory from IBM, hard disks from Seagate, SCSI adapters from Adaptec, tapes from Quantum, just to mention a few. Each hardware component's vendor extensively checks its own products, but still more important are the electrical and mechanical compatibility tests made by the server vendor.

- **Operating system**

  Microsoft extensively tests the Windows operating system and its Service Packs, but due to the low-level communication between some OS components (Hardware Abstraction Layer, device drivers) and the hardware, these tests should be done on exactly the same hardware configuration that will be used for SAP R/3. That means that each server and hardware option (network adapters, RAID adapters, etc.) should appear in the Microsoft Hardware Compatibility List. Moreover the drivers should be the same used during the Microsoft tests.

  With the release of Windows 2000, Microsoft has introduced many enhancements aiming to reduce compatibility problems between drivers and operating system. See 2.3, "Windows 2000 reliability improvements" on page 33 for more information.

Incompatibility problems are typically addressed by the hardware vendor developing driver fixes. The compatibility between hardware and operating system is even more important in a cluster environment.

- **Applications**

  SAP systems, as well as many other software systems, undergo continual development during their product life cycle. Systems are (or at least, should be) carefully tested before put into production, but no time exists for fully testing a software upgrade on the production system after the beginning of the production phase. That's why a three-landscape architecture is strongly recommended:

  > Changes are developed on the (1) development system, transported and then checked on the (2) test system and then moved to the (3) production system.

  This not only applies to SAP fixes and software customizing but also to driver updates, firmware updates, Windows NT Service Packs and so on. To make the test trustable it is fundamental to have identical hardware and software platforms in each of the three phases. Unfortunately this is rarely the case in high-end systems due to the cost of having a Microsoft cluster in the test and development environment. That's not so bad as far as development is concerned, but it is definitely dangerous to have many differences between the test and the production system.

  After installing, often no upgrade, apart from SAP customizing, is made on the production system. The general idea is that we have fully tested the system before going to production, and it worked, so it is better not to change anything. Unfortunately this is not always a good idea. Hardware manufacture's often issue requests to customers asking for immediate replacement of hardware components or updates of drivers, as well as firmware due to the discovery of hardware or software bugs. The same holds true for software products. So at least development and production should be identical.

  But if it is not the case, how do we face a critical upgrade? A good step towards more reliable upgrades is the Windows File Protection contained in Windows 2000 as described in 2.3.2, "Protection against file overwriting" on page 34.

2.1.2 Predictive Failure Analysis

Predictive Failure Analysis (PFA) is a hardware-software technology that can forecast a wide variety of failures. Hardware techniques are used to detect anomalous behavior of hardware components. As a consequence, a software alarm is generated allowing system administrators to change defective parts before the server fails. The following list provides typical examples of components of an Intel-based server protected via PFA:

- **Microprocessors**

  The internal communication channel between CPU and L2 cache (backside bus) is continually examined using an ECC algorithm. Errors are not unusual and are recovered by the ECC mechanism. An excessive amount of errors may be a sign of possible failures to come. If errors exceed a predetermined threshold a software alarm is generated.

- **Memory**

  Errors can happen due to cosmic rays or other factors. When errors exceed a predetermined threshold an alarm is generated.

- **Fans**

  The rotation speed of fans is constant. Only very small deviations are normal. If the speed deviation exceeds a predetermined threshold an alarm is generated.

- **Power supplies**

  Power supplied by the power utilities is often dirty; spikes, surges, sags and any other possible alteration of voltage and frequency are a common experience in almost all countries. That's why UPSes are necessary in order to supply the server with power of a satisfactory quality. One of the main aims of power supplies in any server is to provide stable voltage. Only very small oscillations are allowed. Indeed high oscillation can break internal electronic components. Wide deviations are dangerous and show an anomalous behavior of the power supply. An alarm is then generated allowing you to replace the power supply before stopping the server activity.

- **Voltage regulator modules**

  The Intel Xeon processor complex has as many transistors in the L2 cache as there are in the CPU. To provide sufficient power to these transistors, two different power circuits (voltage regulator modules - VRMs) are necessary. The power coming from the VRMs must have a very stable voltage, so deviations from this voltage are anomalous and an alarm is generated.

2.1.3 Monitoring

Software and hardware errors usually do not appear unexpectedly. Careful monitoring of the system ensures that warnings are detected. Correct interpretation of the warnings lets you forecast possible failures, so as to have the time to plan a stop, replace a failing part or fix a software bug without having to stop the users' activity. Many utilities can be used to monitor the system. The most common one is Windows NT Event Viewer. Every warning or alarm should be examined in conjunction with Microsoft TechNet. Hardware manufacturers such as IBM provide servers with an extended set of monitoring utilities allowing you, for example, to collect warnings and errors on a central server in order to make error checking easier.

2.1.4 Redundancy

Redundancy is usually the most simple and cheapest way to protect a hardware component. The following are a list of the main components that can be protected by making them redundant.

2.1.4.1 Microprocessors

So far, no means exist to protect an Intel-based server from a CPU failure. According to Microsoft, this is a limitation of the Intel-based platform (Microsoft Knowledge Base Q93597):

> Windows NT supports SMP platforms to increase processor power, not for fault tolerance. If a processor fails, Windows NT stops responding ("hangs"). This is not due to a flaw in Windows NT but in the hardware support on 80x86-based SMP machines. At this time, no 80x86-based SMP machine provides the hardware support to recover from a failed processor.

Actually Windows NT does not seem ready for CPU fault tolerance. Indeed the kernel component responsible for thread dispatching and interrupt management cannot be forced to leave the hosting microprocessor. So a failure of this microprocessor necessarily entails a system stop.

Due to these hardware/software limitations microprocessor failures necessarily result in stop screens. Hardware techniques exist on high-end servers that allow you to automatically reboot the server. The failed CPU is electrically isolated and the system continues working with the remaining CPUs.

2.1.4.2 Memory

Memory is protected by means of an Error Checking and Correcting (ECC) algorithm, which detects 2-bit errors and corrects 1-bit errors.

However, standard ECC memory does not recover from more serious errors, such as an entire chip error. A proprietary technology developed by IBM, known as chipkill memory, must be used in order to have better protection. The memory exploits a RAID technology allowing you to recover from one chip error as well as to detect and correct 4-bit errors. For more information, see the white paper *IBM Chipkill Memory* at:

```
http://www.pcco.ibm.com/us/techlink/wtpapers/chipkill.html
```

2.1.4.3 Network adapters

Many adapters exist offering automatic fault tolerance (AFT) capabilities. Two adapters can be configured as a fault tolerant pair, which means that only one IP address is seen externally. One of the adapters is active while the other is passive. In case of failure the activity is quickly and automatically transferred to the passive one. A fraction of a second is necessary for the failover. The broken adapter can often be hot replaced. After the replacement the system automatically fails back the activity to the new adapter. Automatic fault tolerance does not require specific high-end switches. Many data link control technologies exist supporting this feature, including Fast Ethernet, Gigabit Ethernet, token-ring and ATM.

2.1.4.4 Hard disks

The traditional technology allowing you to protect data contained on hard disks is Redundant Array of Independent Disks (RAID). Traditionally RAID technology was classified in 6 levels: RAID 0, 1, ... 5. Newer technologies are now available such as RAID-10 and RAID-5 Enhanced. Minor differences exist between the abilities of the various RAID levels in order to guarantee the availability of the data. Major differences exist between the abilities to guarantee an optimal performance.

2.1.4.5 RAID controllers

High-end systems often offer the ability to have a totally redundant I/O subsystem. This means to have not only full protection of the hard disks data but also a fully redundant I/O chain. This target is reached by doubling any component of the I/O subsystem.

2.1.4.6 Power supplies and fans

Almost every high-end server has redundant power supplies and fans, because almost everybody recognizes that these parts run the higher risks of failure.

2.2 Low MTTR

The main factors in lowering the mean time to repair (MTTR) are described in Figure 3:

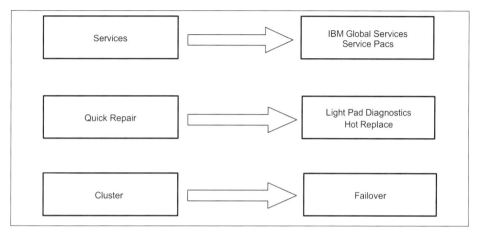

Figure 3. Low MTTR

2.2.1 Services

Any mainstream hardware provider (IBM, Compaq, Hewlett Packard) proviede a wide range of service offerings. According to your budget, you can ask to have a technician on site within one day, eight hours or four hours and to have the server working within four hours. Clearly this last requirement is much more difficult to satisfy. Spare parts must be immediately available, the server must not be too far from the nearest technical support center, and sometimes a ready-to-replace server must be available.

2.2.2 Quick repair

To solve problems with minimal interruption of the customer activity, it is important to provide technicians with easy-to-use diagnostics. For example, IBM's high-end and mid-range servers offer a tool known as *light path diagnostics*.

On the front of the server, a light panel tells you the type of hardware problem you have without having to open the server. If more information is required, by only opening the upper cover it is possible to get access to a second LED panel providing more details on the hardware error. If, for example, you discover by examining this panel that there is a memory problem you can then look at a third-level diagnostic LED. Near each DIMM it is possible to see a small light. The red light allows you to easily detect the faulty component.

A higher quality of service can be provided with hot replace technology. Indeed this technology allows you to repair some faulty parts (RAID adapters, network adapters) without any interruption of the service offered by the server. Hot Replace allow to bypass an important limitation of Windows NT: the necessity to reboot after an adapter installation.

2.2.3 Cluster

What's a cluster? One definition is offered by Hwang-Xu in *Scalable Parallel Computing* (Section 1.4.1):

> A *cluster* is an *interconnected* set of *whole* computers (nodes) that work collectively as a *single system* to provide uninterrupted (*availability*) and efficient (*performance*) services.

The highlighted words are the key terms characterizing clusters. The word *whole* is what makes clusters different from Massively Parallel Processor (MPP) systems. Cluster nodes have a complete operating system, while MPP nodes have only a microkernel. The *single system* image (SSI) is one of the main cluster targets: many nodes but only one administrative console and only one virtual server for clients. *Interconnected* means the high-speed, often dedicated, network used for the communication inside the cluster nodes. *Availability* and *performance* are the ultimate targets.

Dozens of cluster technologies exist and many ways to classify them have been devised in the last 20 years. A very simple classification based on the data sharing is shown below:

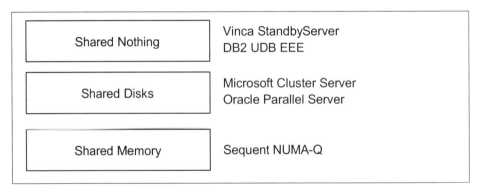

Figure 4. Simple clustering classification

2.2.3.1 Shared nothing

Figure 5 shows a typical example of shared nothing architecture: Vinca StandbyServer for Windows NT.

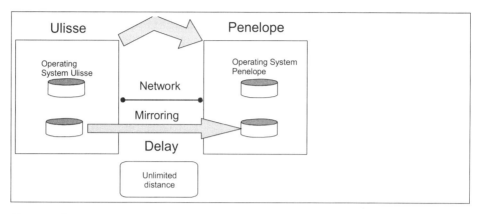

Figure 5. Shared nothing (Vinca StandbyServer)

Two servers are used named Ulisse and Penelope. Each server has its own private disks containing the Windows NT operating system, Vinca StandbyServer software, and any non-clustered software. Each server also has one or more disks. Each time data is written to one of these disks the Vinca software copies the data to its companion on the Penelope server. The Vinca software is then a remote mirroring software. The distance between the servers can be unlimited but delay becomes more and more critical when the distance becomes large. This architecture is called shared nothing because each disk is either owned by server Ulisse or by server Penelope. No disks are shared between the two servers.

2.2.4 Shared disks: Microsoft Cluster Server

Microsoft Cluster Server (MSCS), part of Microsoft Windows NT Server Enterprise Edition, is Microsoft's first major push into the enterprise computing arena. Providing the capability to link servers together to form a single computing resource is one way Microsoft is positioning Windows NT as a viable alternative to UNIX in large-scale business and technical environments.

MSCS is particularly important as it provides an industry-standard clustering platform for Windows NT and it is tightly integrated into the base operating system. This provides the benefits of a consistent application programming interface (API) and a software development kit (SDK) which allow application vendors to create cluster-aware applications that are relatively simple to install.

The first release of MSCS, also referred to as *Phase 1*, links two servers together to allow system redundancy. Even before the release of MSCS, hardware manufacturers such as IBM provided redundancy for many server components, including power supplies, disks, and memory. This, however, would only protect you from component failure and not application failure.

Providing system redundancy means that a complete server can fail and client access to server resources will remain largely unaffected. MSCS extends this by also allowing for software failures at both operating system and application levels. If the operating system fails, all applications and services can be restarted on the other server. Failure of a single application is managed by MSCS individually. This, in effect, means that a failure can occur, but the cluster as a whole remains intact, still servicing its users' requests.

MSCS achieves this by continually monitoring services and applications. Any program that crashes or hangs can be immediately restarted on the same server or on the other server in the cluster.

If a failure does occur, the process of restarting the application on the other server is called *failover*. Failover can occur either automatically, such as when an application or a whole server crashes, or manually. By issuing a manual failover, the administrator is able to move all applications and resources onto one server and bring the first server down for maintenance. When the downed server is brought back online, applications can be transferred back to their original server either manually or automatically. Returning resources to their original server is often referred to as *failback*.

The current MSCS allows only two configured servers, or nodes, to be connected together to form a cluster (Microsoft has stated that future versions will support more nodes). The nodes are made available to client workstations through LAN connections. An additional independent network connection is used for internal housekeeping within the cluster. Both nodes have access to a common disk subsystem. Figure 6 shows the basic hardware configuration to support MSCS:

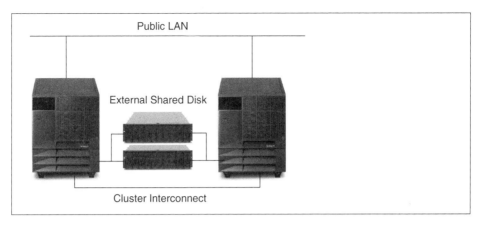

Public LAN

External Shared Disk

Cluster Interconnect

Figure 6. Basic cluster configuration

Common versus shared disk

Two common cluster topologies are *shared disk* and *shared nothing*. From a purely hardware point of view, MSCS is a shared disk clustering technology. But this can be misleading because from a cluster point of view MSCS is a shared nothing technology. Indeed disks are only shared in that they are accessible by both systems at a hardware level. MSCS allocates ownership of the disks to one server or the other. In normal operation, each disk is accessed only by its owning machine. A system can access a disk belonging to the second system only after MSCS has transferred ownership of the disk to the first machine.

In MSCS terminology, the applications, data files, disks, IP addresses, and any other items known to the cluster are called *resources*. Cluster resources are organized into *groups*. A group can reside on either node, but on only one node at any time, and it is the smallest unit that MSCS can fail over.

2.2.4.1 Resources

Resources are the applications, services, or other elements under the control of MSCS. The status of resources is supervised by a Resource Monitor. Communication between the Resource Monitor and the resources is handled by resource dynamic link library (DLL) files. These resource DLLs, or resource modules, detect any change in state of their respective resources and notify the Resource Monitor, which, in turn, provides the information to the cluster service. Figure 7 shows this flow of status data between the cluster service and a cluster's resources:

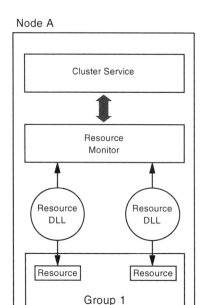

Node A

Cluster Service

Resource
Monitor

Resource
DLL

Resource
DLL

Resource

Resource

Group 1

Figure 7. Communication between the Cluster Service and the resources

2.2.4.2 Resource Monitor

A Resource Monitor watches its assigned resources and notifies the Cluster Service if there is any change to their state. We have shown only a single Resource Monitor in Figure 7, but in fact, each node may run more than one of them. By default, the Cluster Service will start one Resource Monitor to service all resources on a node. You can choose to run a resource under its own separate Resource Monitor when the resource is defined during the cluster installation process. You would normally do this only for resources that are being debugged or if conflicts with other resources have occurred.

The Resource Monitor is separated from the Cluster Service to provide an extra level of security. The resource DLLs are running in the address space of the applications themselves. If the applications fail, the resource DLLs may malfunction, causing the Resource Monitor to fail as well. In these circumstances, the Cluster Service, however, should remain available to the cluster.

2.2.4.3 Dependencies

Dependencies are used within Microsoft Cluster Server to define how different resources relate to each other. Resource interdependencies control the sequence in which MSCS brings those resources online and takes them offline. As an example, we will look at a file share for Microsoft Internet Information Server (IIS).

A file share resource requires a physical disk drive to accommodate the data available through the share. To bind related resources together, they are placed within an MSCS Group. Before the share can be made available to users, the physical disk must be available. However, physical disks and file shares initially are independent resources within the cluster and would both be brought online simultaneously. To make sure that resources in a group are brought online in the correct sequence, dependencies are assigned as part of the group definition.

Other items are required to make a fully functional file share, such as an IP address and a network name. These are included in the group, and so is an Internet Information Server (IIS) Virtual Root (see 2.2.4.4, "Resource types" on page 20 for more information on this resource). The group structure is shown in Figure 8.

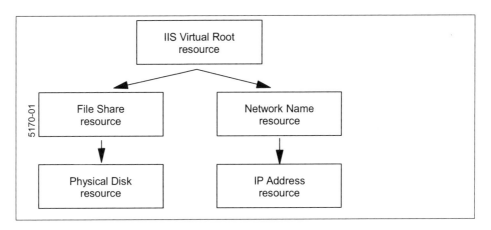

Figure 8. Resource dependencies

This diagram shows the hierarchy of dependencies within the group as a tree structure, where an arrow points from one resource to another resource upon which it depends. We see that the IIS Virtual Root is dependent on two other resources:

- A File Share resource that is itself dependent on a Physical Disk resource

- A Network Name resource that is itself dependent on an IP Address resource

When Microsoft Cluster Server is requested to bring the IIS directory online, it now knows that it must use the following sequence of steps:

1. Bring the Physical Disk and the IP Address resources online.

2. When the Physical Disk becomes available bring the File Share online *and simultaneously,*

3. When the IP Address becomes available bring the Network Name online, *then*

4. When both the File Share and the Network Name become available, bring the IIS Virtual Root online.

As described in 2.2.4.6, "Resource groups" on page 23, all dependent resources must be placed together in a single group and a resource can only belong to one group.

2.2.4.4 Resource types

MSCS defines 12 standard resource types. Other resource types can be offered by third parties if they create suitable resource DLLs using the application programming interface (API) in the Microsoft Platform Software Development Kit (SDK).

- DHCP Server

Documentation error

Although support for this resource type is discussed in the *Microsoft Cluster Server Administrator's Guide*, a DHCP server resource is not supported. Refer to Microsoft Knowledge Base article Q178273.

Since Windows NT Server 4.0 Enterprise Edition does not support the DHCP server, the only way to increase the availability of this service is to create two DHCP servers having disjointed scopes obtained by cutting a subnet in two parts. Windows 2000 cluster will allow you to virtualize the DHCP service making configuration and maintenance easier.

DHCP server resources are typically not configured in SAP clusters.

- Distributed Transaction Coordinator

This resource type allows you to use Microsoft Distributed Transaction Coordinator (MSDTC) in MSCS. Two dependencies are required for this resource: a Physical Disk resource and a Network Name resource.

DTC resources are automatically configured during the SAP R/3 4.5B installation for SQL Server (see 8.9, "Removal of unused resources" on page 232).

- File Share

The File Share resource type lets you share a directory on one of the clustered disks in your configuration to give access to that directory to network clients. You will be asked to enter the name of the share, the network path, a comment, and the maximum number of users that can connect to the share at the same time.

The configuration of a File Share resource type is identical to the configuration of a file share in Windows NT Explorer. File Shares require a Physical Disk resource and a Network Name resource.

- Generic Application

The Generic Application resource type allows existing applications that are otherwise not cluster-aware to operate under the control of MSCS. These applications can then fail over and be restarted if a problem occurs. There are no mandatory resource dependencies.

Microsoft Cluster Server is often demonstrated using the Windows NT clock program. To do so, the clock.exe program is defined to the cluster as a Generic Application.

- Generic Service

This resource type can be used for services running on Windows NT. You must enter the exact name of the service at the creation of the resource. Just as for Generic Applications, the Generic Service resource does not have any resource dependencies.

- IIS Virtual Root

The IIS Virtual Root resource type provides failover capabilities for Microsoft Internet Information Server Version 3.0 or later. It has three resource dependencies: an IP Address resource, a Physical Disk resource, and a Network Name resource.

- IP Address

An IP Address resource type can be used to assign a static IP address and subnet mask to the network interface selected in the Network to Use option during the definition of the resource. IP Addresses do not have any dependencies.

- Microsoft Message Queue Server

  This resource type supports clustered installations of Microsoft Message Queue Server (MSMQ) and is dependent on a Distributed Transaction Coordinator resource, a Physical Disk resource, and a Network Name resource.

- Network Name

  The Network Name resource type gives an identity to a group, allowing client workstations to see the group as a single server. The only dependency for a Network Name is an IP Address resource.

  For example, if you create a group with a Network Name resource called FORTRESS1 and you have a File Share resource with the name UTIL, you can access it from a client desktop entering the path \\FORTRESS1\UTIL. This will give access to the directory on the share regardless of which cluster node actually owns the disk at the time.

- Physical Disk

  When you first install MSCS on your nodes, you are asked to select the available disks on the common subsystem. Each disk will be configured as a Physical Disk resource. If you find it necessary to add more disks after the installation, you would use the Physical Disk resource. This resource does not have any dependencies.

- Print Spooler

  The Print Spooler resource type allows you to create a directory on a common storage disk in which print jobs will be spooled. Two resources are needed to create a Print Spooler resource: a Physical Disk resource and a Network Name resource.

- Time Service

  This is a special resource type that maintains date and time consistency between the two nodes. It does not have any dependencies. The cluster must not have more than one Time Service resource.

- WINS Service

  A new DLL (CLNETRES.DLL) has been introduced with Windows 2000 allowing you to protect the WINS service. Previously it was necessary to create two WINS servers and replicate their DB.

- DHCP Service

  The new Windows 2000 DLL CLNETRES.DLL also protects the DHCP service. Previously it was necessary to create two DHCP servers with disjointed scopes in the same subnet.

2.2.4.5 Resource states

Resources can exist in one of five states:

1. Offline - the resource is not available for use by any other resource or client.

2. Offline Pending - this is a transitional state; the resource is being taken offline.

3. Online - the resource is available.

4. Online Pending - the resource is being brought online.

5. Failed - there is a problem with the resource that MSCS cannot resolve. You can specify the amount of time that MSCS allows for specific resources to go online or offline. If the resource cannot be brought online or offline within this time, the resource will go into the failed state.

2.2.4.6 Resource groups

The smallest unit that MSCS can fail over from one node to the other is a group. Related resources that have been defined from the palette of available resource types are collected together into groups. Dependencies between the resources in a group are then assigned as already described in 2.2.4.3, "Dependencies" on page 18.

Note

Dependent resources must be grouped together.

When one resource is listed as a dependency for another resource, then the two resources *must* be placed in the same group. If all resources are ultimately dependent on the one resource (for example, a single physical disk), then all resources must be in the same group. This means that all cluster resources would have to be on a single node, which is not ideal.

Any cluster operation on a group is performed on all resources within that group. For example, if a resource needs to be moved from node A to node B, all other resources defined in the same group will be moved. Figure 9 depicts how MSCS groups might be distributed between the nodes:

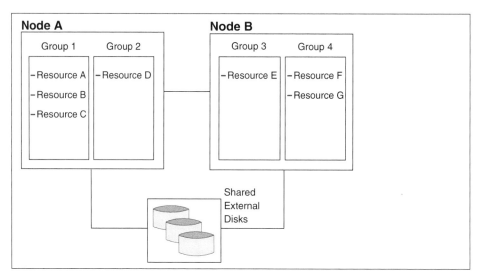

Figure 9. Example of MSCS Groups

Group states

A resource group can be in any one of the following states:

- Online - all resources in the group are online.
- Offline - all resources in the group are offline.
- Partially Online - some resources in the group are offline and some are online.

Virtual servers

A virtual server is a cluster group that contains an IP address and a Network Name resource and optionally a disk and other resources.

Groups that contain at least an IP Address resource and a Network Name resource appear on the network as servers. They appear in Network Neighborhood on Windows clients and are indistinguishable from real servers as far as a client is concerned. These groups are, therefore, sometimes referred to as *virtual servers*.

To gain the benefits of clustering, your network clients must connect to virtual servers and not the physical node servers. For example, if you create a group with a Network Name resource called IIS_Server and then browse your network, you will see an entry (a virtual server) called IIS_Server in the same domain as the physical servers. Although you can browse for the physical server names, you should not use them for connections, because this will circumvent the cluster failover functionality.

2.2.4.7 Quorum resource

One physical disk that is accessible from both nodes is used to store information about the cluster and is called the *quorum disk*. This resource maintains logged data that is essential to maintain cluster integrity and to keep both nodes in synchronization, particularly when the nodes fail to communicate with each other. The quorum disk can be owned by only one node at a time and is used to determine which node will take ownership of cluster resources in certain situations. For example, if the nodes lose contact with each other, the node that cannot contact the quorum disk will withdraw from the cluster while the other node assumes ownership of all cluster resources.

You specify an initial quorum resource when installing the first MSCS node. It must be located on a drive in the common disk subsystem. Therefore, the physical drive used when defining the quorum logical drive must reside in a storage expansion enclosure with the other drives. The drive containing the quorum resource may also contain other applications and data, but this is not recommended.

Note: In the case of IBM's ServeRAID adapters, the quorum resource is temporarily defined on a local disk during installation. By completion, however, the quorum resource has been migrated to one of the common subsystem drives.

2.2.4.8 TCP/IP

MSCS uses TCP/IP to communicate with network applications and resources. Cluster IP addresses cannot be assigned from a Dynamic Host Configuration Protocol (DHCP) server. These include IP Address resources, the cluster administration address (registered at the installation of MSCS), and the addresses used by the nodes themselves for intra-cluster communication.

Note that each node will usually have at least two network adapter cards installed. Although a single network connection can be used, Microsoft recommends using a private network for cluster traffic. One adapter is used to allow communication over the external network for administration and management of the cluster and for user access to cluster resources. The physical server IP addresses assigned to these adapters could be obtained through DHCP, but it is important that users attach to clustered addresses. We recommend the use of static IP addresses for all adapters in your cluster; otherwise, if a DHCP leased address expires and cannot be renewed, the ability to access the cluster may be compromised (see Microsoft Knowledge Base article Q170771).

The second adapter in each machine is for intra-cluster communication, and will typically have one of the TCP/IP addresses that conform to those reserved for private intranets. Table 1 shows the allocated ranges for private IP addresses:

Table 1. Private IP address ranges

IP address range	Description
10.0.0.0 through 10.255.255.255	A single Class A network
172.16.0.0 through 172.31.255.255	16 contiguous Class B Networks
192.168.0.0 through 192.168.255.255	256 contiguous Class C Networks

For more information refer to *TCP/IP Tutorial and Technical Overview*, GG24-3376, and Chapter 3 of *Microsoft Cluster Server Administration Guide*.

Note

You must have TCP/IP installed on both servers in order to use MSCS. Applications that use only NetBEUI or IPX will not work with the failover ability of MSCS. However, NetBIOS over TCP/IP will work.

2.2.4.9 Additional comments about networking with MSCS

- Microsoft SNA Server, Proxy Server and WINS server currently have their own capabilities for high availability and do not use MSCS.

- Clustered servers can be connected to multiple subnets. MSCS additionally supports multihoming configurations using multiple network cards. If we have two subnets connected by a router, however, there is no way to fail over an IP Address resource.

- MSCS cannot use a second network card as a hot backup for the client access. This means that the card may be a critical failure point.

  The problem of redundancy for the client network access must be solved in a network layer below the address assignment by Windows NT. We recommend that you use redundant network adapters. IBM offers fault-tolerant token-ring, fast Ethernet and Gigabit Ethernet adapters.

Cluster problems may arise due to the priority of network adapters in a multihomed Windows NT server. Because each cluster node has adapters connected to at least two different networks (the cluster's private link and the public LAN), each cluster node is also a multihomed host. On such systems, the question, "What is my IP address?" is answered by a list of IP addresses assigned to all network cards installed in the machine. The Windows Sockets API call gethostbyname() is used to obtain these addresses.

Some cluster applications (for example, Oracle FailSafe and SAP R/3) are sensitive about the IP address order in the list returned by gethostbyname(). They require that the IP address of the adapter to which their cluster virtual address will be bound appears on top. This means that the address of the adapter connected to the public LAN must be listed before the address of the cluster's private link adapter. If not, it may be impossible to connect to the application using the virtual address after a failover.

To avoid such problems, you should check the order of assigned IP addresses in the address list before you install MSCS (to ensure that the network assignments are right from the beginning). The two simplest ways to do this are:

- Ping each node from itself. For example, on NodeA you type in a command window:

  ping NodeA

  The address from which the ping is answered must be the address assigned to the adapter card in the public LAN.

- The Windows NT utility ipconfig shows all addresses in the order of the gethostbyname() list.

If the result you get from any of the above methods is in the wrong order, correct it before installing MSCS. When the network adapters are of the same type, then it is sufficient to simply exchange their outgoing cable connections. If you have different adapter types (for example, 10/100 EtherJet for the cluster-private link and redundant FDDI for the public LAN), then you need a way to control the internal IP address order.

Under Windows NT 3.51, the IP address list is in the same order as the TCP/IP network card binding order; therefore, altering the TCP/IP network card binding order (by clicking **Control Panel > Network > Bindings**) will change the IP address order returned by gethostbyname(). Unfortunately, under Windows NT 4.0, the binding order does not influence the IP address order; using the Move Up or Move Down buttons in the Bindings tab of the network control will not work. This is documented in the Microsoft Knowledge Base article number Q171320. To solve the problem, you have to manually add a registry value, DependOnService, to change the IP address order.

Assuming that your two network adapter cards have the driver names
Netcard1 and Netcard2 (the IBM Netfinity 10/100 EtherJet Adapter has the
driver name IBMFE), `PING` and `IPCONFIG` commands show you Netcard1 first,
but your public LAN is on Netcard2. To change the IP address order so that
Netcard2's address is listed first, you must edit the Windows NT Registry as
follows (remember that this can have serious consequences if not done
carefully):

1. Start `REGEDT32` (`REGEDIT` will not work since it cannot add complex value
   types) and select the following subkey:

   `HKEY_LOCAL_MACHINE\SYSTEM\CurrentControlSet\Services\Netcard1`

2. Add a new value with the following specifications:

   Value Name: DependOnService
   Value Type: REG_MULTI_SZ
   Data: Netcard2

3. Exit the Registry Editor and reboot the machine. `PING` and `IPCONFIG` should
   now show you the addresses in the required order.

┌─ **Tip** ──┐

Note that the new registry value, DependOnService, will be deleted
whenever Windows NT rebuilds the network bindings. Thus after each
modification of network parameters you should verify that the order is still
correct. If you change the IP settings frequently, you will save time by
exporting the value to a .REG file for convenient registry merging.

└──┘

2.2.4.10 Domains

The following information specifies the criteria for clustered MSCS servers in
regard to domains:

1. The two servers must be members of the same domain.

2. A server can only be a member of one cluster.

3. The following are the only valid domain relationships between cluster
   nodes:

   - A primary domain controller and a backup domain controller

- Two backup domain controllers
- Two stand-alone servers

Note

For SAP, the servers must be configured as stand-alone.

In general, we recommend that the nodes are set up as stand-alone servers. This will remove the additional workload generated by the authentication chores and the domain master browser role performed by domain controllers. However, there are situations, such as when domain size is small, when it may be appropriate for nodes also to be domain controllers.

2.2.4.11 Failover

Failover is the relocation of resources from a failed node to the surviving node. The Resource Monitor assigned to a resource is responsible for detecting its failure. When a resource failure occurs, the Resource Monitor notifies the Cluster Service, which then triggers the actions defined in the failover policy for that resource. Although individual resource failures are detected, remember that only whole groups can fail over.

Failovers occur in three different circumstances: manually (that is, at the request of an administrator), automatically, or at a specific time as set by IBM Cluster System Manager.

Automatic failovers have three phases:

1. Failure detection
2. Resource relocation
3. Application restart (usually the longest part of the failover process)

An automatic failover is triggered when the group failover threshold is reached within the group failover period. These are configuration settings, defined by the administrator.

Group and resource failover properties

Both groups and resources have failover threshold and period properties associated with them. The functions these properties control, however, depend on whether they are associated with a group or a resource.

---

1. Resource failover settings

   The failover threshold is the number of times in the specified period that MSCS allows the resource to be restarted on the *same* node. If the threshold count is exceeded, the resource and all other resources in that group will fail over to the other node in the cluster.

   The failover period is the time (in seconds) during which the specified number of attempts to restart the resource must occur before the group fails over.

   After exceeding the threshold count of restart attempts, MSCS fails over the group that contains the failing resource and every resource in that group will be brought online according to the startup sequence defined by the dependencies.

2. Group failover settings

   The failover threshold is the maximum number of times that the group is allowed to fail over within the specified period. If the group exceeds this number of failovers in the period, MSCS will leave it offline or partially online, depending on the state of the resources in the group.

   The failover period is the length of time (in hours) during which the group will be allowed to fail over only the number of times specified in Threshold.

For example, consider an application CLOCK.EXE in group CLOCKGROUP. Other resources in the group include a File Share resource and a Physical Disk resource, as shown in Figure 10.

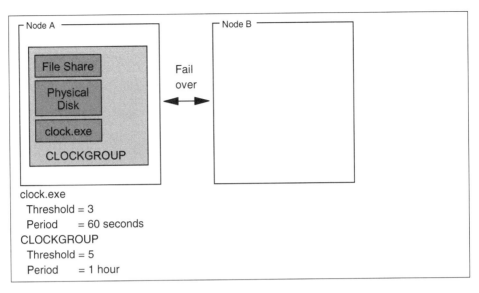

Figure 10. Failover example

The administrator who set up this cluster has assigned a failover threshold of 3 with a failover period of 60 seconds to the clock.exe resource and a failover threshold of 5 with a failover period of one hour to the CLOCKGROUP group.

Consider now the situation when clock.exe continually fails. The program (a Generic Application resource type) will be restarted on Node A three times. On the fourth failure within one minute, it and its group, CLOCKGROUP, will fail over to Node B. This counts as one CLOCKGROUP failover. When CLOCK fails four times (that is, one more than the resource threshold) on Node B, it will fail over to Node A. This counts as the second CLOCKGROUP failover.

After the fifth CLOCKGROUP failover within one hour (Node A->B->A->B->A->B), MSCS will not attempt a restart of CLOCK, nor will it fail over CLOCKGROUP. Instead, it will leave CLOCK in the failed state and CLOCKGROUP will be placed in the partially online state. The other resources in the group will be placed in the failed state if they are dependent on CLOCK; they will remain online if they are not dependent on CLOCK.

2.2.4.12 Failback

Failback is a special case of failover and is the process of moving back some or all groups to their *preferred owner* after a failover has occurred.

A group's preferred owner is the node in the cluster that you have declared as the one upon which you prefer the group of resources to run. If the preferred owner fails, all of its clustered resources will be transferred to the surviving node. When the failed node comes back online, groups that have the restored node as their preferred owner will automatically transfer back to it. Groups that have no preferred owner defined will remain where they are.

You can use the preferred owner settings to set up a simple load-balancing configuration. When both servers are running with failback enabled, the applications and resources will move to their preferred owner, thereby balancing out the workload on the cluster according to your specifications.

When you create a group, its default failback policy is set to disabled. In other words, when a failover occurs, the resources will be transferred to the other node and will remain there, regardless of whether the preferred node is online. If you want failback to occur automatically, you have the choice of setting the group to failback as soon as its preferred node becomes available, or you can set limits so the failback occurs during a specific period, such as outside of business hours.

2.2.4.13 LooksAlive and IsAlive

To determine if resources are available, the Resource Monitor *polls* (requests status information from) the resource DLLs for which it is responsible. Two levels of polling are supported by the Resource Monitor and you can adjust how frequently each of them occurs for each resource. The two levels are called *LooksAlive* and *IsAlive* polling. They are defined as follows:

1. LooksAlive polling:

   The Resource Monitor makes a superficial check to determine if the resource is available.

   If a resource fails to respond to a LooksAlive poll, then the Resource Monitor will notify the Cluster Service. When you create a new resource, you define the interval (in milliseconds) between LooksAlive polling requests. The default interval is 5,000 milliseconds.

2. IsAlive polling:

   The Resource Monitor performs a complete check of the resource to verify that it is fully operational. If a failure is returned, the Cluster Service is immediately notified and, depending on the configuration defined for the resource, the Resource Manager will either terminate the resource or try to bring it back online on the same node or on the other node (as part of a group failover). The default interval is 60,000 milliseconds.

Consider again the Windows NT clock example in Figure 10 on page 31. Assuming that the clock.exe program's Generic Application resource is created with the default parameters, the Resource Monitor calls the LooksAlive function in the resource DLL every five seconds to make a cursory check that the clock is functioning. Every 60 seconds, the IsAlive function is called to perform a more rigorous test to check that the clock is operating correctly.

> **Superficial versus complete checks**
>
> Exactly what constitutes a superficial check or a complete check in the descriptions above is determined by the programmer who wrote the resource DLL. For generic applications such as the clock program, the two tests may be identical. More sophisticated resources such as database elements will usually implement a different test for each entry point.

2.3 Windows 2000 reliability improvements

Windows 2000 contains many improvements aimed at getting rid of the well-known stop screen (also known as the "blue screen of death"). This section discusses these improvements.

2.3.1 Protection of kernel and device drivers

Pentium II processors contain a hardware register in which each thread can register a 2-bit field called Program Status Word (PSW) (see Chapter 6 of Andrew S. Tanenbaum, *Structured Computer Organization,* Fourth Edition). Being a 2-bit field, only four values are possible: 0 (kernel), 1 (system calls), 2 (shared libraries), 3 (user programs). For Windows NT threads, only 0 and 3 are allowed values. If the PSW of a thread is 3, this means that the thread is running in user mode and cannot write on memory pages owned by the threads working in kernel mode (0 value). This hardware protection avoids operating system abends due to badly written user programs corrupting the memory area used by the operating system or device drivers.

While this is a good step towards a really stable operating system, this protection cannot be considered completely satisfactory. No real protection exists against badly written drivers on Windows NT 4.0. Indeed Windows NT 4.0 does not set any limitation to kernel mode threads. That means that a badly written driver (working in kernel mode) can get access to operating system threads memory and corrupt the data. This is a significant hole in Windows NT security: device drivers are often the true culprit of the Windows

NT blue screens as well as of more difficult-to-detect problems such as memory leak.

With Windows 2000, there are definite improvements to this. By default on Windows 2000, a thread working in kernel mode can no longer overwrite the code of other kernel mode threads. That means that kernel mode code cannot corrupt other kernel mode code (see Microsoft Document *Windows 2000 Reliability and Availability Improvements* for more details).

2.3.2 Protection against file overwriting

It is well known that while installing functions from the Windows NT CD-ROM, Service Pack files are overwritten and then at the end of the upgrade Service Packs must be applied again. This is how Windows File protection works as described in Microsoft Document *Windows 2000 Reliability and Availability Improvements:*

> Windows File Protection runs in the background and protects all files installed by the Windows 2000 setup program. It detects attempts by other programs to replace or move a protected system file. Windows File Protection checks the file's digital signature to determine if the new file is the correct Microsoft version. If the file is not the correct version, Windows File Protection replaces the file from the backup stored in the DLLCACHE folder, network install location, or from the Windows 2000 CD.

2.3.3 Driver signing

As described in 2.3.1, "Protection of kernel and device drivers" on page 33, the real enemies of Windows NT 4.0 stability are badly written drivers. Besides the kernel-mode write protection previously described, *driver signing* has been introduced in Windows 2000 in order to avoid the well-known stop screens.

Drivers should be used only if fully tested by Microsoft. With NT 4.0 there was no easy way to discover if the drivers were not Microsoft certified.

When a driver submitted to Microsoft for compatibility testing passes the test, a catalog (.CAT) file is generated that is digitally signed by Microsoft. Any change made to the binary file of the driver after the testing makes this catalog flle invalid. If you try to load an untested driver on a Windows 2000 server, you get a warning message asking you if you really want to do that.

2.3.4 Memory leak

One of the most difficult Windows NT problems to detect is memory leak. Badly written drivers can allocate memory and then fail to release it. This software bug can slowly exhaust specific memory areas, like the non-paged pool memory and eventually hang the system. Windows 2000 introduces a new feature called "Pool Tagging" which aims to help developers to write better code.

Chapter 3. SAP R/3 and high availability

In this chapter, we consider the special issues with SAP R/3, including the following:

- Critical elements of SAP R/3 systems
- How Microsoft Cluster Server (MSCS) can be used with SAP R/3
- Alternate approaches to high availability

Because the focus of this redbook is on MSCS, the alternative solutions will not be covered in detail. For the following discussion we assume that you are familiar with the basic components of R/3 systems as described in the following books:

- Liane Will, *SAP R/3 System Administration*, Sybex, ISBN 0782124267l

- Hartwig Brand, *SAP R/3 Implementation with ASAP*, Sybex, ISBN 0782124725

- Diane Bullock et al., *DB2 Universal Database and SAP R/3 Version 4*, IBM, SC09-2801

- Robert E. Parkinson et al., *Basis Administration for SAP*, Prima Tech, ISBN 0761518878

- Thomas Schneider, *SAP R/3 Performance Optimization*, Sybex, ISBN 0782125638

- The IBM redbook *Optimizing IBM Netfinity Servers for SAP R/3 and Windows NT*, SG24-5219.

3.1 SAP R/3 architecture

The SAP R/3 software has a conventional client/server architecture and can operate in either a two-tier or a three-tier configuration. An SAP R/3 system consists of one database server, several application servers, and many front-end or presentation servers. These latter servers are, in fact, the client workstations but are referred to as servers in SAP R/3 terminology.

All the logic and data of an SAP R/3 system is stored within the database managed by the central database server. Application servers communicate with the database server and execute the SAP R/3 programs. The front-end servers (usually desktop client systems) are connected to the application servers and provide the interface for users of the system. Solutions using terminal servers for the front-end servers, or connections over the Internet using a browser, may also be implemented.

In a two-tier system, the central server operates as both database and application server whereas a three-tier system is configured with these functions executing on separate physical machines. These structures are illustrated in Figure 11:

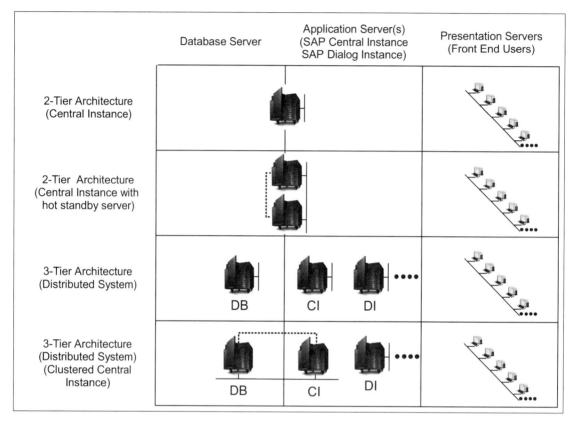

Figure 11. Two-tier and three-tier configurations

3.2 SAP R/3 system landscape

In a typical SAP environment, several SAP R/3 systems are connected together in an overall configuration termed a *landscape*. These individual systems allow ongoing development while the business uses the production system. The individual systems might be as follows:

- A development system, which is used for creating new elements of the overall business system and for testing the correct operation of these new elements.

- A quality assurance system, which allows newly developed elements to be incorporated into the existing configuration without risking the main production system.

- A production system, which carries the live business data. New elements are only introduced into this system when testing and consolidation activities have guaranteed a low risk of problems.

Each system has its own database and may need its own backup processes.

A typical system landscape is shown in Figure 12:

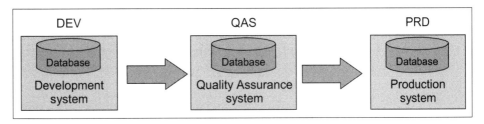

Figure 12. Standard SAP R/3 system landscape

Each system in an SAP R/3 landscape has a three-character system identifier (SID). Our example landscape has three systems, DEV, QAS and PRD. New SAP R/3 applications are designed and developed on the development system, then validated in a non-production environment on the quality assurance system before being transported into the regular production environment.

More complex system landscapes are possible, and these may include legacy systems that were in use by the customer prior to the implementation of SAP R/3.

3.3 SAP R/3 components

SAP R/3 has features to improve system availability:

- Automatic reconnecting
- Automatic restart of processes
- Redundancy by multiple instances

Most R/3 services have the ability to reconnect dynamically if the corresponding process is restarted. This means automatic recovery is possible from many problems that affect only individual processes or connections between them.

For example, if the SAP graphical user interface (SAPGUI) loses connection to its corresponding dialog process on the application server because of a network outage, it asks the user to reconnect. The user context is not preserved on the application server. Thus all transactions that were not committed are cancelled. Data changes from committed transactions remain persistent in the database.

This feature will not help if the process at the other site fails. But most R/3 processes are restarted automatically by the dispatcher after process failure. This includes all work processes (dialog, update, enqueue, batch, spool) and the R/3 gateway process. Only the processes of the SAPGUI, message services and dispatcher services are not restarted automatically. The SAPGUI can be recovered manually by simply restarting it on the workstation.

Most of the R/3 application services (such as dialog, update, batch, gateway, and spool) can all be configured redundantly on multiple servers to provide improved availability.

There are three critical R/3 system components that cannot be made redundant by configuring multiple instances of them on different machines:

- DBMS
- Enqueue service
- Message service

Thus these three components are single points of failure in the SAP R/3 architecture.

```
┌─ ATP server ──────────────────────────────────────────────────┐
```

As of Release 4.0 the materials availability check used in the R/3 logistics
modules can be performed using a dedicated R/3 service running on an
R/3 instance, the ATP server. Instead of checking the materials availability
on the RESB and VBBE tables, work processes check the materials
availability in the export/import buffer.

The ATP server is responsible for the synchronization between this buffer
and the contents of the DB tables. To start the ATP server the R/3 profile
parameter rdisp/atp_server must be set to the name of the R/3 instance
hosting the ATP server.

If you plan on using an ATP server, keep in mind that this is a single point of
failure also. Therefore it has to be configured to run on the cluster node
with the central instance. See T. Schneider, *SAP R/3 Performance
Optimization,* Chapter 8 for further details.

Thus the R/3 components can be divided into two groups, depending on their
importance for system availability:

- Services that are R/3 system-wide single points of failure

  The enqueue and the message processes, and the DBMS cannot be
  configured redundantly and require human intervention for recovery.
  These services should be centralized to reduce the number of servers
  requiring additional protection against failure.

- Services that are not single points of failure

  These services may be configured redundantly and should be distributed
  on several servers.

The following table summarizes the elements of an R/3 system and their
recovery characteristics:

Table 2. Redundancy and recovery of SAP R/3 services

R/3 services	Number per R/3 system	Recovery
ATP server	n = 0 or n = 1	Automatic restart by dispatcher
Batch	$n \geq 1$	Automatic restart by dispatcher
Database	$n = 1$	Manual restart (and recovery, if necessary) by system administrator
Dialog	$n \geq 1$	Automatic restart by dispatcher

R/3 services	Number per R/3 system	Recovery
Dispatcher	$n \geq 1$	Manual restart of application service by system administrator
Enqueue	$n = 1$	Automatic restart by dispatcher
Gateway	$n \geq 1$	Automatic restart by dispatcher
Message	$n = 1$	Manual restart by system administrator
Sapgui	$n \geq 1$	Manual restart by user; reconnect to previous context may be used
Saprouter	$n \geq 0$	Manual restart by system administrator
Spool	$n \geq 0$	Automatic restart by dispatcher
Update	$n \geq 1$	Automatic restart by dispatcher

Note: Automatic restart by the dispatcher assumes that the dispatcher itself is not affected by the failure. It is possible that locks held by one user may be simultaneously granted to another user.

A second group of critical resources comes from the network environment. The two file shares SAPLOC and SAPMNT must be available. Some installations use an Internet Domain Name Service (DNS) or Windows Internet Name Service (WINS) for name resolution. DNS or WINS are also single points of failure. Additionally, a Windows NT domain controller is needed to log on to the R/3 service accounts.

To summarize, the following components must be protected to make the R/3 system highly available:

- DBMS
- R/3 application service on the enqueue/message host (central instance)
- File shares SAPLOC and SAPMNT
- Name resolution service (DNS or WINS)
- Windows NT domain controller

The domain controller will be made redundant by configuring multiple domain controllers as primary and backup controllers. In a similar fashion, there are ways to provide redundant DNS or WINS. The details are out of the scope of this book. Protecting the R/3 central instance (services and file shares) and the database is discussed in the remainder of this chapter.

3.4 Using MSCS with SAP R/3

With the release of Microsoft Cluster Server, SAP—for the first time in its history supporting different operating systems—has begun to support a cluster integration for R/3, called R/3 Cluster for Windows NT. This is the cluster-aware version of the R/3 software on Windows NT. The R/3 system (mainly the R/3 kernel and the installation procedure) has been extended with components that integrate R/3 with MSCS. The R/3 processes, services, disks, addresses, and shares are configured as cluster resources and monitored by MSCS.

SAP supports a configuration based on a two-node cluster in an active-active mode as shown in Figure 13. The database runs on one node and the central instance of the R/3 system runs on the other node. In the event of a failure, the surviving node continues to provide both services: database and central instance. MSCS monitors the R/3 and database resources for a failure and switches over services in the event of a failure. Thus the critical R/3 components, as shown in Table 2 on page 41, are made highly available. This default configuration is shown in Figure 13.

The situation where both services, database and central instance, are running on the same node is considered a special case that occurs after a failover of all resources to one node, during planned maintenance, or for other reasons.

A typical MSCS-based SAP R/3 system has the following structure:

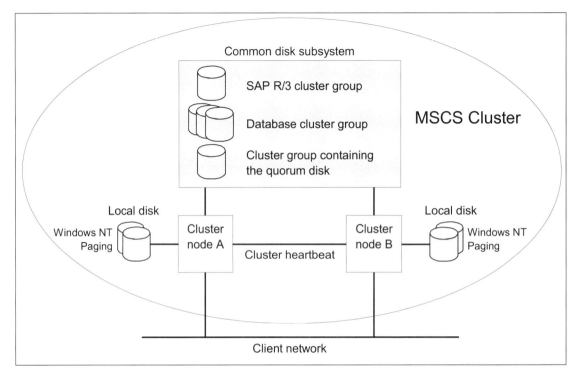

Figure 13. Typical MSCS configuration for SAP R/3

Supported MSCS configuration

This cluster configuration (database server and central instance of the same R/3 system on two cluster nodes with mutual failover) is the only one supported by SAP. There is no support for other possible combinations (for example, failover of a central production system to a test server, or failover of the central instance to another application server, or running an additional application server on the DBMS machine).

A special cluster combination may work. But the R/3 installation procedure is not prepared to handle it, and there will be no support from SAP for daily operations or release upgrades.

A supported SAP R/3 cluster configuration has to fulfill the following conditions:

- The hardware must adhere to any hardware vendor-specific and MSCS-specific certification programs. In the case of IBM hardware it has to be IBM Server Proven. For a complete list of IBM-tested Netfinity MSCS solutions, go to the Web site:

`http://www.pc.ibm.com/us/netfinity/cluster_server.html`

- The hardware must be in the Microsoft Hardware Compatibility list. Note that such approval includes:

  - Both servers
  - The shared disk subsystem between them (controllers and storage expansions)
  - The cluster-private network connection (only for long distance configurations)

  For a complete list of Microsoft-certified hardware MSCS solutions, go to the Web site:

  `http://www.microsoft.com/hwtest/hcl/`

- The hardware must be certified for SAP R/3, as for every R/3 system. For a list of certified configurations, see the Internet Web site:

  `http://www.r3onnt.de/`

Note

See 4.2, "Certification and validation of hardware" on page 73 for more details on the certification processes.

- The operating system release, the Windows NT Service Pack release, the DBMS release and the SAP R/3 release are supported by SAP. To check if your SAP R/3 version supports MSCS you should obtain the latest update of the OSS Note 0106275, *Availability of R/3 on Microsoft Cluster Server*. At the time of writing, the following support was available or planned with Intel-based Windows NT servers:

Table 3. MSCS support for Intel-based Windows NT servers with different SAP R/3 releases

DBMS	R/3 V3.1I	R/3 V4.0B	R/3 V4.5A	R/3 V4.5B
Oracle 7.3	Supported	No	No	No
Oracle 8.0.4	Supported	Supported	Supported	No
Oracle 8.0.5	Supported	Supported	Supported	Supported
Microsoft SQL 6.5	Supported	No	No	No
Microsoft SQL 7.0	Supported	Supported	Supported	Supported
Informix	Supported	Supported	Supported	Supported

DBMS	R/3 V3.1I	R/3 V4.0B	R/3 V4.5A	R/3 V4.5B
Adabas	No	No	Supported	Supported
DB2	No	No	No	Supported

Note: Refer to OSS Note 0106275, Availability of R/3 on Microsoft Cluster Server for the latest support matrix.

3.5 Alternative approaches to SAP R/3 high availability

Using MSCS may not be the only possible solution in your business case to achieve high availability for SAP R/3. Here, we discuss the advantages and disadvantages of some other approaches. For a more complete discussion see the excellent book *Windows NT Microsoft Cluster Server* by Richard R. Lee.

There are several other failover solutions available for Windows NT, for example:

- Vinca CoStandbyServer for Windows NT
- Veritas First Watch
- NCR LifeKeeper
- Legato/Qualix FullTime Cluster
- Compaq/Digital Cluster Plus for Windows NT
- Compaq/Tandem NSK-Lite
- Legato Octopus HA+
- NSI Software Double-Take

Note: This is not a complete list. It does not intend to express the significance of the products mentioned, nor their compliance with a particular R/3 release tested by IBM or SAP.

Even if the description of the product may lead to the assumption that it works with MSCS, this does not say anything about the functionality with SAP R/3. Failover products are inherently complex. Setting up R/3 and the DBMS to fail over correctly is a tremendous task including the handling of registry keys, DLLs, environment variables, failover scripts, and other objects that may be undocumented and changed with the next release of the R/3 or DBMS software. Thus you should always ensure that you get appropriate support, comparable with that provided by SAP for MSCS, from the vendor over the full lifetime of your system.

3.5.1 Cold standby server

The idea to improve availability with a so-called cold standby server is to completely exchange the production server if it fails. For that purpose, you need to configure an additional server identical to the production machine. This means that all components (especially I/O adapters) should be of the same type and in the same slots in both machines. However, the standby server does not contain any disks with an operating system or data. When the production server fails, an operator moves all disks from the production server to the standby server. Because of the identical configuration, the copy of the operating system from the production machine will boot without problems on the standby server too. Then the R/3 instance or DBMS can be started. After doing some checks in the R/3 system, the standby machine can be made available to the users with the same addresses and services as the production machine.

To move the disks quickly, all disks should be installed in an external storage expansion enclosure. Then moving the disks means only recabling the storage expansion. For smaller configurations it may be sufficient to have the disks as hot-swap drives in the production machine, without an additional storage expansion enclosure.

This looks primitive. But despite its simplicity, there are some advantages especially for a small business:

- The solution can be provided by almost any vendor with arbitrary hardware, which does not need to be approved for a cluster solution like MSCS. The only restriction about server models, disk technology, and other components is the certification for SAP R/3.

- No special cluster support is required from the vendor or SAP. All R/3 and DBMS releases work in the usual way.

- There is no need for splitting the production system into separate servers for the DBMS and the R/3 central instance. The additional server may act as cold standby for multiple production servers (of the same hardware configuration) from different R/3 systems, or a test machine may be used.

- There are no cluster-related restrictions for using hardware or software RAID.

The disadvantages are obvious:

- Human intervention is necessary to recover from a server failure. This requires monitoring of the system and an appropriate reaction time. Moving the disks, and starting and checking the system should be done by trained operators. If the system is used only during normal office hours, that may be acceptable. But batch jobs during the night or weekend or any other kind of 24x7 usage requires automatic reaction to system outages.

- Only hardware-related failures are covered. If there is a problem with the operating system on the production machine (for example, driver failures or wrong network setup), then this will happen on the standby machine also.

- The same hardware configuration of the machines must always be kept, in all details. When the standby machine cannot be used otherwise, maintaining a large machine only as a big spare part may be too expensive.

Thus a cold standby server is worth considering if the sizing of your SAP R/3 systems leads to a central installation with production R/3 services and DBMS on the same machine, and if the restrictions about service availability are acceptable in your business.

3.5.2 Replicated database

This section discusses ways to achieve high availability by replicating the database using DBMS features. Note that this technique differs from RAID and from replicated DBMS servers:

- Replicating the database is maintaining a (not necessarily complete or actual) copy of data that is under the control of the DBMS.

- Replicating the DBMS server means running an additional, fully functional DBMS in parallel. This is discussed in 3.5.3, "Replicated DBMS server" on page 53.

- RAID protects data (inside or outside the database) against disk failures. Server or DBMS failures are not covered.

Replicated databases are sometimes referred to as *shadow* databases. There are several solutions available from the DBMS vendors:

- Oracle Standby Database
- Symmetric Replication from Oracle
- High-availability Data Replication (HDR) from Informix
- SQL Server Replication from Microsoft
- Replicated Standby Database for DB2/UDB from IBM

The idea is to have a second DBMS in standby mode on a different node that continuously receives information about database changes made on the production node. Then the standby DBMS can apply (replicate) these changes. If the initial data were identical on both nodes, and if no change information has been lost, then the standby DBMS maintains an exact copy of the production database. When the production node fails then the R/3 system can be connected to the standby node.

The following are among the issues that you should consider when selecting a strategy for database replication:

- Synchronous versus asynchronous replication

  Synchronous replication considers a transaction as completed only when the remote DBMS also committed successful execution of all changes. Asynchronous replication performs the remote updates at a later time. Thus asynchronous replication schemes may suffer transaction loss in the case of failure, while synchronous replication schemes by definition guarantee no transaction loss.

- Log-based versus statement-based replication

  Log-based replication evaluates or copies the redo logs of the DBMS to get the change information for the remote node. Log-based implementations tend to be asynchronous, while statement-based implementations are mostly synchronous.

- Level of replication

  Some solutions provide replication at the schema or table level, while others perform replication at the database level. Schema level replication is more flexible but requires extra effort in that the system administrator has to define the list of tables, either whole tables or subsets (rows or columns), to be replicated.

- BLOB handling

  There may be limitations for the replication of binary large objects (BLOBs).

From the solutions mentioned above, Oracle Standby Database, Replicated Standby Database for DB2/UDB (both at the database level), and Microsoft SQL Server Replication (at the schema or table level) implement asynchronous log-based replication. Symmetric Replication from Oracle is statement based and may be synchronous or asynchronous at the schema or table level. Informix High-availability Data Replication (HDR) offers asynchronous and synchronous log-based replication at the database level.

There are different ways to use data replication for R/3 high availability, including the following:

1. Maintain complete, hot standby database

   The R/3 system switches to the standby database and continues to function without any loss of transactions. Synchronous replication is required. From the products above, only Informix HDR in synchronous mode may be used for this purpose. This can be considered as an alternative to remote mirroring of the database disks.

2. Maintain an incomplete, warm standby database

   If it is sufficient to have a warm standby database (loss of some transactions is acceptable) rather than a hot standby, then any of the log-based replication schemes may be used.

3.5.2.1 Standby database example: Oracle
This section uses the Oracle DBMS as an example.

To explain the concepts of a warm standby database, we outline the configuration of Oracle Standby Database. The hardware architecture and the operating system must be the same on both nodes. The version of the Oracle software on the standby node must be the same or higher as on the production node.

1. Take a complete backup of the data files of the production server.

2. Create a standby database control file.

3. If the backup was not an offline backup, then archive the current online redo log of the production database.

4. Transfer the backed up data files, the control file, and all archived redo log files to the standby machine.

5. To begin with actual replication, start the DBMS on the standby machine, mount the database in standby mode, and let the DBMS operate in recovery mode.

6. To keep the update gap between the production and the standby database as small as possible, you have to ensure that the archived redo log files from the production system are transferred to the standby system as soon as possible.

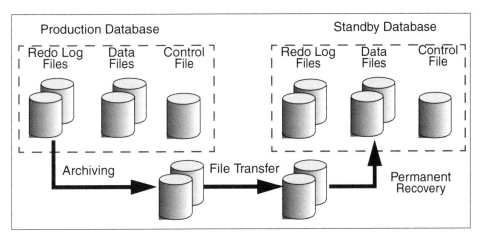

Figure 14. Oracle standby database

The greatest advantage of this approach, compared with clustering, is the more distant separation of the production system and the standby system. Even geographic distribution is simple because only a network connection with moderate bandwidth is needed for redo log file transfer. There are no cluster-related restrictions on which kind of hardware to use.

The greatest disadvantage is that only the Oracle database is protected. Failures of the R/3 central instance services or file shares are not covered. If you plan to prepare a standby central instance on the standby database node also, keep in mind that changes in non-database files (like R/3 profiles) are not replicated. Other disadvantages are:

- The standby Oracle database is in recovery mode and always lags slightly behind the production database. The loss of transactions during the failover may include all changes stored in up to three redo log files:

  - One because it was the last active file
  - A second because of incomplete archiving
  - A third because of incomplete transfer to the standby server

  After work resumes using the standby database, all users have to be made aware that transactions may be lost and that they have to check whether the last changes they made are still available.

- Oracle does not provide anything to transfer the archived redo logs from the primary node to the standby node. However, Libelle Informatik of Germany provides a third-party tool. See:

  http://www.libelle.de

- The remote Oracle database is mounted in standby mode and cannot be used in any way other than for recovery.

- An Oracle database mounted in standby mode cannot be opened in the standard way. This prevents an accidental opening, which would invalidate the standby state of the database. But if the production database becomes unavailable, the standby database has to be activated, shut down, and then opened for normal use. This procedure should be performed by an experienced system administrator. Automating this procedure may give unexpected results if, for example, only a network outage or a reboot of the production server suspends a log file transfer.

- It is complicated and time-consuming to fail back to the original production database because of the risk of losing transactions. Basically the same procedure as for setting up the standby database is needed for failback.

- Structural database changes such as adding or dropping data files, or modifying parameters stored in the INIT.ORA file, are not propagated to the standby database.

- If there are failures on the standby system, then inconsistencies may result, and tablespaces may be lost. In this situation, the only way is to set up the standby database from scratch again.

In addition, you have to consider the effects on the R/3 application servers connected to the Oracle database, when failover to the standby database is performed. Because the standby node must have its own network addresses for receiving the log files, the R/3 processes cannot reconnect to the address known as the DBMS service. This may be solved by a restart using different R/3 profiles to connect to the standby database or by using an alias name for the DBMS node and remapping the alias with DNS.

There are third-party products available that resolve problems in daily operations of a replicated database. For example, the Libelle Database Mirror (for Oracle only, see http://www.libelle.de/) helps create the replica, controls the transfer of the archived redolog files, and detects and replicates structural database changes. Without such DBMS-specific tools, a replicated database should be considered only if the system administrator has detailed knowledge and experience with the DBMS used. Of course, such tools don't change the basic architectural principles of the database replication (long distance, hot standby versus warm standby with time delay and possible loss of transactions) which are the criteria to decide if such a solution is appropriate (or may be combined with MSCS).

Note: The contents of this section, 3.5.2.1, "Standby database example: Oracle" on page 50 only applied to Oracle. Similar functionality is available in DB2 UDB and SQL Server

3.5.3 Replicated DBMS server

As mentioned in 3.5.2, "Replicated database" on page 48, replicating the complete DBMS server means running an additional DBMS in parallel with the production system. This includes replication of the database itself and increases the availability of the R/3 system.

This section explains the basic concept of the replicated database with Oracle Parallel Server as an example. IBM DB2 UDB Enterprise Edition and Microsoft SQL Server provide similar functionality. For information on DB2 UDB check out the document *DB2 Replication Guide and Reference* which is available in the online documentation or through the IBM Web site (http://www.ibm.com). For additional information on database replication with SQL Server, check the Microsoft SQL Server Web site (http://www.microsoft.com/sql).

3.5.3.1 Example: Oracle Parallel Server

As an example of a replicated DBMS server, we describe the functionality of Oracle Parallel Server (OPS).

An operational Oracle DBMS used by an application such as SAP R/3 consists of several main components. There are files that form the database (data files, redo log files, control files), other objects such as the system global area (SGA, the buffer area in memory), and a set of database background processes (log writer LGWR, database writer DBWR, and others). SGA and background processes are called the Oracle instance. Each instance has a private set of online redo log files. A normal installation has only one instance per database. With OPS it is possible to have multiple Oracle instances on different machines providing access to the same database.

This provides protection against DBMS failures. If one instance fails, a surviving instance performs the recovery. Transactions open at the time of the instance failure are rolled back, and committed transactions are reapplied. The surviving instance continues to provide database access. Application processes connected to the failed instance can reconnect to any surviving instance. OPS can also be used to enhance the DBMS performance, using multiple active instances concurrently. OPS is implemented on the shared workload cluster model, in contrast to MSCS, which is based on the partitioned workload cluster model. With OPS, the failure of one database server is only a special case in permanent load balancing between instances.

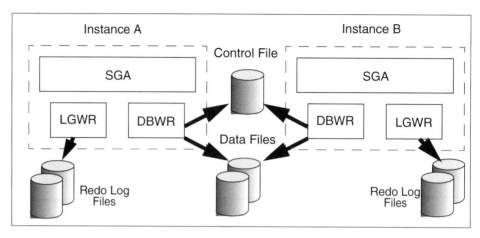

Figure 15. Architecture of Oracle Parallel Server on Windows NT

Oracle Parallel Server is available on Windows NT beginning with Version 7.3.3 on certified hardware platforms with between two and eight DBMS nodes. For more detailed information about the OPS implementation for Windows NT and the hardware, go to the the following Web site:

`http://www.oracle.com/nt/clusters/`

The availability of the R/3 system with OPS depends on the hardware platform and R/3 release. SAP supports OPS only for approved installations. You must ensure that you have this approval before going into production. Only the setup with an idle instance is currently supported. If two instances are configured, all R/3 processes connect to the same instance. The other instance is idle and acts as a hot standby. If the production instance fails, the R/3 processes reconnect to the standby instance.

Compared with a replicated database, this approach has some advantages:

- In the event of failure, no committed transactions are lost.
- There is no operator intervention necessary to fail over the DBMS.
- Setup and failback are easier because no backup and restore are necessary.

Some of the disadvantages of OPS when used with SAP R/3 are the same as for replicated databases:

- OPS protects against DBMS failures only. Problems of the SAP R/3 central instance services or file shares are not covered.

- Compared to SAP R/3, OPS imposes more restrictions on the hardware that may be used.

- Because all instances must have direct (shared) access to all database disks, a network connection is not sufficient. There must be a shared disk subsystem between all database servers. Thus the options for the separation of the nodes are limited by the shared storage technology.

- OPS for Windows NT is incompatible with MSCS. Both products cannot be on the same nodes.

3.5.4 Multiplatform solutions

With SAP R/3, the DBMS and the R/3 application processes may reside on machines with different operating systems. The R/3 processes need only TCP/IP connections to a DBMS with a compatible version according to the requirements for that R/3 release. If the DBMS is configured as highly available on another operating system platform, then only the critical R/3 processes of the central instance and the file shares must be protected under Windows NT. Other high-availability platforms are:

- HACMP (High Availability Cluster Multi-Processing) for AIX
- HAGEO (High Availability Geographic Cluster) for AIX
- Oracle Parallel Server on HACMP for AIX
- OS/390 Parallel Sysplex (with DB2)

For more information see the following redbooks available from http://www.redbooks.ibm.com:

- *Disaster Recovery with HAGEO: An Installer's Companion*, SG24-2018

- *Bullet-Proofing Your Oracle Database with HACMP: A Guide to Implementing AIX Databases with HACMP*, SG24-4788

- *Oracle Cluster POWERsolution Guide*, SG24-2019

- *High Availability Considerations: SAP R/3 on DB2 for OS/390*, SG24-2003

To protect the Windows NT server with the R/3 central instance, an MSCS configuration, a cold standby server, or an alternate failover solution can be used. When using MSCS, keep in mind the restrictions of R/3 support for MSCS (see 3.4, "Using MSCS with SAP R/3" on page 43). There are plans for cluster configurations with the central instance on one node and another application server of the same R/3 system (with a different system number) on the other node running the database (no failover of this second instance). At the time of writing, the failover of the central instance to the database node with another R/3 instance running on it is not supported by SAP.

This approach has advantages for large installations. If a cluster configuration for AIX or mainframe systems already exists, then the R/3 database may be integrated easily and fast. Additional infrastructure for high availability (network environment, appropriate operating service, disaster recovery planning) is available immediately. Because the DBMS exploits a cluster implementation that is more mature than MSCS, there are more choices for the configuration, and the cluster can also be used to boost database performance (Oracle Parallel Server for AIX or DB2 UDB Extended Enterprise Edition).

If there is no AIX or mainframe cluster available, then a multi-platform approach may be more expensive than a pure Windows NT environment. The costs include hardware, software and training. Because of the variety of platforms, maintenance is more complicated and requires more specialists. Multi-platform solutions are favored primarily for large installations with strong performance requirements.

3.6 Microsoft Cluster Server and SAP R/3

In order to give a general idea of how SAP R/3 works with Microsoft Cluster Server, we shall analyze the general structure of the cluster groups for the SAP R/3 4.5B installation. This section aims to provide only a general description of the extensions introduced in SAP R/3 in order to allow it to work in a Microsoft Cluster environment. More details can be found in the SAP document *SAP R/3 in a Microsoft Cluster Environment Technical Overview.*

3.6.1 SAP R/3 extensions

Two DLLs have been developed in order to make SAP R/3 a cluster-aware application: SAPRC.DLL and SAPRCEX.DLL. The first DLL allows the Microsoft Cluster Server Resource Monitor to check the status of the SAP R/3 system and to start and stop the SAP services in case of failover. The second DLL is necessary in order to allow the Cluster Administrator to manage the SAP resource.

The SAP R/3 resource DLL implements the following functions (as described in *SAP R/3 in a Microsoft Cluster Environment Technical Overview*):

* SaprcOnline — Start the R/3 service and work processes.

- SaprcOffline — Stop the R/3 service and work processes.
- SaprcTerminate — Stop the R3 service without stopping R/3 beforehand. This function is only for testing purposes.
- SaprcIsAlive — IsAlive status check for the R/3 system.
- SaprcLooksAlive — LooksAlive status check for the R/3 system, which is identical to IsAlive.

Other specific extensions are:

- The program INSAPRCT.EXE has been added in order to create the SAP R/3 resource type
- The program CRCLGRP.EXE has been added in order to create the cluster group SAP R/3 <SID>
- The program COCLGRP.EXE has been added in order to create the resource SAP R/3<SID> and put it in its own group.

3.6.2 Cluster Group

Figure 16 shows an example of the dependencies that relate the resources in the cluster group at the end of an SAP R/3 installation with Oracle DBMS:

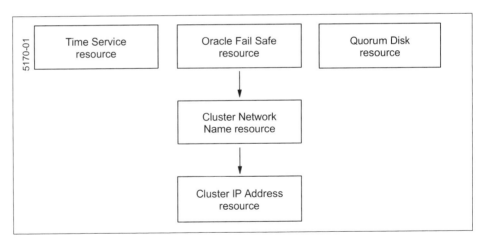

Figure 16. Oracle cluster group

A slightly different group is created during the DB2/UDB installation as shown in Figure 17:

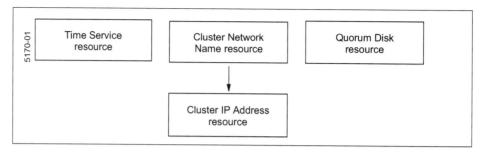

Figure 17. DB2 cluster group

Figure 18 shows the group created during the SQL Server installation:

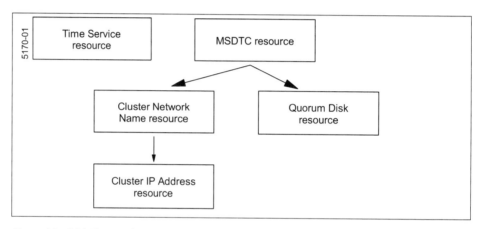

Figure 18. SQL Server cluster group

The MSDTC dependencies must be removed and then the resource must be deleted as described in 8.9, "Removal of unused resources" on page 232.

3.6.3 Group SAP-R/3 <SID>

The SAP MSCS resource group is database-independent. Thus the group for the R/3 instance has the same structure with an SQL Server database as with Oracle. Figure 19 shows the dependencies that relate the resources in the SAP-R/3 ITS group.

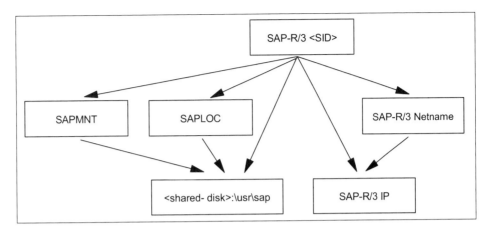

Figure 19. SAP-R/3 ITS group dependencies

3.6.4 Database resource group

In order to make the Oracle database cluster aware, Oracle has implemented some extensions. The main extensions are the creation of the FSODBS.DLL and FSODBSEX.DLL resource DLLs. FSODBS.DLL allows the cluster to bring the Oracle database online or offline. Moreover it checks the database through IsAlive polling. The FSODBSEX.DLL is used by Microsoft Cluster Administrator to display the properties of the database resource.

Figure 20 shows the dependencies that relate the resources for the Oracle ITS group.

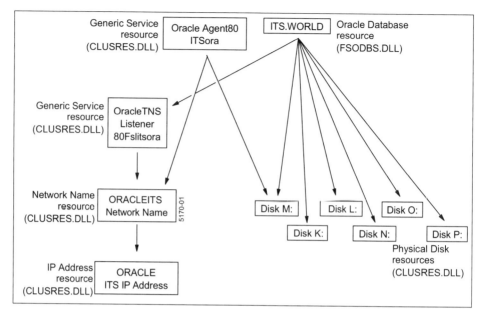

Figure 20. Oracle cluster dependencies

In order to make the DB2 UDB DBMS cluster aware, IBM has implemented some extensions. One of the main extensions is the creation of the DLL DB2WOLF.DLL. This resource DLL implements the DB2 resource type functions to start and stop a clustered DB2 database instance on either node and also implements the IsAlive and LooksAlive functionality required by MSCS.

Note

The resource DLL does not use the Force flag when stopping the database instance. The DB2 resource will therefore not go offline as long as active connection exists to a database controlled by this database instance.

Figure 21 shows the dependencies in the DB2 group:

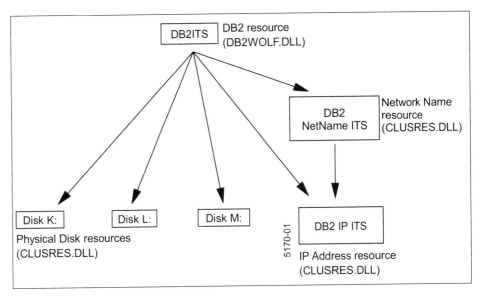

Figure 21. DB2 cluster dependencies

Many extensions have been introduced in SQL Server 7.0 Enterprise Edition in order to make the DBMS cluster aware. The main extension are the creation of the SQAGTRES.DLL and SQLSRVRES.DLL.

Figure 22 shows the dependencies in the SQL Server group.

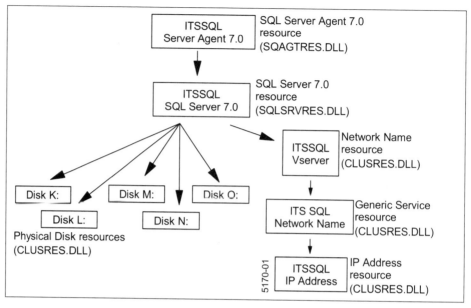

Figure 22. SQL Server cluster dependencies

3.7 Backup and recovery

Clustering with Microsoft Cluster Server (MSCS) offers significant benefits in terms of availability of your server resources. Implementing a clustered configuration allows operations to continue even when many hardware failures occur. Integrity of your data, however, cannot be guaranteed by clustering alone. User error or multiple hardware failures, for example, can compromise your systems. So, even in a clustered environment, a good backup process remains an important part of your data protection strategy. Backup and recovery processes similar to those used for stand-alone systems may be used, but additional factors and constraints have to be considered due to the unique characteristics of MSCS clustered systems.

Just as for a standard Windows NT system, you can use local tape drives or a central backup server as backup devices for your cluster. Tape drives, however, cannot be defined as MSCS cluster resources to allow coordinated access by both nodes of the cluster, and a tape drive attached to one node cannot directly back up the local system disk of the other node. If you decide on local tape drives you should attach the same number and type to each server in the cluster.

Microsoft Cluster Server (MSCS), with its common disk subsystem, causes some difficulties for backup and recovery that we will discuss in this section. Specific characteristics of MSCS that are relevant include:

- A backup program running on a single cluster node may not be able to access all disks in the common disk subsystem.
- Tape devices cannot be cluster resources.
- Drives in the common disk subsystem are accessible from both nodes, but only one node at any given time. Which node has access to a particular drive at a particular time is controlled without reference to backup software.
- Files on the common disk subsystem need to be identified in a unique fashion.
- Taking databases and applications offline requires special care.
- Files unique to MSCS may not be handled correctly by backup software.

3.7.1 Complete backup of a cluster

The complete backup of a cluster includes the operating system files and other local drives on each node as well as all shared disks. During normal operation of an MSCS cluster, only a subset of the total number of disks in the common disk subsystem may be accessible from an individual node. A backup taken from one node will not include data from those disks the node cannot access.

To overcome this difficulty and ensure that all of your data is backed up, one of these three approaches is often used:

- Move all resources to one node before beginning the backup.
- Run backup jobs on both nodes.
- Run backup jobs on the physical nodes to protect the data on their local disks, but back up the data on the common disk subsystem by running jobs on the virtual servers that own the disks.

3.7.1.1 Moving resources to a single node

Moving all resources automatically before and after each backup operation requires that the backup program can launch pre- and post-backup procedures containing cluster commands (alternatively, Netfinity Manager or Netfinity Director may be used to schedule cluster actions). This may be an option if the availability requirements are moderate and the resulting scheduled interruptions in service are acceptable. Keep in mind, however, that failing over SAP R/3 or DBMS resources from one node to the other in an MSCS cluster causes in-process transactions and batch jobs to be aborted.

3.7.1.2 Local tape drives

Running backup jobs on both nodes avoids any interruptions in service and also allows the local disks on both cluster nodes to be backed up regularly. If each node has its own local tape drive, however, you will have to keep track of which set of backup tapes belong to each machine and ensure that sets from each node are kept in step so that a complete cluster recovery can be performed.

Also, because you do not know, in general, which particular node owns a specific disk in the common subsystem, each node has to attempt to back up all disks. This will cause backup failure messages for those disks that cannot be accessed from a particular system.

3.7.1.3 Dedicated backup server

Another approach is to implement a centralized network backup process using a dedicated backup server. This, however, creates a problem with unique file identification for data residing on the common disk subsystem.

In this configuration, the network backup software, consisting of a backup client on each cluster node that communicates with a central backup server, catalogs each saved file using the relevant client's network name and the path in the client's disk and file system. In this manner, the backup process regards file H:\DIR_X\FILE_Y from node A as different from H:\DIR_X\FILE_Y from node B.

This is the case even if H: is one of the clustered disks that could be assigned to either node A or node B. Because of this, a backup copy of H:\DIR_X\FILE_Y could be created from node A one day and from node B the next. These two copies of the same file would be cataloged as backups of different objects because of the different backup client names.

This is not just inconvenient if you are looking for all copies of a specific file or for a complete backup listing of a specific day. More importantly, incremental backup schemes, such as the one used by Tivoli Storage Manager, break down. The two copies of H:\DIR_X\FILE_Y are not considered to be sequential generations of the same file and so the incremental backup process fails. This is illustrated in Figure 23:

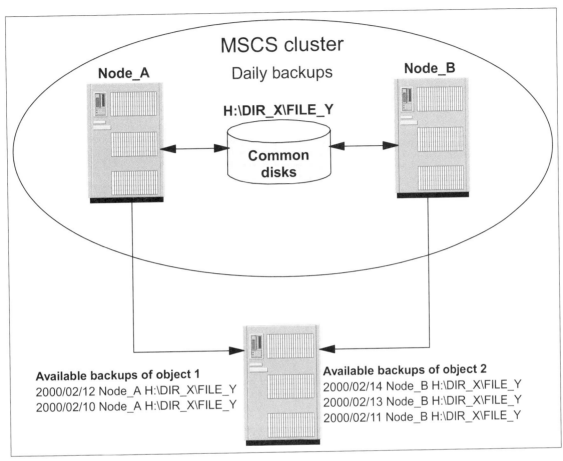

Figure 23. Incremental backup process failure in a clustered environment

There are two practical approaches that overcome this problem and guarantee consistency:

- Alias definitions at the backup server

  By defining that files from node A's disk H: are to be considered as identical to files from node B's disk H: ("NODE_A\\H: is an alias for NODE_B\\H:"), the backup software will track changes to files on this disk. Aliases have to be defined at the level of individual disks because a general alias valid for all disks ("node A is an alias for node B") would also merge local disk backups. This function would typically be provided by the backup server software.

- Using virtual names for backup clients

  To use this method, each clustered disk has to belong to a resource group with at least one virtual network name. In an SAP R/3 system, clustered disks belong either to the database group (with a virtual database name) or to the R/3 group (with a virtual R/3 name). The quorum disk may belong to any group (the cluster group with the cluster virtual name is the default). Now we configure three backup clients on each cluster node:

    - Client 1 using the physical node name to identify itself
    - Client 2 using the virtual database name
    - Client 3 using the virtual R/3 name

  The first of these clients backs up the local disks of the particular node on which it is installed. Each of the other clients performs a backup only for those disks that belong to the corresponding resource group. Now, because the backup client that saves the file H:\DIR_X\FILE_Y is known to the backup server by a virtual name, all backup copies of H:\DIR_X\FILE_Y are kept under this name. Thus all files on shared disks are cataloged on the backup server in a unique manner, independent of which cluster node owned the data when the backup was made.

  For example Tivoli Storage Manager uses a special option for the backup client to identify cluster disks and then implements this second approach using the cluster name in the backup file catalog. See the IBM Redbook *Using Tivoli Storage Management in a Clustered NT Environment,* SG24-5742 for more information.

  It is important that clients 2 and 3 back up both the files and the database using the name of their respective virtual servers, not the name of the physical node.

3.7.2 Backing up clustered disks

In some cases, a backup of data held on clustered disks may be made without active backup client software by simply defining file shares with virtual names. As explained in *Microsoft Cluster Server Administrator's Guide,* Microsoft document X0327902, hidden administrative shares are useful for this purpose. For example, you might use the New Resource wizard in the Windows NT Cluster Administrator to create a \\<virtual_name>\HBACKUP$ file share for the root directory of partition H:. This share does not appear in the Windows NT browse list (thanks to the trailing $ symbol in its name) and could be configured to allow access only to members of the Backup Operators group. Then the backup server connects to the share and performs a network drive backup without regard to which node owns the share.

In an SAP R/3 cluster you may use this technique to back up files of the SAP R/3 disk (directory \USR\SAP). But you cannot perform an online database backup in the same way because the database files are open and database operations would interfere with backup access, leading to inconsistent data in the backup files.

3.7.2.1 Offline backups

In a clustered SAP R/3 environment, the database service is a monitored cluster resource. Stopping the database with the usual commands (using Oracle as an example, this would be the svmgr30 command) to allow an offline backup procedure will not work in a cluster. This is because the cluster resource monitor detects loss of the database processes and restarts them immediately on either the same or the other cluster node and the offline backup consequently fails.

To stop the database service the appropriate cluster command has to be issued rather than the normal database management utility. The cluster command should affect only the database service, not the entire database resource group; the disks must stay online so that the data to be backed up can be accessed.

3.7.3 MSCS unique files

In an MSCS cluster, the system maintains files that contain information about cluster configuration and resource status. These include:

- Several files in directory \MSCS on the quorum disk
- Two files CLUSDB and CLUSDB.LOG in the directory %WINDIR%\CLUSTER

These files are permanently open and, at present, no standard procedures will allow you to back them up. To protect these files, a workaround is necessary.

The cluster information on the quorum disk may be restored if the configuration information on the nodes itself (in the CLUSDB file) is correct. Procedures to recover from a failed quorum resource or corrupted quorum log are described in *Microsoft Cluster Server Administrator's Guide,* Microsoft document X0327902, and in Microsoft Knowledge Base, articles Q172951 and Q172944. Thus you should maintain backup copies of at least CLUSDB and CLUSDB.LOG. To make these copies, there are three workarounds:

- By booting the second copy of Windows NT, you can do a complete offline backup of the production installation of Windows NT, including the special files. Because the emergency system should not have an MSCS installation (to avoid any problems in the case of emergency restore), this requires you to separate the cluster node from the shared bus (or to shut down the other node).

- The two files contain the registry branch that sits below the key HKEY_LOCAL_MACHINE\Cluster. You can export this tree using one of the standard Windows NT registry utility programs and recover by importing it back into the registry.

- By using Tivoli Data Protection for Workgroups with its logical replication to duplicate the files for backup.

The following table summarizes the MSCS backup and recovery issues and the proposed solutions.

Table 4. MSCS: resolving backup and recovery related issues

MSCS backup and recovery issue	Resolution
A backup program running on a cluster node may not be able to access all shared disks.	A scheduler resource exists within each MSCS resource group (virtual server), which is invoked externally from a backup server.
Tape devices cannot be shared cluster resources.	An external system is implemented as a backup server using a tape library.
Files on the shared disks need to be identified in a unique fashion.	A scheduler resource exists within each MSCS resource group (virtual server).
Bringing databases and applications offline requires special care.	Scripts containing cluster.exe commands are used to control these elements.
Additional MSCS files may not be handled correctly by the backup software.	Tivoli Data Protection for Workgroups' object replication mechanism is used to back up these files.

Chapter 4. Hardware configuration and MSCS planning

Before starting an SAP R/3 project, the following main technological choices must be made:

- Operating system (Windows NT, Windows 2000 and Linux on Intel-based servers; AIX, HP-UX, Solaris/SPARC etc. on RISC platforms; OS/400; OS/390, etc)

- Database Management System software (Oracle, DB2 UDB, Microsoft SQL Server, Informix, etc.)

- SAP R/3 Release (3.1I, 4.0B, 4.5B, etc) (operating system, DBMS and SAP Release must be compatible; see OSS note 0085841 for 4.5B)

All these choices are fundamental in order to get the expected business benefits from the SAP R/3 system. In this chapter, we shall not examine these big problems, but we shall try to explain how to get the best configuration given the following choices:

- Windows NT 4.0 or Windows 2000
- Oracle or DB2/UDB or MS SQL DBMS
- SAP R/3 4.5B
- SCSI or FCAL storage

Having chosen the operating system, the DBMS and the SAP R/3 release in a consistent way, the configuration phase can begin. The main steps are the following:

- Sizing (see 4.3, "Hardware sizing" on page 78 for details).

- Choice of the hardware platform. Until the end of 1999, this meant a choice between Intel and Alpha processor-based servers; now it only means to choose the hardware manufacturer. The complete hardware configuration must be certified:

    - By the server manufacturer for hardware compatibility
    - By Microsoft for operating system compatibility
    - By SAP for SAP R/3 compatibility (see 4.2, "Certification and validation of hardware" on page 73 for more details)

- Storage technology (viable choices are SCSI, SSA, FCAL, FCS, ESS, etc). The two main storage technologies, SCSI and FCAL will be thoroughly discussed in 4.5, "Typical SCSI RAID controller configurations" on page 101 and 4.6, "Fibre Channel configurations" on page 104.

- Network technology (Fast Ethernet, token ring, Gigabit Ethernet, ATM, etc.) and network configuration (fully redundant network connections or not, see 4.7, "Network configurations" on page 110 for details)
- Disk layout (see section 4.4, "Disk layouts" on page 84 for details)

4.1 Checklist for SAP MSCS installation

In this section, we discuss what you need and what you should be aware of before the installation of SAP R/3. All the specific information will be explained in detail later in this chapter.

4.1.1 Minimum cluster hardware requirements

To provide high availability to your SAP R/3 system you must configure your hardware carefully. You need two identical Netfinity servers certified for use on Windows NT. For details regarding the certification process and how to choose your hardware see 4.2, "Certification and validation of hardware" on page 73. Keep in mind that your platform must be certified to be sure that you will have support from your hardware vendor, Microsoft and SAP in case you experience trouble.

- RAM. Each server must have at least 256 MB. You will also need significant disk space for paging files (four to five times the amount of RAM installed, as described in 5.6.2, "Page file tuning" on page 137).
- SCSI RAID controller and/or Fibre Channel controller for internal disks and/or the external shared disks. For Fibre Channel configurations, you need at least one Fibre Channel adapter in each machine connected via hubs to a Fibre Channel RAID controller. The external disks are then connected to the RAID controller.
- Network. For the network configuration, you need at least two network adapters in each server. One is dedicated to the private network (called the "heartbeat"). This is usually a crossover Ethernet connection. The other adapter is for the public network, used for data communication with clients. An additional third adapter dedicated to server communications (called a backbone) is also recommended.

Table 5 lists minimum hardware requirements assuming you are using IBM Netfinity servers:

Table 5. Minimum hardware requirements

Configuration	Minimum requirements
Devices	• Two identical servers, certified for clustering
Memory	• At least 256 MB of RAM
SCSI	• Two SCSI RAID adapters, each with at least one internal and one external SCSI channel (for example an IBM ServeRAID-3HB) with the latest BIOS and firmware levels • External disk enclosure
Fibre Channel	• Two SCSI RAID adapters with an internal SCSI channel (for example an IBM ServeRAID-3L or 3HB) with the latest BIOS and firmware levels for internal disk connectivity • Two Fibre Channel host adapters • One Fibre Channel RAID controller • One Fibre Channel hub with at least four GBICs • External disk enclosure
Network	• Two network cards for private network communications • Two network cards for public network communications • Four physical IP addresses for the network cards • Three additional IP addresses for the R/3 and DB cluster resources

4.1.2 Minimum cluster software requirements

From the software point of view, the requirements for the system are common to both the SCSI and the Fibre Channel configuration. Microsoft Windows NT 4.0 Enterprise Edition Service Pack 4 plus the component needed for Y2K compliance (Microsoft Internet Explorer 4.01 Service Pack 1 and Microsoft Data Access components 2.0 Service Pack 1) are required, but it is better to install the latest Service Pack from Microsoft. For SAP R/3, which Service Pack you install depends on which database you want to use. Refer to OSS note 30478 for details.

Y2K compliance

If you plan to install Windows NT Service Pack 5 or 6a (SP5, SP6a) without installing Service Pack 4 (SP4) first, you should remember to install the additional components in SP4 for Y2K compliance. These include Microsoft Internet Explorer 4.01 Service Pack 1 and Microsoft Data Access Components 2.0 Service Pack 1. Alternatively, install SP4 first, then SP5 or SP6a.

Refer to SAP OSS Note 0030478 to get latest information about Service Packs and SAP R/3. Currently, the situation with MSCS is as follows: for R/3 systems using MSCS, SP4 may only be used if the Microsoft hot fixes are imported according to OSS Note 0144310 (for SQL Server 7.0 only hotfix "RNR20.DLL" is required). If possible, you should immediately implement Service Pack 5 or 6a. For the application of Service Packs in cluster systems, you must read Note 0144310. The use of Service Packs is also described in 5.8, "Service pack and post-SP installation steps" on page 142.

The minimum space requirements on the local disks and the shared disks are summarized in Table 6:

Table 6. Minimum space requirements

Component	Minimum space requirement
Internal drives capacity on each node	• 500 MB for Microsoft Windows NT 4.0 Enterprise Edition, Service Pack 4, Microsoft Internet Explorer 4.01 Service Pack 1, and Microsoft Data Access Component 2.0 Service Pack 1 • 3 MB for MSCS • 10 MB for SAP cluster files • 4-5 x RAM size for Windows NT page file • Oracle: 600 MB for Oracle server software RDBMS 8.0.5, 10 MB for Oracle FailSafe V 2.1.3 • DB2: 100 MB for DB2 UDB V5.2 • SQL: 65 MB for MS SQL Server 7.0 EE program files
SAP R/3: shared volumes requirements (external enclosure)	• 1 GB for SAP R/3 executable files
Oracle: shared volumes requirements (external enclosure)	• 100 KB for Cluster quorum resource • 10 GB initially for SAP R/3 data files • 120 MB for Online redo logs set A • 120 MB for Online redo logs set B • 120 MB for Mirrored online redo logs set A • 120 MB for Mirrored online redo logs set B • 4 GB for archived online redo logs • 2 GB for SAPDBA directories
DB2: shared volumes requirements (external enclosure)	• 100 KB for Cluster quorum resource • 11 GB initially for SAP R/3 data files • 100 MB for DB2 database instance files • 1 GB (at least) for DB2 log files • 4 GB for DB2 archived log files

Component	Minimum space requirement
Microsoft SQL: shared volumes requirements (external enclosure)	• 100 KB for Cluster quorum resource • 6 GB initially for R/3 data files • 45 MB for SQL server master DB • 300 MB for SQL server temp DB • 1 GB minimum for the transaction log files (log device) **Note**: There are no archived log files with SQL Server. You need to back up the active log file regularly and reduce the log file afterwards.

4.2 Certification and validation of hardware

All hardware vendors providing Windows NT server hardware must obtain certification and validation of hardware configurations by iXOS Software AG (iXOS) and Microsoft. The IBM Netfinity ServerProven and ClusterProven programs will not be addressed in this book since SAP currently does not participate in these IBM membership programs.

As an independent assessor, iXOS performs certification of all Windows NT server platforms offered by hardware vendors competing for shares of the SAP R/3 market. SAP will not support an R/3 installation on a hardware platform not certified by iXOS or the hardware vendors themselves.

Microsoft maintains a validation program for testing the compatibility of vendor server hardware and associated drivers with Windows NT. As part of its hardware validation program, Microsoft maintains a program specifically for validating vendor server hardware in a clustered configuration using MSCS. Microsoft will not support an MSCS installation on a hardware platform that is not validated by Microsoft.

4.2.1 iXOS

iXOS Software AG (iXOS), in close cooperation with SAP, has developed a server hardware certification process for the purpose of investigating the performance and stability of SAP R/3 on Windows NT platforms. This certification is essential for all hardware manufacturers. Since 1993, the R/3 NT Competency Center (R3 NTC) of iXOS has exclusively performed the certification process, as an independent assessor, for a large number of Windows NT platform hardware vendors.

SAP corporation now allows server hardware vendors to self-certify their respective platforms using Microsoft Windows operating system products

(Windows NT and Windows 2000). Each hardware vendor is obliged to secure approval from SAP in order to conduct self-certification for R/3.

If a hardware vendor meets SAP's defined requirements, then the hardware vendor will be allowed to perform the certification tests on its own at its own facility. The following criteria are prerequisites:

- The tests must be performed in a dedicated space (known as "laboratory" by SAP) at the hardware vendor's facility. The hardware involved in the certification must be permanently located in this "laboratory" with each server having its configuration (firmware, BIOS, drivers, etc.) at the latest level available. It is assumed that these systems run SAP R/3 regularly and are tested with the R/3 application.

- The hardware vendor must name the manager responsible for the certification activities.

- The "laboratory" must be maintained by at least two employees of the hardware vendor. Each of these employees must be named and each must be certified as an SAP R/3 Technical Consultant. The "laboratory" must be occupied by at least one of these employees during normal work hours.

- SAP, in conjunction with iXOS, will verify the hardware vendor's compliance with these criteria.

The audit of the test results provided by the hardware vendor will be performed by iXOS. The certification will not be officially announced until a successful audit is completed. Once a successful audit is completed, the hardware vendor's server system will be posted as a certified platform on the following Web page:

http://www.R3onNT.com

Note that SAP supports the operation of certified R/3 systems only.

There are five different hardware certification categories in place as developed by iXOS in conjunction with SAP. The hardware certification testing is executed by iXOS as follows:

1. Initial certification: The first, and only the first, Windows NT server offering from a hardware vendor must undergo the initial certification. A very detailed test sequence is performed.

2. Ongoing certification: All server offerings for R/3 on Windows NT currently offered to the market are subject to the process of the ongoing certification. Twice a year, the ongoing certification tests are repeated on each server offering. The ongoing certification is executed to validate the

operation of the system in conjunction with a new release of Windows NT or an upgrade of hardware or firmware by the hardware vendor.

3. Ongoing controller certification: This level of certification allows for a set of reduced tests to be performed in order to certify I/O controllers offered by hardware vendors. Once an I/O controller is certified by iXOS in one Windows NT server product offered by a hardware vendor, it is certified for use in all the hardware vendor's Windows NT server products that have been certified by iXOS.

4. S/390 certification: This certification requires reduced tests to be performed against an already certified NT platform that is to have access to a DB2 database on a System/390. For this certification category, it is the connectivity type that is certified. Each connectivity type (for example, FDDI, Fast Ethernet, ESCON) must be certified once per hardware vendor.

5. Outgoing certification: Hardware platforms no longer being sold for R/3 on Windows NT, but still used by customers in a production environment, are subject to an outgoing certification.

To enter the SAP R/3 on Windows NT market, a hardware vendor must secure an initial certification for its server platform. The first server offering and all subsequent server offerings a hardware vendor may supply to the market are subject to the ongoing certification until they are no longer offered for SAP R/3 on Windows NT.

4.2.1.1 Hardware components

According to the iXOS certification process a hardware platform consists of three different types of components:

1. Critical components

   - The chip set: A platform is defined by its chip set and corresponding chip set extensions that enable the data transfer between processor, memory, and I/O. Changing the chip set requires that a Windows NT server system must undergo an ongoing certification.

   - The I/O controller: A particular I/O controller must be certified once for each hardware vendor. If an I/O controller has been successfully tested with one Windows NT server offering supplied by a hardware vendor, it is certified with all other iXOS certified Windows NT server offerings supplied by the vendor (if supported by the vendor).

   The same applies to the certification of S/390 connectivity types.

2. Peripheral components

The hardware vendor is obligated to provide a list of all peripheral components associated with the server system to be used in support of SAP R/3 on Windows NT. The hardware vendor guarantees function and support of the components listed. If any of the peripheral components are replaced, the list is to be updated by the hardware vendor and no new certification is necessary. Peripheral components are:

- Hard disks
- Memory
- Network adapter
- Backup device

3. Non-critical components

All components that are not defined as critical components or peripheral components are defined as *non-critical components*. Changing non-critical components does not affect the certification of the platform. Non-critical components are, for example:

- Monitor
- Graphic adapter
- Mouse
- Others

I/O subsystems

SAP R/3 certification rules do not require the certification of I/O subsystems. However, iXOS offers to vendors of I/O subsystems special tests that validate the stability and measure the I/O performance of the storage solution.

4.2.2 Microsoft

Microsoft evaluates hardware compatibility using the Windows NT Hardware Compatibility Tests (HCTs). The HCTs are run for the purpose of testing the interaction between device drivers and hardware. These tests issue the full range of commands available to applications and operating systems software, and are designed to stress hardware beyond the level of most real-world situations. At the Windows Hardware Quality Labs (WHQL), Microsoft personnel run the HCTs and report results to the hardware manufacturer. Hardware that passes testing is included on the Windows NT Hardware Compatibility List (HCL). The HCL may be viewed by visiting http://www.microsoft.com/hcl/. A validated cluster configuration can potentially include any server that is on the Microsoft HCL for Windows NT server. For validating hardware in a cluster configuration, the Microsoft Cluster HCT is executed.

The most important criteria for MSCS hardware is that it is included as a validated cluster configuration on the Microsoft HCL, indicating it has passed the Microsoft Cluster HCT. Microsoft will support MSCS only when it is used on a validated cluster configuration. Only complete configurations are validated, not individual components. The complete cluster configuration consists of two servers and a storage solution.

Microsoft allows hardware manufacturers to run the Microsoft Cluster HCT at their own facilities. The result of a successful test is an encrypted file that is returned to Microsoft for validation. Validated cluster configurations may be viewed by selecting the Cluster category at:

`http://www.microsoft.com/hcl/`

IBM currently tests MSCS solutions with the Netfinity 10/100 Ethernet Adapter and a crossover cable as cluster interconnect. This is the configuration submitted to Microsoft for certification, and it is recommended that you follow this practice. The MSCS certification rules allow replacement of the interconnect cards with another 100% compliant NDIS PCI card listed on the HCL (see `http://www.microsoft.com/hwtest/sysdocs/wolfpackdoc.htm`). Consult with the Netfinity ServerProven list to be sure that the alternate card is listed as one that is tested and supported on Netfinity servers.

Cluster component candidates

The Microsoft HCL also has the categories *Cluster Fibre Channel Adapter*, *Cluster/SCSI Adapter*, *Cluster/RAID*, *Cluster RAID Controller*, and *Cluster RAID System*.

It is important to note that inclusion of these components on the HCL does *not* qualify a component for MSCS support services unless the component was included in a validated cluster configuration. Make sure you consult the Cluster category on the HCL to view the validated configuration with the storage adapter included. These other cluster categories are intended for vendors, system integrators, and test labs that are validating complete cluster configurations.

4.2.3 Certification of SAP R/3 and Windows 2000

SAP is planning to release R/3 for Windows 2000 at the launch time of Windows 2000. Currently, Microsoft is running R/3 tests with every major Windows 2000 build.

Because of this situation the following rules for hardware certification for R/3 on Windows 2000 will apply:

- Customers and partners can install R/3 on Windows 2000 if the hardware:
    - Has been certified by iXOS for Windows NT (is listed on iXOS Web page)
    - Is also listed on the Microsoft Hardware Compatibility List (HCL) for Windows 2000 (on the Microsoft Web page)
    - Is officially supported for SAP installations on Windows 2000 by the hardware partner.
- The hardware partner must test and support all peripherals (including network adapter, tape device, graphic adapter and so on) that will be used by SAP customers for Windows 2000.
- New hardware must be certified by iXOS as before. Hardware partners must notify SAP and iXOS as to which hardware will be supported by Windows 2000. iXOS will add a Windows 2000 list to the Web page with all qualifying hardware platforms.

4.3 Hardware sizing

This section will help you understand the general approach to sizing the hardware for use with SAP R/3 with Microsoft Cluster Server. It explains the mechanism currently used to provide an accurate hardware configuration.

While most of this section is hardware vendor independent, you will see a few references to IBM methods. Other hardware vendors may use different methods and you will need to get additional information from them for successful hardware sizing.

4.3.1 Terms and definitions

First of all, you should be aware that the configuration resulting from an SAP sizing process is a matter of definitions. The customer and the hardware vendor have to agree on the definition of the words used and on the assumptions concerning the future configuration. This is the first step of the sizing.

- SAP Application Performance Standard (SAPS)

  SAPS is a definition of throughput developed by SAP capacity planning and performance testing personnel. It describes machine capability at 100% load condition. It does not reflect customer-allowable response time conditions, nor should it be used for sizing because response times as a function of load are non-linear.

  - 100 SAPS are defined as 2,000 fully business-processed order line items per hour in the standard SAP SD (sales/distribution) application benchmark. This is equivalent to 6000 dialog steps and 2000 postings to the database per hour.

  - With SAPS, you measure the maximum (at 100% CPU utilization) number of dialog steps on a particular model of machine. This means you can express the maximum throughput of each model in a total number of SAPS, independent of response time.

  - SAPS is valid for a theoretical SD load only.

- Users

  - Named users: The users that have an account in the R/3 system.

  - Connected or logged-on users: The users that are connected or logged on to the system at one point in time. The percentage of named users simultaneously connected to the system varies from customer to customer.

  - Active users: The users that are connected/logged on and putting load on to the system. The default assumption recommended by the IBM/SAP International Competency Center (ISICC) is that 65% of the logged-on users are active. Active users can further be divided into three workload categories (power/high, standard/medium, and occasional/low).

4.3.2 What is to be sized?

Here are the components that have to be sized before choosing any hardware configuration:

- CPU processor capacity: Mainly depends on the version of SAP, the database system chosen, and the number of active users (including multisession users).

- Main memory: Mainly depends on the software version, the number of instances installed on the system, and the number of logged-on users (including multisession users).

- Internal disks: Mainly depends on the operating system and the main memory (for the pagefile).

- External disks: Mainly depends on the database software, the number of named users, and the level of security/performance expected.

- Backup capacity: Based on the amount of data to be stored/restored and the time frame given for storage operations.

- Network load: Mainly depends on the number of users and the type of network.

- Client for the SAP GUI: Only depends on the SAP software version.

Figure 24 shows the major influencing factors that should be considered and discussed with the team in charge of hardware sizing.

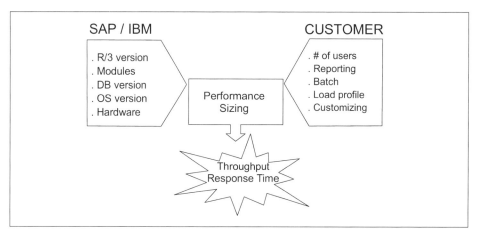

Figure 24. Influencing factors

4.3.3 Sizing methodology

A sizing estimate result includes recommendations for CPU(s), memory, and disks required to run the basic SAP R/3 application suite. Most likely, there will be software, server, and network requirements that are not addressed by this sizing estimate. For example, many SAP R/3 installations run software for system management, EDI translation, file transfer, help desk management, etc. To determine the total hardware and software configuration required for any R/3 implementation, we recommend that customers work with an SAP R/3 consultant who will help to develop the overall system architecture.

Sizing the hardware requirements for each customer's SAP R/3 implementation is an iterative process, which may be refined and repeated a number of times. In the early stages of planning, customers have limited information about their planned SAP R/3 environment. In this case, the sizing estimate can be completed with general information about the numbers of users the IBM SAP R/3 system needs to support. Further along in the R/3 implementation planning, customers will know more about SAP R/3, the R/3 applications they plan to use, and their potential R/3 transaction activity. At that time, another sizing estimate should be requested based on more detailed information.

It is important to understand that the sizing estimate is a presales effort, which is based on benchmark performance data; it should not replace capacity planning for installed systems. The sizing estimate can be used for preinstallation planning. However, during the process of implementing R/3, customers should work with a hardware vendor/SAP capacity planning consultant to monitor and predict the ongoing resource requirements for the production R/3 system.

The IBM/SAP sizing methodology is continually reviewed and revised to provide the best possible estimate of the IBM hardware resources required to run SAP R/3. Guidelines for sizing R/3 come from a number of sources, including SAP, SAP R/3 benchmarks, and customer feedback. Based on information from these sources and the sizing questionnaire completed by the customers, the IBM ERP sales team will analyze the SAP R/3 requirements and recommend an IBM hardware configuration with a target CPU utilization of 65%.

There are basically two different methods for interactive sizing: user-based sizing and transaction-based sizing.

- In general, *user-based sizing* determines the total interactive load of an SAP complex by summing up the total number of mathematical and financial operation type users. The method then makes a processor recommendation based on a 65% (IBM) loading condition of these mathematical operation users. This allows significant capacity for peak interactive conditions, batch loads, report generation, and other forms of complex loading.

- The *transaction-based sizing* methods developed and used by IBM sums up the total amount of normalized financial (FI) transactions an SAP system will see, and then, assuming an average amount of dialogs per transaction, computes a total normalized dialog load. The new transaction-based method developed by SAP and the hardware partner council is based on measurements that have been achieved on a reference machine for every single transaction evaluated at this time (one to three transactions per module).

Both user-based sizing and transaction-based sizing have advantages and disadvantages. In fact, we recommend that you obtain both user data and transaction data from a customer when doing a sizing (per the sizing questionnaire). This will allow you to have the data to cross check the user-based sizing with transaction sizing.

The objective of the IBM/SAP sizing methodology is to estimate the hardware resources required to support the peak hour of business processing. The IBM sizing philosophy is that if we size the hardware to provide acceptable response time for the peak application workload, then all workloads outside of the peak hour should also provide acceptable response time.

The peak hour is the busiest hour of activity from an information-processing standpoint. It is the hour in which the CPU utilization is the highest. In identifying the peak hour, you should consider how your processing volumes vary throughout the year and select a peak hour during the busiest time of the year. A survey in the user departments of the various SAP R/3 modules may be helpful. Typically, the peak hour occurs somewhere between 8:00 a.m. and 6:00 p.m., but this can vary. In Figure 25, the thick line shows the transaction volumes for all of the SAP R/3 modules used in one organization, with the peak hour occurring from 10:00 a.m. to 11:00 a.m.

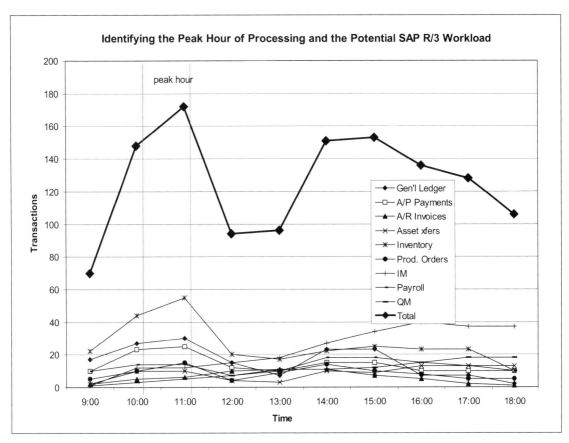

Figure 25. Identifying the peak hour of processing and the potential SAP R/3 workload

The SAP R/3 functions that will be in use during that hour (refer to Figure 25) have to be determined also. For user-based sizing, it will be the R/3 modules that will be active during the peak hour and the numbers of users of each module. For transaction-based sizing, we will break down the modules by transaction type and specify the number of transactions to be processed during the peak hour. For example, in user-based sizing, customers could indicate that 20 Financial Accounting (FI) users will be active; for transaction-based sizing, customers would specify some number of A/P Payments, A/R Invoices, GL Postings, etc. It is important to understand that every SAP R/3 module/transaction to be used by the organization should not be included. Instead, only those R/3 modules/transactions that will be active during the peak hour should be reported.

The batch processing workload should also be identified. For user-based sizing, the batch volume is a percentage of the total system workload. By default, we recommend that 20% of the total workload during the peak hour is batch processing. For transaction-based sizing, it is the batch transaction volumes for the peak hour.

For further information, you can contact your hardware vendor. For IBM customers, contact the IBM national ERP Solutions team or the IBM/SAP International Competency Center (ISICC) in Walldorf, Germany.

Three electronic sizing tools are available to help IBM sales team, partners, and customers.

- The *SAP QuickSizer* is accessible from the Internet on the SAPNET Web site (http://sapnet.sap.com, OSS user ID, and password are required).

- The second tool is the *ISICC R/3 Sizing Tool*, available on the ISICC Lotus Notes Server accessible only by IBM employees at the time of writing. To access this server, please review the instructions on the ISICC intranet Web site http://w3.isicc.de.ibm.com.

- The third tool, called *IBM Insight for R/3*, is available to anyone at http://www.ibm.com/erp/sap/insight. This tool can be used to verify the sizing of hardware currently running R/3 and/or provide input for the resizing of the hardware of a currently running R/3 instance. The customer runs this tool for several days in his environment and sends the resulting data to the IBM sizing team. There the data is analyzed and a report is generated, which is then sent back to the customer. The tool is independent of the hardware used and also supports mixed environments including OS/390 and AS/400. Check http://www.ibm.com/erp/sap/insight for additional information.

4.4 Disk layouts

One of the basic differences between a non-clustered SAP installation and a clustered SAP installation is strict separation of R/3 files and DBMS files on different shared disks. MSCS uses the *shared nothing* architecture, which means that each system accesses its own disk resources (that is, the systems logically share nothing at any time). Because DBMS and R/3 services run on different nodes during normal operation, their disk space must not intersect. Thus more disks are needed in clustered R/3 systems where DBMS and R/3 directories must reside on different disks.

Throughout this redbook, the term *Windows NT disk n* means the *disk n* we observe in the Windows NT Disk Administrator window. This may be:

- A single physical disk (not recommended)
- A RAID disk array

- A subdivision of a RAID disk array (so-called logical drive or logical unit)

For more details on specific advantages and limitations of SCSI or Fibre Channel disk subsystems, please refer to 4.5, "Typical SCSI RAID controller configurations" on page 101 and 4.6, "Fibre Channel configurations" on page 104.

Only the local disks contain the operating system and page file. Data redundancy for local disks may be achieved with hardware RAID. MSCS currently does not support software RAID for shared disks, so a certified cluster solution with hardware RAID must be used. Shared disks are needed for:

- MSCS quorum
- R/3 files
- DBMS data and log files (here the details differ for the specific DBMS)

> **Convention**
>
> Throughout this book, you will find references to the usual conventions; <SID> denotes the three-character SAP system identification code.

4.4.1 Operating system

MSCS requires that the operating system files (including page files) are placed on non-shared disks. We recommend you configure two separate Windows NT disks for the following reasons:

- R/3 assumes large page files (four times the amount of RAM for a standard installation, five times the amount of RAM for a cluster installation). Separating page file I/O from system file access may improve performance.
- For fast system repair and recovery, a second copy of the operating system (so-called emergency system) should be installed.

At a minimum, you should use four hard disk drives in two separate RAID-1 arrays:

- Because page files have a write/read ratio of 50% or more, placing them on RAID-5 arrays would decrease performance.
- To ensure fast recovery even in the case of losing more than one hard disk drive, the second copy of Windows NT should be installed on a RAID array different from that of the production system.

Using only two large hard disk drives or combining all drives in a single RAID array would not reach our objectives. For these disks, hardware RAID must be used for SCSI clustering configuration and Fibre Channel configuration.

> **Windows NT page file**
>
> SAP recommends you create a combined Windows NT page file of four times the RAM amount for non-cluster configuration, and five times the amount for cluster configuration. However, on Windows NT, as well as on Windows 2000, each page file has an upper size limit of 4 GB. You therefore may need multiple page files on different disks. For performance reasons, it is recommended that you install each page file on a separate physical disk.

According to these considerations, we should have the following disk layout on both cluster nodes (Table 7):

Table 7. Windows NT disk layout recommendations

Disk Name and Letter		Purpose	Disk Type
Windows NT disk 0	C:\ (4 GB)	• Windows NT 4.0 EE production operating system • Oracle: complete software in \ORANT • Microsoft SQL Server: client software • DB2 UDB software in \SQLLIB • Client for backup software (production) • System management software • SapCluster directory	Two internal disk drives 9.1 GB in a RAID-1 array with two logical drives
	E:\ (5 GB)	Page file #2 (up to 4 GB)	
Windows NT disk 1	D:\ (4 GB)	• Second copy of operating system • Client for backup software (recovery)	Two internal or external disk drives 9.1 GB in a RAID-1 array with two logical drives
	F:\ (5 GB)	Page file #1 (up to 4 GB)	
Windows NT disk 2	G:\ (4 GB)	Page file #3 (up to 4 GB)	9.1 GB internal or external disk drives in RAID-1 array
Windows NT disk 3	H:\ (4 GB)	Page file #4 (up to 4 GB)	
Windows NT disk 4		Additional disk for Page file #5 (up to 4 GB) if you follow the five-times-RAM recommendation.	
No Name		Hot Spare	9.1 GB disk drive

According to Microsoft terminology we must distinguish the system partition, that is the partition containing NTDETECT.COM, NTLDR, BOOT.INI, from the boot partition, that is the partition containing NTOSKRNL.EXE as well as many other files.

During Windows NT installation, it is not possible to create a system partition larger than 4 GB. One way around this problem is to install the physical disk in another server already running NT, format a partition on the disk with the NTFS file system and then move the disk back to the cluster node. Then you can use the newly created partition as the system partition. Why would a system partition larger than 4 GB be required? If Windows NT has a kernel mode stop error and the setting write debugging information to: %SystemRoot%\memory.dmp is enabled, as a consequence of a stop screen the contents of memory is written to the pagefile and after the reboot the content of the pagefile is copied to the MEMORY.DMP file. This file can then be examined in order to understand what happened to the system.

It is very important in a high availability environment to be able to determine the reason for the stop screen, because problems should be understood, not simply bypassed. In order to allow the memory dump process to work a page file as large as the RAM (plus 1 MB) must exist on the system partition (see Knowledge Base article Q197379).

Hence if the server has a very large memory, for instance 4 GB, a page file of 4 GB should be created on the system partition. Large partitions can be created exploiting the above-described workaround, but due to limitations of the partition table, PC Architecture (BIOS INT 13), and Windows NT, the system partition cannot be larger than 7.8 GB (see Knowledge Base article Q114841). This limitation can be overcome exploiting the extended translation feature available on some RAID adapters.

Not all the Windows NT disks described in Table 7 on page 87 have to be created always. The configuration will depend on the hardware model and RAM amount installed. Each model has a different number of hot-swap bays for hard disk drives and a different maximum RAM size.

Windows NT disk 0

- Partition C:

  We use this primary NTFS partition for the production Windows NT 4.0 Enterprise Edition operating system (called boot partition).

Partitions

To avoid any confusion with the drive letter assignment for each partition, we recommend you use only primary partitions. The Windows NT 4.0 installation procedure does not allow a second primary partition on Windows NT disk 0.

You first create a primary partition (C:) on Windows NT disk 0 to be used as system partition for the Standby OS, and a primary partition (D:) on Windows NT disk 1 to be used as boot partition for the Standby OS. Then you install the Standby OS on D:. Using the Standby OS you can create a second primary partition on Windows NT disk 0 (E:) and a second primary partition on Windows NT disk 1 (F:).

Then you can reboot and install the Active OS on drive C. This partition will be the system partition as well as the boot partition for the Active OS.

- Partition E:

  This partition contains only a second page file (the primary page file is stored on the F: partition). It will be used if the page file total size has to be greater than the 4 GB installed on F:.

Windows NT disk 1

- Partition D:

  We use this drive as an emergency (or backup) Windows NT (NTFS, primary partition). Configuring an emergency Windows NT is good installation practice and recommended by SAP. To avoid as many problem sources as possible, this system should be configured as a stand-alone NT server, and it should not contain any software that is not absolutely necessary for basic recovery operations.

- Partition F:

  This drive contains the primary page file up to 4 GB. If the page file size has to be greater, partition E: has to be used for a total size up to 8 GB. Beyond this value, more disks in RAID-1 arrays have to be added.

The advantages of using two Windows NT installations on two different disks are higher availability and faster recovery. If disk 0 fails we can boot from (the already present and configured) disk 1 (with a Windows NT formatted diskette and some necessary, basic Windows NT files). We are able to fix driver, registry, and other problems on disk 0, or we immediately start a full restore from a previous offline backup to disk 0. For more details on Windows NT availability and recovery, see the redbook *Windows NT Backup and Recovery with ADSM*, SG24-2231.

4.4.1.1 Overcoming the 4 GB RAM barrier

Being a 32-bit operating system, each Windows NT 4.0 process has a 4 GB virtual address space. The Windows NT executive component Virtual Memory Manager maps this virtual address space to the available physical RAM and if required, parts of the page files. Due to limitations of the original Pentium architecture, no more than 4 GB of physical memory has been accessible to the Window NT operating system.

Moreover, in each process, only kernel mode threads can get access to the entire 4 GB virtual memory space, while user mode threads can get access only to 2 GB of virtual memory (3 GB, if 4 GB tuning is used on Windows NT 4.0 Enterprise Edition;, see 5.6.3, "4 GB tuning" on page 138).

This is a severe constraint for applications that require large amounts of memory for buffering as in ERP and Data Warehouse environments. To bypass this limitation, more recent Intel microprocessors (such as the Xeon) offer a 36-bit address mechanism allowing up to 64 GB of RAM. The problem is that Windows NT Virtual Memory Manager is not able to address memory above 4 GB, because it is still based on 32-bit addresses.

In order to exploit the extra memory offered by modern servers, Intel has developed a driver, called PSE36 driver, allowing Windows NT 4.0 to use all the memory available on the server (up to 64 GB). The driver works by intercepting memory requests and copying the memory pages above 4 GB into an address range below 4 GB. This is clearly an expensive activity for the CPU. A faster access to memory above 4 GB will be available with Windows 2000. Indeed, the new release of the Microsoft operating system will be able to exploit Intel Page Address Extensions (PAE) architecture. That means that the server will be able to use up to 64 GB of RAM.

It is important to understand that Windows 2000 is still a 32-bit operating system and that each process still has a 4 GB virtual address space, but now the Virtual Memory Manager can map the virtual memory areas of all the processes to a physical memory of up to 64 GB.

Due to commercial policy choices made by Microsoft, the Windows 2000 Advanced Server operating system will be able to exploit no more than 8 GB of RAM. The high-end version of Windows 2000 (Windows 2000 Datacenter Server) will be able to exploit up to 32 GB of RAM. No technical reasons exist for the 32 GB constraint. This limitation seems to be due to the lack of servers based on the Intel microprocessor platform that support 64 GB RAM. So with the Datacenter Server release we can expect to be able to exploit up to 64 GB RAM. For details on how the Windows NT 4.0 Virtual Memory Manager works, see the Intel presentation *Beyond 4GB: Extended Server Memory Architecture* (available from http://www.intel.com) and David A. Salomon, *Inside Windows NT*, 2nd Edition.

The described memory constraint is now the main limitation of the Intel-Windows platform. The unsatisfactory performance on integer and floating point calculations of Intel microprocessors, compared to RISC microprocessors, is relevant only for few applications (for instance scientific applications and OLAP servers), while the memory limitation is especially a constraint on ERP and Data Warehouse systems. This limitation will be largely overcome with the next release of Intel IA-64 architecture and Windows 64-bit operating systems.

These servers with large physical memory create new problems for SAP systems. It becomes more and more difficult to satisfy the page file requirements with about five times RAM - particularly due to the limitation of

Windows NT/Windows 2000 not allowing you to create a page file larger than 4095 MB on a single partition.

The size of the pag efile is a very controversial topic. According to Robert E. Parkinson, author of *Basis Administration for SAP* by Prima Publishing:

> Sizing swap space is a very controversial subject. Three times the available memory is sometimes too much and other times not enough. SAP suggests a minimum of 1 GB of swap space. It is confusing. The bottom line is you do not want the system run out of swap space. Remember always to configure enough swap space for extraordinary circumstances, not for the norm. Play it safe: For systems with less than 512 MB memory install a minimum of 1 GB swap space; use the three-times-memory formula for systems with memory up to 2 GB, and for systems with more than 2 GB it will mostly depend on the behavior of the application. Only add swap space if the system needs it and you are sure that the system will consume all the available swap space. A formula you can use for systems with more than 2 GB memory is *Memory+2 GB*.

Drive letters in Windows NT

Whatever the database or the disk subsystem technology used, only a limited number of Windows NT partitions can be created, one for each of the 26 letters of the alphabet. This can be a critical weakness for a very large database, as half of the letters are already in use by system files, SAP software, or database logs.

Therefore, the Windows NT partitioning and number of arrays for the data files should be created carefully, taking into consideration the limitation of both SCSI and Fibre Channel. See 4.5, "Typical SCSI RAID controller configurations" on page 101 and 4.6, "Fibre Channel configurations" on page 104 for detailed explanations about these limitations.

4.4.2 Shared external drives

The shared disks are configured as follows.

4.4.2.1 Quorum

MSCS requires a shared quorum disk to arbitrate for access in the case of connection loss between the cluster nodes. Quorum and log information is stored in the directory tree \MSCS. Per the SAP R/3 installation guide, SAP recommends that no R/3 or data files should be stored on the quorum disk for safety reasons (so as not to put the disk offline by accident and not to have space problems if the data files grow too large). The ownership of the quorum disk determines which node is the master of the cluster and controls the cluster configuration.

When using a Fibre Channel RAID controller, as the quorum files are very small (100 KB), it is possible to create two logical units (LUNs) on the same RAID-1 array, if the controller supports this. The MSCS quorum file can be stored on the first LUN, and the SAP software (\USR\SAP) can be installed on the other LUN without any problem. This configuration may not be possible when a SCSI RAID controller is used. It is, for example, not supported in an IBM ServeRAID configuration, since you cannot have multiple logical drives configured in a shared RAID array.

4.4.2.2 SAP R/3 files

The R/3 files (system-global software and profile directories, instance-specific directories, and central transport directory) must reside on a shared Windows NT disk different from the quorum and the data files disks.

The main directory on this disk is \USR\SAP. The cluster File Share resources SAPMNT and SAPLOC, which are part of the SAP cluster group, point to this directory.

In an MSCS environment, you cannot store any database related files on this disk, because this disk is a requirement for the SAP application server.

4.4.2.3 Oracle files

The DBMS data and log files must reside on shared Windows NT disks different from the quorum and the R/3 disk. There are recommendations for Oracle and SQL Server and DB2 to distribute the files over several RAID arrays for security and performance reasons. These are discussed in the following sections.

The Oracle software home directory (default is \ORANT) will be installed locally on each cluster node. A natural choice for placing this directory is the production Windows NT operating system partition (in our disk layout, C: on Windows NT disk 0). The redo log files and the Oracle FailSafe repository are on shared disks.

Redo logs are fundamentally Oracle transaction logs. Oracle organizes logs in redo log groups containing identical copies of the logs. One of the copies is the original log while the other is the mirrored log. The Oracle LGWR (Log Writer) process writes simultaneously on both files. The purpose is to have a backup of log files to be used if there is any problem with the original logs.

Since both these log files are continuously written by the LGWR process it is important that they be put on different disks.

Once Oracle fills one of the log files, a log switch is performed, that is, the LGWR process starts to write to the log files in another log group. Simultaneously the ARCH (Archiver) background process starts to copy the logs from the filled redo log group to the archive directory (SAP archive). The archiving is necessary because when the LGWR has exhausted all the redo log groups, the next log switch brings it back to the original redo log group and then it begins to overwrite the original log. Thus, to avoid losing the data in the logs, it is necessary to archive them. Since the ARCH process reads the data from the log directories while the LGWR is writing to the log directories, it is important to have more than one redo log group. In this way while ARCH is reading from one log file on one disk, the LGWR is writing to a second log file on a different disk. For the same reason, it is important to have a dedicated SAP archive. The ARCH can write data on the archive disk without competing with the LGWR for the I/O resources.

During the installation, R3Setup creates four redo log groups having the structure shown in Table 8:

Table 8. Redo log groups

Redo Log Group name	Log files
11	ORILOGA MIRRORLOGA
12	ORILOGB MIRRORLOGB
13	ORILOGA MIRRORLOGA
14	ORILOGB MIRRORLOGB

For the reasons explained above, it is important to have at least groups 11 and 13 in a separate physical disk from the one containing groups 12 and 14.

For further details see:

- *Oracle Architecture* by S. Bobrowski, Chapter 10
- *Oracle 8 Tuning* by M. J. Corey et al., Chapter 3

The Oracle DBWR (Database Writer) process gains access to data and indexes simultaneously. Hence it is fundamental to create different tablespaces for data and indexes and store them on different disks. Besides this basic tuning rule, a second fundamental rule says that you must try to put the most often used tables on different disks. SAP R/3 4.5B tries to satisfy these requirements by creating 27 different tablespaces scattered among the six SAPDATA directories.

If you have exactly six different disks for the SAPDATA directories, the data and indexes are correctly distributed according to the above-mentioned rules. If you have more space available, you can further improve the default distribution.

If you have less than six disks you can try to improve the R3Setup distribution of tablespaces. If large amount of customer data is expected, SAP recommends that you store at least the four following tablespaces on separate disks:

Table 9. Tablespaces

Tablespace	Default data file
PSAPSTABD	SAPDATA5
PSAPSTABI	SAPDATA6
PSAPBTABD	SAPDATA3
PSAPBTABI	SAPDATA6

If, for performance reasons, you need a nondefault data file distribution, you can customize the configuration manually by modifying the R3Setup control file CENTRALDB.R3S.

For further details see:

• *Oracle 8 Tuning* by M. J. Corey et al., Chapter 3

To ensure that no data is lost in a single disk or RAID array failure, the following three groups of Oracle files should be on different shared RAID arrays:

• Data files (tablespace files)
• At least one set (original or mirrored) of online redo log files
• Archived redo log files

In its OSS notes, SAP still recommends Oracle software mirroring for the database online redo log files, even if hardware mirroring is already provided. The technical reason for this recommendation is unknown and may be just a relic from the times when hardware mirroring was not available or not affordable. To avoid controversy and because of support implications, we advise using Oracle mirroring of online redo log files.

Another Oracle-specific directory that has to reside on a shared Windows NT disk is the Oracle FailSafe Repository (directory \ORANT\FailSafe). It is used to store information (50-100 MB) about the Oracle databases in the cluster that are configured for failover (in an SAP MSCS cluster, this is only the R/3 database). Because of cluster resource dependencies, the Oracle FailSafe Repository must reside on a disk that will belong to the Oracle cluster resource group. The OracleAgent80<virtual_DB_name> MSCS resource depends on the Oracle FailSafe Repository as well as on the Oracle <SID> Network Name resource. Thus the Oracle FailSafe Repository disk belongs to the Oracle resource group.

You may place this directory on any Windows NT disk used for Oracle data or log files, or configure a separate shared disk for clarity.

For more details on different configurations see the SAP manuals *R/3 Installation on Windows NT-Oracle Database, Release 4.5B* (SAP product number 51005499, May 1999) and *Conversion to Microsoft Cluster Server: Oracle, Release 4.0B 4.5A 4.5B (SAP product number 51005504) (May 1999)*.

Recommended disk configuration

The following disk configuration is not the only possible layout, but is an optimal one based on Oracle, SAP and Microsoft recommendations for excellent level of security and performance.

Table 10. Oracle / MSCS recommended disk layout

Disk Name and Letter		Purpose	Disk Type
Windows NT disk 4	I:\ Quorum	\MSCS	2 disk drives in a RAID-1 array with 1 logical drive[1]
Windows NT disk 5	J:\ SAPExe	\USR\SAP	2 disk drives in a RAID-1 array with 1 logical drive
Windows NT disk 6	K:\ DBLog	\ORACLE\<SID>\orilogA \ORACLE\<SID>\mirrorlogB \ORACLE\<SID>\sapbackup \ORACLE\<SID>\sapcheck	2 disk drives in a RAID-1 array with 1 logical drive

Disk Name and Letter		Purpose	Disk Type
Windows NT disk 7	L:\ ArchLog	\ORACLE\<SID>\orilogB \ORACLE\<SID>\mirrlogA \ORACLE\<SID>\sapreorg \ORACLE\<SID>\saptrace	2 disk drives in a RAID-1 array with 1 logical drive
Windows NT disk 8	M:\ SAPArch	\ORACLE\<SID>\saparch \ORANT\FailSafe	2 disk drives in a RAID-1 array with 1 logical drive
Windows NT disk 9,....etc	N:\ ,...etc Data	\ORACLE\<SID>\sapdata1	Number of drives depends on the database size: RAID-1, RAID-1E, RAID-5 or RAID-5E
		\ORACLE\<SID>\sapdata2	
		\ORACLE\<SID>\sapdata3	
		\ORACLE\<SID>\sapdata4	
		\ORACLE\<SID>\sapdata5	
		\ORACLE\<SID>\sapdata6	
No Name		Hot Spare	Same disk drives as the larger one
Note: 1 For Fibre Channel disk subsystems, see note " Logical units and MSCS" on page 109			

Ten disk drives, organized in five arrays, are used for installing the MSCS quorum, SAP R/3 files, and all the online and archived redo logs. The DB data files can be stored on as many drives as necessary, depending on the database size.

For better performance, we recommend you create only RAID-1 arrays when using SCSI RAID controllers, rather than RAID-5. If your RAID controller supports write-back cache for shared disks, you can use RAID-5 arrays as well for the database data files.

When using Fibre Channel controllers, with mirrored caches external to the servers (and cache consistency is ensured independent of server failures), RAID-5 performance with write-back caching is comparable to RAID-1 when using large RAID-5 arrays.

Log files

Database data files and both sets of online redo log files should always be distributed over different physical disks. As the online redo logs are written synchronously, they produce the most I/O activity of all database files.

In large configurations, this activity can become critical. The recommendation is then to add two new RAID-1 arrays to physically separate the active online logs A and B, as well as the mirrored logs A and B.

4.4.2.4 IBM DB2 files

DB2 UDB Enterprise Edition has to be installed locally on both nodes. The standard directory is C:\SQLLIB. The conversion into a clustered database is done after the regular R/3 installation. The clustered DB2 instance stored in the directory \DB2PROFS and the databases <SID> and ADM<SID> all need to be installed on a shared drive.

The database data files, the active database logs, and the archived database logs have to be stored on different NT disks to avoid that data is lost or at least the amount of data lost is minimized in the case of a RAID array failure.

The disk holding the active database logs is the disk with the largest number of synchronous disk writes. Try to connect this disk to a channel or adapter with low load. We recommend that you separate this disk at least from the one storing the archived database logs, because every time the DB2 user exit process is started, a log file is copied from the active log files disk to the archived log files disk, while the database is writing new log file data to the active log files disk.

In a cluster configuration, it is not possible to store the archived database logs on the same drive as the R/3 executables, as is often done in non-clustered R/3 installations with DB2. The DB2 user exit process, responsible for moving log files to the archived log directory, is always started on the machine running the database instance. If the R/3 server is running on the other node, the DB2 user exit process has no access to the drive with the R/3 executables.

Figure 26 shows this configuration. The DB2 RDBMS runs on Node B and controls the database <SID>, the active database log files, and the invocation of the DB2 user exit (DB2UE). When a database log file becomes inactive, the RDBMS calls the DB2UE (1). The DB2UE in turn copies the database log file from the active logs disk to the archived logs disk (2) and notifies the

DBMS of the successful copy operation. The DBMS then deletes the original database log file (3) when it is not needed any more.

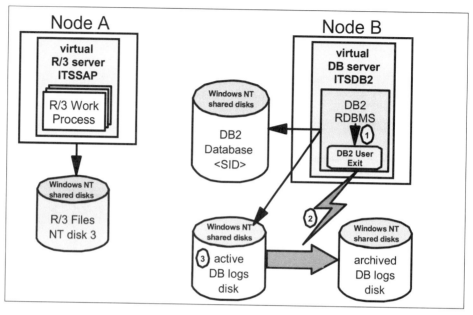

Figure 26. Database log archives must be separate from R/3 binaries

Recommended Disk Configuration

The maximum number of RAID-1 arrays to be configured for the database data should not exceed six for a new installation, because R3Setup offers only the distribution of SAPDATA1-SAPDATA6 to different Windows NT disks. You can add additional drives later as needed.

If you want to use more than six disks you can also edit the R3Setup file CENTRDB.R3S to redistribute the tablespaces to match your planned disk layout, but this requires some expertise.

One possible, optimal distribution of database data on different Windows NT disks is shown in Table 11:

Table 11. DB2 UDB MSCS recommended disk layout

Disk name and letter		Purpose	Disk type
Windows NT disk 4	I:\ Quorum	\MSCS	Two disk drives in a RAID-1 array with one logical drive[1]
Windows NT disk 5	J:\ SAPExe	\USR\SAP	Two disk drives in a RAID-1 array with one logical drive
Windows NT disk 6	K:\ DBLog	\DB2\<SID>\log_dir	Two disk drives in a RAID-1 array with one logical drive
Windows NT disk 7	L:\ ArchLog	\DB2\<SID>\log_archive \DB2<SID>\saprest \DB2\<SID>\sapreorg \db2rsd \DB2PROFS\db2rsd \DB2\<SID>\saparch	Two disk drives in a RAID-1 array with one logical drive
Windows NT disk 8, etc.	M:\ ,etc. Data	\DB2\<SID>\sapdata1	Number of drives depends on the database size: RAID-1, RAID-1E, RAID-5 or RAID-5E
		\DB2\<SID>\sapdata2	
		\DB2\<SID>\sapdata3	
		\DB2\<SID>\sapdata4	
		\DB2\<SID>\sapdata5	
		\DB2\<SID>\sapdata6	
No Name		Hot Spare	Same disk drives as the larger one

Note:
1 For Fibre Channel disk subsystems, see note " Logical units and MSCS" on page 109

For large databases, two Fibre Channel RAID controller units may be useful.

4.4.2.5 SQL Server 7.0 files

The DBMS data and log files must reside on shared Windows NT disks different from the quorum and the R/3 disk.

The SQL Server database software consists of a *server* and a *client* part. The client software must be installed locally on each cluster node (default directory: \MSSQL). A natural choice for placing this directory is the production Windows NT operating system partition (in our disk layout, C: on Windows NT disk 0). The server part of the software (default is another \MSSQL directory), the SQL Server master database, and the container files with application data and logs (called SQL Server *devices*) are on shared disks.

To ensure that no data is lost in a single disk or RAID array failure, the following three types of SQL Server devices should be on different shared RAID disk arrays:

- Data devices
- Log devices
- TEMP device

Table 12. SQL Server 7 MSCS recommended disk layout

Disk name and letter		Purpose	Disk type
Windows NT disk 4	I:\ Quorum	\MSCS	Two disk drives in a RAID-1 array with one logical drive[1]
Windows NT disk 5	J:\ SAPExe	\usr\sap	Two disk drives in a RAID-1 array with one logical drive
Windows NT disk 6	K:\ SQLSrv	\MSSQL \TEMPDB\TEMPDB.DAT	Two disk drives in a RAID-1 array with one logical drive
Windows NT disk 7	L:\ SQLLog	\<SID>LOG<n>\<SID>LOG<n>.DAT	Two disk drives in a RAID-1 array with one logical drive
Windows NT disk 8,etc.	M:\ ,etc. Data	\<SID>DATA<n>\<SID>DATA<n>.DAT	Number of drives depends on the database size: RAID-1, RAID-1E, RAID-5 or RAID-5E
		\<SID>DATA<n>\<SID>DATA<n>.DAT	
		\<SID>DATA<n>\<SID>DATA<n>.DAT	
		\<SID>DATA<n>\<SID>DATA<n>.DAT	
		\<SID>DATA<n>\<SID>DATA<n>.DAT	
		\<SID>DATA<n>\<SID>DATA<n>.DAT	
No Name		Hot Spare	Same disk drives as the larger one
Note: 1 For Fibre Channel disk subsystems, see note " Logical units and MSCS" on page 109			

Four arrays are necessary for the software installation on the shared disks. For large databases, two Fibre Channel RAID controller units may be useful.

4.4.2.6 FTP area

Some systems need an FTP area to be used to download files from the
legacy systems. FTP transfers can be done using Microsoft Internet
Information Server. Since this application is cluster aware, it can be installed
on the shared drives in order to exploit Microsoft Cluster Server protection.
For performance and security reasons, we recommend you use dedicated
drives for this activity.

4.5 Typical SCSI RAID controller configurations

This section introduces the MSCS configuration using a SCSI RAID disk
subsystem. We only provide the configuration plan.

4.5.1 SAP R/3 disk configurations

With respect to the rules for R/3 cluster configuration as explained in 4.4,
"Disk layouts" on page 84, usage of different disk types makes sense.

- Since SAP recommends that no R/3 or data files be stored on the MSCS
  quorum disk (as described in 4.4.2.1, "Quorum" on page 91), small drives
  are appropriate. The quorum disk has no influence on cluster performance
  during normal operation. MSCS data takes up few megabytes. Thus a
  RAID-1 array of two 4.5 GB disks is sufficient.

- For the volume containing the \USR\SAP directory tree, a 4.5 GB or 9.1
  GB RAID-1 array fulfills the needs. Using fast disks (10,000 RPM) may
  improve performance on R/3 systems with many context switches (rollfile
  and page file usage).

- The database online log files are not large but critical for security and
  response time. Thus these volumes should be placed on RAID-1 arrays of
  fast disks. The size depends on any additional database directories placed
  there.

- Database archived log files are only written once in background. Disk
  speed will influence R/3 performance only if a very large amount of log
  data must be archived quickly. The disk space necessary depends on the
  number of transactions between scheduled backups. Heavy loaded

systems without daily full backup require large archives. A RAID-1 array of the necessary size should be configured.

- Data files may be stored on RAID-1 or RAID-5 arrays. Because of the large database size in R/3 systems, 9.1 GB and 18.2 GB disk drives are preferred. The number of physical disk drives used for the data files should be as large as possible for optimum performance, but should be small enough to allow for easy extension of available disk space in the case the database size is outgrowing the available disk size.

- Other cluster-specific restrictions for the SCSI RAID adapters may need to be considered. As an example, the restrictions of the IBM ServeRAID adapter are shown here. SCSI RAID adapters from other hardware vendors will have different restrictions.

  - The unit of failover is the physical array. Only one ServeRAID logical drive can be created per shared physical array.

  - The maximum number of logical drives per adapter is eight before or after a failover. A failover will not complete if this number is exceeded. Note that this limit includes shared and nonshared logical drives. Thus the maximum number of shared logical drives per adapter pair is eight minus the largest number of nonshared logical drives from the adapters.

  - RAID-0 and RAID-1 logical drives may fail over in normal or critical state. But the ServeRAID adapters do not allow failover of RAID-5 logical drives that are in critical state (that is, one drive in the RAID-5 array has failed). For this reason, you should not use RAID-5 for the quorum disk.

  - Hot-spare drives are not shared between the adapters in a pair. Each ServeRAID adapter must have its own hot-spare drive(s) defined. All hot-spare drives must be connected to shared channels so that, if the hot-spare is used to replace a failed shared disk, the disk can be accessed from either node in case a failover occurs later.

  - Compared with a non-clustered SAP R/3 installation with ServeRAID adapters, as a rule of thumb, in a cluster you will need two additional RAID-1 arrays with two disks each, and you have to double the number of hot-spare drives.

4.5.2 Cluster configuration

Figure 27 shows a sample of a SCSI-based Microsoft Cluster Server configuration using the IBM ServeRAID-3 and the IBM EtherJet (Ethernet 10/100) adapter:

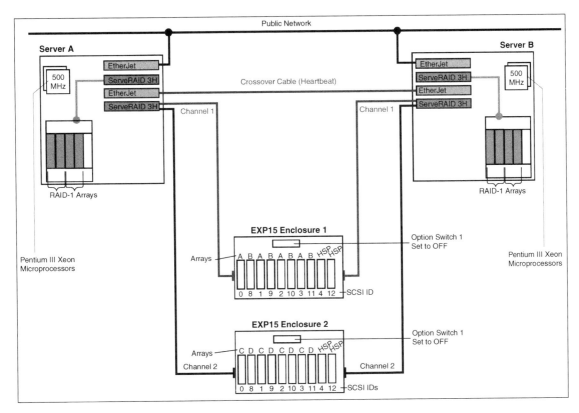

Figure 27. SCSI-based MSCS configuration

There are two network adapters configured in Figure 27, but there can be more, depending on your networking requirements. We discuss this in 4.7, "Network configurations" on page 110.

4.5.3 SCSI tuning recommendations

This section presents some suggested optimization parameters for the SAP cluster to achieve its optimum performance.

The SCSI RAID controllers have tuning parameters that have significant impact on database server performance. SAP R/3 requires mirroring of the redo logs and defaults to additional software mirroring in the case of Oracle. An array controller can implement mirroring and therefore offload the CPU from performing those tasks. The stripe size of the controller must closely match the block size of the application. For example, an Oracle database can use 2 KB, 4 KB, or 8 KB blocks for the tables and would give the best performance using 8 KB stripe size on the controller.

Turning the Read Ahead function off on the array controller will also benefit users in the SAP R/3 write-intensive workload.

Additionally, performance improvements can be achieved with the following settings, if they are available on the SCSI RAID adapter used:

- Configure two separate SCSI RAID adapters:

    - One for the local disks containing the operating system and page files
    - One for the shared disks containing the database files

- Set the stripe sizes as follows:

    - 64 KB for the local disks containing the page files (best performance for the page files)
    - 8 KB for the shared disks or larger depending on the native database block sizes used

- Set Read Ahead as follows:

    - On for the local disks
    - Off for the shared disks, especially for the disks containing the database files

- Set the cache policy as follows:

    - Write-through for all shared disks (set it to write-back if your RAID controller supports this in a cluster configuration)
    - Write-back for all local disks

Please refer to 10.3, "Database tuning" on page 259 for a discussion on how to tune the RDBMS being used in the installed SAP R/3 environment:

4.6 Fibre Channel configurations

Fibre Channel is an emerging storage technology that overcomes many of the limitations of SCSI. Like SSA and Enterprise Systems Connection (ESCON), S/390 channel connectivity, Fibre Channel is based on the idea of storage networks to which servers may attach, avoiding the problems of traditional bus topologies. Fibre Channel received great market awareness even when it was not available for production usage. It is considered the future solution for large-scale storage requirements.

Fibre Channel supports data transfer rates of 100 Mbps on copper and optical interfaces. A copper interface is used for short connections (less than 30 meters); a multimode short-wave optical interface is used for intermediate distances (less than 500 meters); and a single-mode long-wave optical interface is used for long distances (up to 10 kilometers). Three topology types are defined:

- Point-to-Point. Two Fibre Channel nodes (for example, server and storage subsystem) are directly connected.
- Arbitrated Loop (FC-AL). Up to 126 Fibre Channel devices may be attached.
- Switched Fabric. Multiple FC-ALs may be served by a switch.

4.6.1 Components of a Fibre Channel solution

Fibre Channel solutions consist of the following key components:

- Fibre Channel PCI adapters
- Fibre Channel RAID controller units
- Fibre Channel Hub, Gigabit Interface Converter (GBIC) options (short-wave and long-wave), short-wave optical cables
- External disk subsystem controlled by the Fibre Channel RAID controller unit

4.6.1.1 Fibre Channel PCI adapter

The adapter is necessary to connect Netfinity servers to the Fibre Channel network. But in contrast to the SCSI RAID adapter, the Fibre Channel PCI Adapter does not provide any RAID functionality. All RAID functions are performed by the Fibre Channel RAID controller unit.

4.6.1.2 Fibre Channel RAID controller unit

The Fibre Channel RAID controller unit provides the RAID functionality. It controls and owns the physical disks, either in SCSI or native Fibre Channel technology.

Each RAID array is shown to the servers as one or more *logical units* (LUN=logical unit number). LUNs are parts of a RAID array. A LUN is, from the operating system's point of view, similar to a logical drive on a SCSI RAID array, although the implementation at the SCSI protocol layer is different. Windows NT treats the LUN as one Windows NT disk.

Each LUN can fail over independently from other LUNs sharing the same RAID array. All LUNs are completely independent.

4.6.1.3 Fibre Channel hub

A Fibre Channel hub is required when more than two devices (also called *nodes*) should be connected as a Fibre Channel Arbitrated Loop (FC-AL).

Without a hub, failure of one device would break the loop because there is no redundancy in an FC-AL. The hub ensures that the loop topology is maintained. Each hub port receives serial data from an attached Fibre Channel node and retransmits the data out of the next hub port to the next node attached in the loop. This includes data regeneration (both signal timing and amplitude) supporting full distance optical links. The hub detects any Fibre Channel loop node that is missing or is inoperative and automatically routes the data to the next operational port and attached node in the loop.

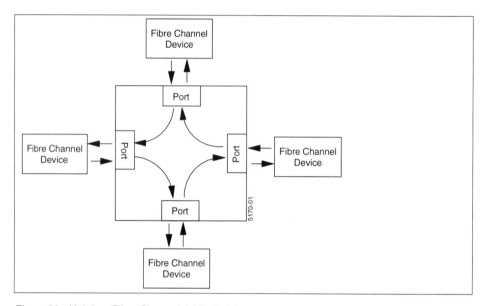

Figure 28. Hub in a Fibre Channel Arbitrated Loop

4.6.2 Cluster configurations with Fibre Channel components

The basic cluster configuration using Fibre Channel consists of two servers and a RAID controller unit connected to a hub. Figure 29 shows a typical complete configuration using IBM Netfinity hardware. Solutions from other hardware vendors will differ, but the basic required parts will be the same.

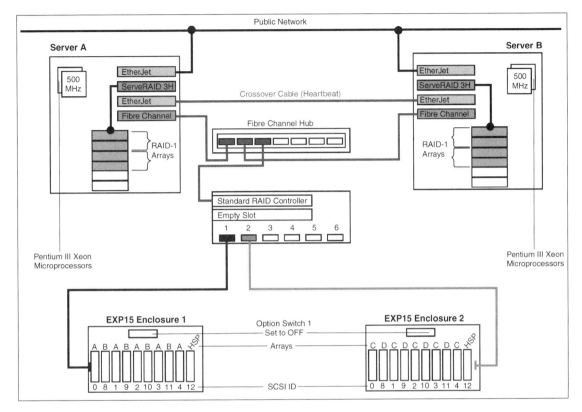

Figure 29. Simple Fibre Channel/MSCS configuration

Note: There are three single points of failure in this configuration:

- The RAID controller unit
- The hub
- The Fibre Channel cable between the hub and RAID controller unit

Because all access to the shared disks is operated by these components, which exist only once in the cluster, a failure of one of these components would cause both cluster servers to lose access to the shared disks. Thus all cluster disk resources would fail, and the DBMS and the R/3 processes would fail also.

The first step to avoid such situations is adding a redundant Fibre Channel FailSafe RAID Controller in the controller unit. Attaching this second controller to the hub would eliminate the first single point of failure only. To avoid having the hub or any FC cable as the critical point, a second hub is needed. With two hubs, each hub forms a separate FC loop. The RAID controllers are connected to different loops, while the servers are connected to both loops. This gives the configuration as shown in Figure 30 on page 108.

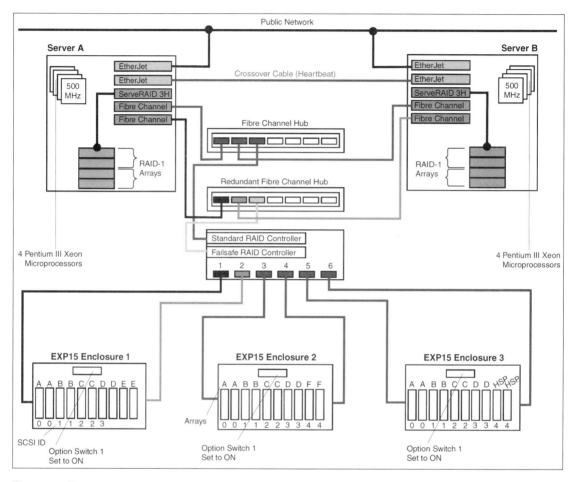

Figure 30. Fully redundant Fibre Channel/MSCS configuration

Without special precautions, the operating system would not recognize the disk access paths provided through the two Fibre Channel adapters as redundant paths to the same common set of LUNs. To ensure that the second FC adapter is considered an alternate path to the LUNs accessed by the first adapter (and vice versa), the SYMplicity Storage Manager software adds a redundant disk array controller (RDAC) driver and a resolution daemon.

This software supports a fully redundant I/O path design (adapter, cable, and RAID controller) with host-level failure recovery, transparent to applications.

The RDAC driver is not a kind of RAID software — it does not mirror between the FC loops. It ensures only Fibre Channel link integrity in the case of failure. The failing path or I/O initiator will be detected, and the backup RDAC will take its place. Because any mirroring is done by the Fibre Channel RAID Controllers between SCSI channels, this is not a method for disaster protection using FC. The maximum distance between disk drives in the same RAID-1 array is limited by LVDS SCSI cable length.

This configuration combines large disk space, high performance, and high safety. When both RAID controllers in each controller unit are set as an active/active pair, then any bottlenecks in the controllers or FC paths are avoided.

Logical units and MSCS

The concept of LUNs allows very effective use of disk space. We can combine several smaller Windows NT disks on the same RAID array using different LUNs. Because all LUNs are completely independent, these Windows NT disks may even belong to different cluster resource groups. But you should not combine such Windows NT disks as LUNs of the same RAID array, that need to be separated for data security. Failure of an array (because of multiple disk failures) causes all LUNs of that array to fail. Thus we never provide LUNs with data files and LUNs with log files from the same array.

The Fibre Channel LUNs will be configured in three different MSCS resource groups, which may fail over independently. The R/3 group (disk with the \USR\SAP directory tree), the Database group (containing all Windows NT disks with a \ORACLE\<SID> tree or \DB2\<SID> tree or the MSSQL directories, and the Oracle FailSafe Repository), and the Cluster Group (containing the Cluster Name, Cluster IP Address, and the Time Service). The Oracle FailSafe Repository may be located on any Oracle disk or on a separate partition, should not be installed on the quorum disk, as per OSS note 0112266.

The only FC topology that guarantees that no cluster component constitutes a single point of failure is using two independent loops with redundant RAID controllers, as shown in Figure 30 on page 108.

4.6.3 Fibre Channel tuning recommendations

The IBM Netfinity RAID controller unit, for example, has the following tuning parameters that have significant performance on database servers. For non-IBM controllers, check your hardware documentation for similar parameters.

- **Segment size**. You can configure the segment size (stripe size) from 16 KB up to 128 KB. The segment size of the controller must be matched closely to the block size of the application. For example, an Oracle database can use 2 KB, 4 KB, or 8 KB blocks for the tables and would give the best performance using 16 KB stripe size on the controller. However, the SAP R/3 application logic may write in 64 KB blocks and would be optimized with the array controller set to 64 KB stripes. Note that the segment size is set at the LUN level.

- **Active/active mode**. If you are using the Fibre Channel FailSafe Controller, you should set the two controllers in active/active configuration. By default, they are set up in active/passive mode, which means that the second controller is used as a passive hot-spare. We recommend active/active because it allows you to benefit from the load balancing between the controller. This feature is an advantage of the Fibre Channel technology. The 128 MB cache is split in half and mirrored between the two "sides". You can balance the LUN ownership between controllers in order to distribute the I/O for better performance.

- **Write cache**. As R/3 is a write intensive application, the write cache usage parameter should always be activated. When using the FailSafe controller, you should also consider activating the write cache mirroring (these parameters are the default).

4.7 Network configurations

In this section we introduce the basic elements of the network for a SAP installation in a Microsoft clustering on IBM Netfinity servers. This is only to provide guidelines on the general concepts and not a box-by-box description.

For an understanding of Microsoft Cluster Server (MSCS) concepts, review the chapter "Microsoft Cluster Server Concepts" in the *Microsoft Cluster Server Administrator's Guide*, \SUPPORT\BOOKS\MSCSADM.HLP on the Windows NT 4.0 Enterprise Edition CD 1.

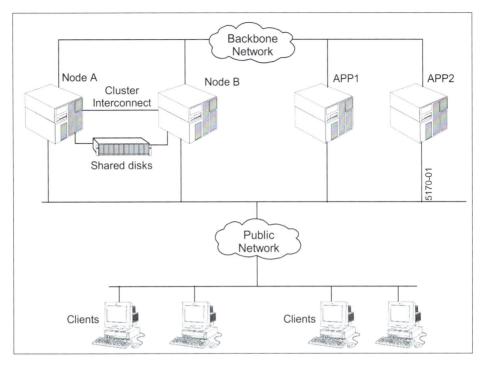

Figure 31. Network cluster configuration example

4.7.1 Components

The components that make up the network are:

- **Backbone network**

  In large R/3 systems the network adapters can cause bottlenecks and therefore the use of multiple network interface cards is recommended. The backbone network terminology is used to describe the LAN on which interserver traffic will be concentrated. This is a very fast network segment with a transport capacity of 100 Mbps or more.

  This is the preferred path for local traffic between the SAP application servers and the database server. See Chapter 9, "Backbone network" on page 233, where a more complete description can be found.

- **Public network**

  All servers and clients have a direct connection or route to this network. This will be in a routed, switched, subnetted, or bridged environment. The whole enterprise uses this network for everything from file server access to print servers, e-mail, etc. To maximize the bandwidth of the R/3 system traffic between the sapgui and dialog instances, we must be aware of the total usage and capacity of this network. In a TCP/IP network, the ideal way to handle this situation is by creating Virtual LANs (VLANs). See *Switched, Fast and Gigabit Ethernet* by Robert Breyer and Sean Riley for details on how to create a VLAN.

- **Private network**

  The term *private network* is used in many different ways. This example refers to the crossover-connected (100BaseT) heartbeat (or *interconnect*) cable. MSCS is constantly checking the status of the two nodes. The server that is in passive mode uses this cable to poll the other server as to the status of all the resources being managed in the cluster. Provided we've configured the public network to accept all communications traffic (that is, client and interconnect traffic), if this interconnect link goes down, the cluster will use the public network to do polling instead. In this way, we have two redundant paths (public and backbone) for the cluster heartbeat. If a resource fails on the active node, then through the use of this cable, the cluster knows when to fail over.

All Windows NT nodes are members of the same domain, SAPDOM. For the two Windows NT servers forming the MSCS cluster, five network names and seven static IP addresses are needed as shown in Table 13. We have also mentioned four more static IP addresses to show the connection to the backbone network:

Table 13. Network parameters for MSCS nodes

Server	NetBIOS name	DNS host name	Description	TCP/IP addresses
Windows NT server 1 (Node A)	SERVERA	servera	Preferred node for R/3 central instance (CI)	Public network: 192.168.0.1
		serverai		Private network: 10.0.0.1
		serverab		Backbone network: 172.16.0.1
Windows NT server 2 (Node B)	SERVERB	serverb	Preferred node for DBMS	Public network: 192.168.0.2
		serverbi		Private network: 10.0.0.2
		serverbb		Backbone network: 172.16.0.2
Virtual server	SAPCLUS	sapclus	Cluster alias (for MSCS administration)	Public network: 192.168.0.50

Server	NetBIOS name	DNS host name	Description	TCP/IP addresses
Virtual server	ITSSAP	itssap	R/3 alias (for connecting to the R/3 services)	Public network: 192.168.0.51
	ITSSAPB	itssapb		Backbone network: 172.16.0.51[1]
Virtual server	ITS<DBMS>	its<dbms>	DBMS alias (for connecting to the DBMS services)	Public network:192.168.0.52
	ITS<DBMS>B	its<dbms>b		Backbone network: 172.16.0.52[1]

Note 1: Details on when and how to configure the backbone addresses are provided in 5.14, "Backbone configuration" on page 162 and Chapter 4, "Hardware configuration and MSCS planning" on page 69.

Server names

The MSCS part of the SAP installation manuals uses the names *Node A* and *Node B* for the two MSCS nodes. It does not matter which node is called A and which is called B. We used the real computer names SERVERA and SERVERB from our test installation. This convention makes it easier to understand the screen captures throughout this book.

The TCP/IP HOSTS file (in directory \WINNT\SYSTEM32\DRIVERS\ETC) was used for naming resolution, containing entries for all five IP addresses on the public network.

Note that the cluster-private LAN (crossover Ethernet connection) is used for the MSCS communication only. The virtual names ITSSAP and ITS<DBMS> on the public LAN are used for user access and communication between R/3 work processes and the database. Thus the public network in our example has to handle the SAPGUI traffic (which is usually of lower volume) and the database traffic (from R/3 application servers to the DB server, which may be of very high volume). Additional bandwidth is required if backups are done via a remote backup server. A small bandwidth network will not be appropriate.

A common practice in large SAP R/3 environments is to separate the user's network (small-bandwidth public LAN) completely from the network for database access (large-bandwidth SAP backbone). You configure the SAP backbone as additional network, thus having three network interface cards in each cluster node and two network interface cards in additional R/3 application servers.

SAP recommends that during installation all settings be restricted so the entire communication runs via the normal public network. The SAP installation documentation is also formulated under this assumption. After the installation is completed, you can reconfigure the cluster so that the communication to the database is carried out via the backbone network. See 5.14, "Backbone configuration" on page 162 and Chapter 9, "Backbone network" on page 233 for details.

4.7.2 Different name resolution methods

The three most common methods used for name resolution in a Windows NT environment are:

- **DNS**

  Domain Name System (DNS) can map very complex hierarchical tree structures with a large number of host systems. This method is decentralized in its implementation. That means the entire list of all hosts are not kept on one system, only a portion of the entries, making it feasible for a search request to reply in a reasonable amount of time. A good example of the scalability of DNS is its use in the management of the Internet.

- **WINS**

  Windows Name Service (WINS) is used to dynamically map NetBIOS names (computer names) to IP addresses. The same function can be performed in the absence of a WINS server with LMHOSTS files, but these files are static and do not incorporate dynamic changes. WINS is suited to a pure Microsoft Windows environment. The advantage of WINS is its simplicity, robustness, and flexibility. The disadvantage is that WINS is only suited for smaller, flatly structured homogeneous networks.

- **HOSTS file**

  The HOSTS file is an ASCII text file that statically maps local and remote host names to IP addresses, located in %WINDIR%\system32\drivers\etc. This file is read from top to bottom and as soon as a match is found for a host name, the file stops being read. The HOSTS file is a reliable and simple solution, since all the information that is needed to resolve a name to an IP address is stored on the computer. This local administration gives very high performance. The cost of this performance is the need for a lot of maintenance if the environment is constantly changing. An example is:

  `192.168.0.1 servera node1`

  where node1 is the name of the alias.

The use of a second (mirrored) WINS or DNS server is strongly recommended.

Hint: When using a DNS server or HOSTS file with fully qualified names (for example, `server1.company.com`), you should enter the DNS domain in the Domain Suffix Search Order for the TCP/IP protocol in the Network Control Panel applet.

4.7.3 Resolve IP address to the correct host name

You now need to check which IP address will respond when SERVERA or SERVERB is pinged. Having two or more network adapters in the same server can lead to address requests resolving to the wrong IP address. In our lab setup, we assigned an IP address of 192.168.0.1 to SERVERA in the HOSTS file. When the command `PING SERVERA` is entered from a command prompt, the IP address that may be returned is 10.0.0.1, which is incorrect. The correct address should be one from the public network.

For systems with Service Pack 4 or later installed, perform the following steps on both nodes to correct the problem, as described in Microsoft Knowledge Base entry Q164023:

1. Open the Network applet in the Control Panel.

2. Click the **Bindings** tab, select **Show bindings for all protocols.** Expand **TCP/IP protocols**. This will display all network interface cards installed.

3. The solution is to change the order so the public network interface card is displayed before the private network interface card. Use the **Move Up** and **Move Down** buttons to change the order of the cards.

4. Repeat this procedure for any other TCP/IP protocols installed.

We recommend that you install Service Pack 4 or later for this reason. If you have Service Pack 3 or earlier installed, upgrade to later ones.

Note: This workaround only applies to Windows NT 4.0 computers that have multiple network adapters installed and only when it is querying the local host name. It has no effect when querying other computers on the network.

4.7.4 Redundancy in the network path

The nodes of an MSCS cluster must be connected by one or more physically independent networks (sometimes referred to as interconnects). Although MSCS clusters can function with only one interconnect, two interconnects are strongly recommended and are required for the verification of MSCS OEM systems that include both hardware and MSCS software.

Redundant, independent interconnects eliminate any single point of failure that could disrupt communication between nodes. When two nodes are unable to communicate, they are said to be partitioned. After the two nodes became partitioned, both nodes start an arbitration process for the quorum resource. This process is based on a challenge-response protocol using SCSI device reservations for the quorum disk. Because only one node can finally hold a SCSI reservation for a disk on the shared bus, this node will be the winner of the arbitration process. We cannot determine in advance which node will be the winner as it depends on the timing at the moment of partitioning. The other node will stop the cluster service (the node is still running but doesn't bring any cluster resources online).

For example, if each node has only one network adapter, and the network cable on one of the nodes fails, each node (because it is unable to communicate with the other) attempts to take control of the quorum resource. There is no guarantee that the node with a functioning network connection will gain control of the quorum resource. If the node with the failed network cable gains control, the entire cluster is unavailable to network clients. Each network can have one of four roles in a cluster. The network can support:

- Node-to-node communication, referred to as private networks
- Only client-to-cluster communication
- Both node-to-node communication and client-to-cluster communication
- No cluster-related communication

Networks that support client-to-cluster communication (either with or without supporting node-to-node communication) are referred to as public networks. We recommend that you configure the public network to be both the node-to-node and the client-to-cluster communications for added network redundancy.

Before you install the MSCS software, you must configure both nodes to use the TCP/IP protocol over all interconnects. Also, each network adapter must have an assigned static IP address that is on the same network as the corresponding network adapter on the other node. Therefore, there can be no routers between two MSCS nodes. However, routers can be placed between the cluster and its clients. If all interconnects must run through a hub, use separate hubs to isolate each interconnect.

Note: MSCS does not support the use of IP addresses assigned from a Dynamic Host Configuration Protocol (DHCP) server for the cluster administration address (which is associated with the cluster name) or any IP Address resources. You should use static IP addresses for the Windows NT network configuration on each node.

4.7.5 Auto-sensing network adapters

The latest types of Ethernet network adapters are now able to automatically sense the speed of the network. The typical speed is 10/100 Mbps and operation mode of half or full duplex. A poor cable installation can cause some ports on a 10/100 switch to have different speeds.

The solution is to not use auto-sensing and to manually configure the network interface cards to the setting of the network, for example, 100 Mbps/full duplex. The switches and hubs must be able to support the 100 Mbps full duplex type of configuration. See Knowledge Base article Q174812 for more information.

4.7.6 Redundant adapters

The use of redundant adapters is highly recommended for the public LAN connections.

Various Fast Ethernet and token-ring adapters support adapter fault tolerance (AFT), allowing two adapters to be paired inside a server in an active/passive configuration. If there is a failure of the cable, connector or primary adapter, then the backup adapter is automatically brought online to handle the traffic. This failover typically occurs in a fraction of a second, minimizing lost data and virtually eliminating down time due to adapter or cable failures.

The behavior of MSCS in the case of cable or adapter failure depends on the nature of the failure. If the adapter fails completely (in Windows NT, you will no longer see the adapter when issuing an IPCONFIG command), then the IP resources bound to that adapter also fail and will be moved to the other node, causing the group to be moved. However, disconnecting a cable doesn't constitute an adapter failure (see Microsoft Knowledge Base articles Q175767 and Q176320) and will not force MSCS to fail over any resource. This may produce a situation where all cluster resources are still online but cannot be reached by the clients.

In theory, connection loss because of cable failure may lead an application process to fail, thus forcing MSCS to follow the restart/failover policy defined for this process. But as explained in Chapter 3, "SAP R/3 and high availability" on page 37, R/3 processes will go into reconnect status. For database processes, this depends on the type of the database.

The exact behavior of a R/3 cluster in the case of a cable or adapter failure is undefined. You should always configure redundant adapters for the public LAN connections.

However, we do not recommend the use of redundant adapters for the cluster heartbeat, because the cluster heartbeat can be configured at the MSCS layer to fail over to the public LAN. Redundant heartbeat adapters could confuse the cluster. When Node A fails, the redundant adapters on Node B try to reconnect both ways. Alternately, after some timeouts one adapter will remain the primary. If Node A restarts, then the adapter on the other cable may be the primary heartbeat adapter of A. Thus both servers will not establish a connection automatically, which would require operator intervention to reset the primary/secondary adapter definitions. Again the exact behavior depends on the adapter's chipset and driver. To avoid any problem, you should not configure redundant adapters for the cluster heartbeat, but fail over to the public LAN instead.

4.7.7 Load balancing

Adapters that support load balancing enable the server to add scalable bandwidth as traffic demands grow. This feature balances outgoing server traffic across as many as four adapters of the same type, enabling server bandwidth to scale up to 800 Mbps in a full-duplex switched environment. This allows you to add bandwidth to your server as you need it using proven, cost-effective Fast Ethernet technology.

Network adapter performance can be strongly improved by using link aggregation, that is by using more network cards as a single network path. The Netfinity Ethernet Adapter for example provides two link aggregation techniques: Automatic Load Balancing (ALB) and Fast EtherChannel (FEC).

ALB allows you to use up to four network cards as a single virtual network adapter. What you get is not only link aggregation but also load balancing of the traffic. That means situations in which one card manages 90% of the traffic while the other only has 10% are avoided by the adapter driver. The ALB guarantees link aggregation and load balancing only for outgoing packets. Any Fast Ethernet switch can be used.

FEC is a proprietary Cisco technology allowing load balancing both for incoming and outgoing traffic. Again up to four adapters can be configured as a single virtual card. Only Cisco FEC switches like those of the Catalyst 5000 family can be used. Similar considerations hold for the Gigabit Ethernet adapters. They also provide two link aggregation techniques: Automatic Load Balancing and Gigabit EtherChannel (GEC). Similar considerations hold: up to four adapters can be configured as a single virtual card, but ALB only balances outgoing packets. GEC is a Cisco proprietary technology requiring Cisco switches.

Chapter 5. Installation and verification

In this chapter we describe the installation of SAP R/3 4.5B on a Microsoft cluster (Windows NT) with three main database management systems (DBMS): Oracle, DB2 UDB, and Microsoft SQL Server. The installation is described using flow charts and tables.

Windows 2000 installation

For additional information regarding the installation of SAP R/3 on Windows 2000 check the following OSS note:

0169468 - Windows 2000 support

For major references to the installation, we have used the SAP R/3 publications and OSS notes. The intent of this chapter is not to replace the original SAP documentation — rather we only want to make the installation as simple as possible. In each step we will refer to the relevant documentation.

This chapter contains a general description of the installation from the very first planning step to the final tuning phase. We provide, as much as possible, the details that are DBMS independent. DBMS-dependent installation steps are contained in the following three chapters:

- Chapter 6, "Installation using Oracle" on page 171
- Chapter 7, "Installation using DB2" on page 193
- Chapter 8, "Installation using SQL Server" on page 221

5.1 General overview of the installation process

The structure of the chapter is shown in Figure 32:

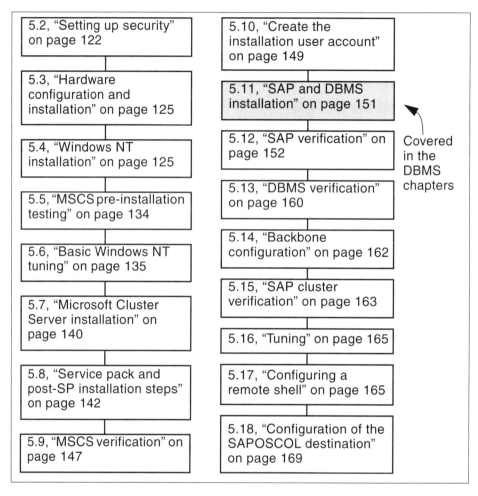

Figure 32. Overall installation process

In sections 5.4 to 5.16, the installation process is further divided into 30 steps as shown in Figure 33. Step 24 is highlighted indicating it is covered in the database chapters.

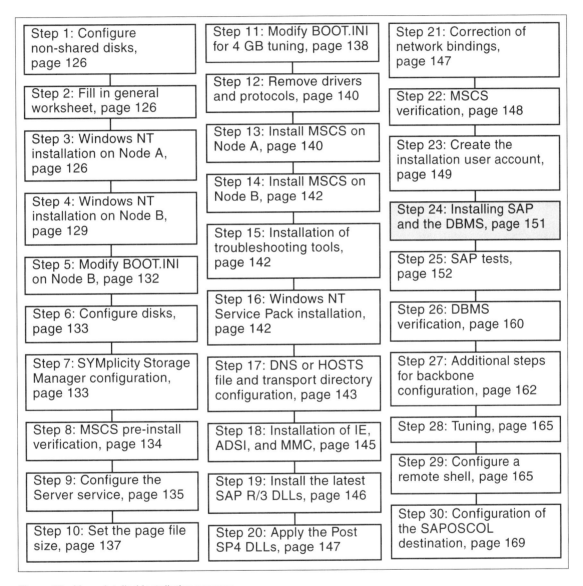

Figure 33. More detailed installation process

5.2 Setting up security

When a company decides to implement SAP its success strongly depends on how the SAP system works. The database of the SAP system is the main repository of sensitive data about customers, sales, financial activities, etc. To get into the SAP database means to have a privileged view of company activities. This can be an invaluable tool for marketing, sales, and management, but it can also be very dangerous if adequate security policies are not defined. Security is quite an obscure and delicate subject involving these main components:

- The Windows NT account databases
- The Windows NT file system
- The SAP security system
- The DBMS security system
- The network configuration

This section provides general hints and tips about the subject of planning the security of an SAP environment.

5.2.1 Windows NT security planning

As a general reference publication to be used to configure Windows NT in a secure environment, we recommend *Windows NT Security Guidelines* by Steve Sutton. Updated information about security problems in Windows NT can be found at the following Web sites:

http://www.microsoft.com/security
http://ntsecurity.ntadvice.com
http://www.trustedsystems.com

5.2.2 SAP R/3 security planning

The steps to configure SAP R/3 in a Windows NT environment to achieve the maximum level of security are fully described in the three volumes of the SAP publication, *SAP R/3 Security Guide.* As described in the second volume of the *SAP R/3 Security Guide,* it is recommended you create two different Windows NT domains. In this redbook, we call them the USERS and SAPDOM domains. The two domains are used to:

- Create the user and PC accounts in the USERS domain

- Create the SAP and DBMS fundamental server accounts in the SAPDOM domain

A broad summary of the architecture of the system with indications on network connections is shown in Figure 34:

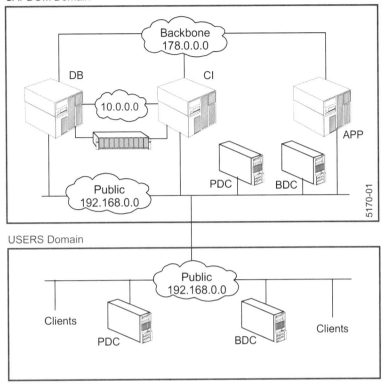

SAPDOM Domain

Backbone
178.0.0.0

DB

CI

10.0.0.0

APP

PDC

BDC

Public
192.168.0.0

5170-01

USERS Domain

Public
192.168.0.0

Clients

PDC

BDC

Clients

Figure 34. Domain layout

5.2.3 DBMS security planning

Detailed information on how to improve the security of the DBMS is provided in Chapter 2, "Database Access Protection" of the *R/3 Security Guide: Volume II, R/3 Security Services in Detail*. This chapter includes a specific section on Oracle and DB2 under Windows NT.

The accounts that must be created during the installation are described in the following tables. Table 14 shows the accounts common to all the DBMSs.

> **Attention: Case is important**
>
> Throughout this chapter and the rest of the redbook, take note of the case of parameters such as accounts, groups, and variables. The way they are written is case sensitive. For example if <sid> is "its", then:
>
> - <SID> equates to ITS
> - <sid> equates to its
>
> Failure to adhere to the case of the parameters will likely result in a broken installation.

Table 14. Accounts common to all DBMSs

Account	Where	Details	Lab values
Cluster service account	Domain controller of the SAPDOM domain	User ID name[2]	SAPDOM\ClusSvc
User who administers the R/3 system	Domain controller of the SAPDOM domain	<sid>adm[1,3]	SAPDOM\itsadm
SAP service account	Domain controller of the SAPDOM domain	SAPService<SID>[1,4] (for DB2 UDB, it is sapse<sid>)	SAPDOM\SAPServiceITS (for DB2, sapseits)
Global group of SAP administrators	Domain controller of the SAPDOM domain	SAP_<SID>_GlobalAdmin[1]	SAPDOM\SAP_ITS_GlobalAdmin
Local group of SAP administrators	Local account on SAP application servers and DB server	SAP_<SID>_LocalAdmin[1]	SAP_ITS_LocalAdmin
CI server account	Domain controller of the SAPDOM domain	NetBIOS name unique in the USERS and SAPDOM domain[5]	SERVERA
DB server account	Domain controller of the SAPDOM domain	NetBIOS name unique in the USERS and SAPDOM domain[5]	SERVERB
Other SAP application servers account	Domain controller of the SAPDOM domain	NetBIOS name unique in the USERS and SAPDOM domain[2]	SERVERC

Account	Where	Details	Lab values

Notes:

1 The case of the parameter must be exactly as specified.

2 The cluster service account must be a domain user and belong to the local Administrators group in both nodes of the cluster. Moreover, the account must have the following rights: Backup files and directories; increase quotas; increase scheduling priority; load and unload device drivers; lock pages in memory; logon as a service; restore files and directories.

3 The <sid>adm account must be a domain user and belong to the Domain Admins, Domain Users, and SAP_<SID>_Global Admin groups. Besides the account must have the following rights: Replace a process level token; increase quotas; act as a part of the operating system. After the installation it is recommended to remove the <sid>adm account from the Domain Admins groups to improve security.

4 The SAP service account must be a domain user and have the following rights: Logon as a service.

5 We recommend using only alphabetic and numeric characters and not to use more than eight characters.

5.3 Hardware configuration and installation

A description of how to configure and install the hardware is included in the following sections:

- 4.3, "Hardware sizing" on page 78
- 4.2, "Certification and validation of hardware" on page 73
- 4.4, "Disk layouts" on page 84
- 4.5, "Typical SCSI RAID controller configurations" on page 101
- 4.6, "Fibre Channel configurations" on page 104

We recommend you also plan the distribution of the adapters in the PCI slots before beginning the installation. This distribution can have a major impact on the performance of your system. For information, see *Netfinity Performance Tuning with Windows NT 4.0*, SG24-5287.

5.4 Windows NT installation

This section contains a general description of the installation process of Windows NT for an SAP server. We strongly recommend, before beginning the installation, you review 4.5, "Typical SCSI RAID controller configurations" on page 101 if you are working with a SCSI cluster and 4.6, "Fibre Channel configurations" on page 104 if you are working with a Fibre Channel cluster. See also the continually updated OSS note 0112266 *R/3+MS Cluster Server: Frequent Questions and Tips*.

Step 1: Configure non-shared disks

Configure the non-shared disks as described in 4.5, "Typical SCSI RAID controller configurations" on page 101. Relevant information on how to configure the disks is also contained in 4.4, "Disk layouts" on page 84.

Step 2: Fill in general worksheet

Before starting the installation it is useful to gather information that could be relevant during the setup. Table 15 should be filled out with the relevant data:

Table 15. General worksheet

Parameters	Lab values	Your values
Windows NT domain for SAP and DB servers	SAPDOM	
PDC of SAP domain NetBIOS Name	SAPPDC	
PDC of SAP domain IP address	192.168.0.10	
PDC of SAP domain subnet mask	255.255.255.0	
Windows NT domain for user accounts	USERS	
PDC of USERS domain NetBIOS Name	USERSPDC	
PDC of USERS domain IP address	192.168.0.120	
PDC of USERS domain subnet mask	255.255.255.0	

Step 3: Windows NT installation on Node A

Installation begins with Node A. Before installing, fill inTable 16.

First you install the Standby OS and then the Active OS. You first create a primary partition (C:) on Windows NT disk 0 to be used as a system partition for the Standby OS and a primary partition (D:) on Windows NT disk 1 to be used as a boot partition for the Standby OS. Then you install the Standby OS on D. Using the Standby OS you can create a second primary partition on Windows NT disk 0 (E:) and a second primary partition on Windows NT disk 1 (F:).

Then you can reboot and install the Active OS on drive C. This partition will be the system partition as well as the boot partition for the Active OS.

At the end of the installation install Service Pack 3. (More recent service packs are installed in step 16 on page 142).

Table 16. Node A worksheet

Parameters	Restrictions and recommendations	Lab values	Your values
Standby OS drive	The Standby operating system must be installed before the Active one.	D:	
Active OS drive	The Active operating system must be installed after the Standby one.	C:	
Windows NT directory for Standby OS	Change the default value \WINNT only if you are installing the Standby operating system in the same logical drive in which the Active operating system is installed.	\WINNT	
Windows NT directory for Active OS	Use the default value \WINNT.	\WINNT	
Computer name	The maximum is eight characters. Only letters, numbers, and the "-" symbol are allowed. The last character cannot be a "-" symbol.	SERVERA	
Administrator built-in account password	Follow the general recommendations about passwords in a secure environment.	ibm	
Domain role	The server cannot be a PDC or a BDC.	Stand-alone server	
Components to install	Leave default.	Default components	
RAS installation	Do not install RAS.	No	
Microsoft IIS	Do not install IIS.	No	
Network protocols	MSCS only supports TCP/IP.	Only TCP/IP	
Dynamically assigned address	Only static addresses should be used with MSCS.	No	
IP address (private network)	Private network must be a separate subnet. The use of the IANA reserved network 10.0.0.0 is good practice. Use a different network only when this network is already used for other purposes.	10.0.0.1[1]	

Parameters	Restrictions and recommendations	Lab values	Your values
Subnet mask (private)		255.255.255.0	
Default gateway (private)	Must be blank.	Blank	
IP address (public)		192.168.0.1[1]	
Subnet mask (public)		255.255.255.0	
Default gateway (public)		192.168.0.100[1]	
IP address (backbone)		172.16.0.1[1]	
Subnet mask (backbone)		255.255.255.0	
Default gateway (backbone)	Must be blank.	Blank	
DNS domain name		itso.ral.ibm.com	
DNS Service search order	List of DNS servers.	192.168.0.101[1]	
DNS suffix search order	List of DNS suffixes. Should contain own domain.	None	
Primary WINS server (private network)	Leave empty.	None	
Secondary WINS server (private network)	Leave empty.	None	
Primary WINS server (public)	IP address of the primary WINS server.	192.168.0.101	
Secondary WINS server (public network)	IP address of the secondary WINS server.	None	
Primary WINS server (backbone network)	Leave blank or configure a WINS server for the backbone network.	None	
Secondary WINS server (backbone network)	Leave blank or configure a WINS server for the backbone network.	None	
Enable DNS for Windows resolution		Checked	
Enable LMHOSTS lookup		Checked	

Parameters	Restrictions and recommendations	Lab values	Your values
Domain name	Name of the SAP domain.	SAPDOM	
SAP Domain administrator User ID		Administrator	
SAP Domain administrator account password		ibm	
Note: The IP address used in our lab is reserved for private use. However, this is not necessary for your installation except where noted.			

Important

At the end of the installation when the administrator logs on for the first time the Windows NT Enterprise Edition Installer is automatically started. Do not try to configure the cluster now. The cluster will be installed later.

Step 4: Windows NT installation on Node B

After installing Service Pack 3 on Node A, the installation of Windows NT EE on Node B can begin. Before installing fill in Table 17. You must first install the Standby OS and then the Active OS as described in Step 3 on page 126. At the end of the installation of Node B, Service Pack 3 must be installed:

Table 17. Node B worksheet

Parameters	Restrictions and recommendations	Lab values	Your values
Standby OS drive	The Standby operating system must be installed *before* the Active one.	D:	
Active OS drive	The Active operating system must be installed *after* the Standby one.	C:	
Windows NT directory for Standby OS	Change the default value \WINNT only if you are installing the Standby operating system in the same logical drive in which the Active operating system is installed.	\WINNT	
Windows NT directory for Active OS	Use the default value \WINNT.	\WINNT	

Parameters	Restrictions and recommendations	Lab values	Your values
Computer name	The maximum is eight characters. Only letters, numbers, and the "-" symbol are allowed. The last character cannot be a "-" symbol.	SERVERB	
Administrator built-in account password	Follow the general recommendations about passwords in a secure environment.	ibm	
Domain role	The server cannot be a PDC or a BDC.	Stand-alone server	
Components to install	Leave default.	Default components	
RAS installation	Do not install RAS.	No	
Microsoft IIS	Do not install IIS.	No	
Network protocols	MSCS only supports TCP/IP.	Only TCP/IP	
Dynamically assigned address	Only static addresses should be used with MSCS.	No	
IP address (private network)	Private network must be a separate subnet. The use of the IANA reserved network 10.0.0.0 is good practice. Use a different network only when this network is already used for other purposes.	10.0.0.2[1]	
Subnet mask (private)		255.255.255.0	
Default gateway (private)	Not required for the private network.	Blank	
IP address (public)		192.168.0.2[1]	
Subnet mask (public)		255.255.255.0	
Default gateway (public)		192.168.0.100[1]	
IP address (backbone)		172.16.0.2[1]	
Subnet mask (backbone)		255.255.255.0	
Default gateway (backbone)	Not required if all the application servers are in the same site.	None	

Parameters	Restrictions and recommendations	Lab values	Your values
DNS Domain name		itso.ral.ibm.com	
DNS Service search order	List of DNS servers.	192.168.0.101[1]	
DNS suffix search order	List of DNS suffixes.	None	
Primary WINS server (private)	Leave empty.	None	
Secondary WINS server (private)	Leave empty.	None	
Primary WINS server (public)	IP address of the primary WINS server.	192.168.0.101[1]	
Secondary WINS server (public)	IP address of the secondary WINS server.	None	
Primary WINS server (backbone)	Leave blank or configure a WINS server for the backbone network.	None	
Secondary WINS server (backbone)	Leave blank or configure a WINS server for the backbone network.	None	
Enable DNS for Windows resolution		Checked	
Enable LMHOSTS lookup		Checked	
Domain name	Name of the SAP domain.	SAPDOM	
SAP Domain administrator User ID		Administrator	
SAP Domain administrator account password		ibm	
Administrator built-in account password		ibm	

Note:
1 The IP address used in our lab is reserved for private use. However, this is not necessary for your installation except where noted.

At the end of the installation when the administrator logs on for the first time the Windows NT Enterprise Edition Installer is automatically started. Do not try to configure the cluster now. MSCS will be installed in step 14 on page 142.

At the end of the installation remember to configure either the DNS server, WINS server, or the HOSTS file. If you plan to use the HOSTS file, it is important to remember that the file is case sensitive. See Knowledge Base article Q101746 "TCP/IP Hosts File Is Case Sensitive" for details. It is also important not to install Service Packs 4 or 5 at this point. SP4 and SP5 are installed after MSCS is installed.

You should also reference the following Knowledge Base articles:

- Q195462 "WINS registration and IP address behavior for MSCS" (general information about how to use)
- Q193890 "Recommended WINS configuration for MSCS" (disable WINS client from the private LAN)
- Q217199 "Static WINS entries cause the network name to go offline" (do not use static entries in WINS for clustered computers)

Step 5: Modify BOOT.INI on Node B

Modify the BOOT.INI file of Node B to avoid simultaneous contention of shared drives. This can be obtained by adding a different boot timeout in the servers:

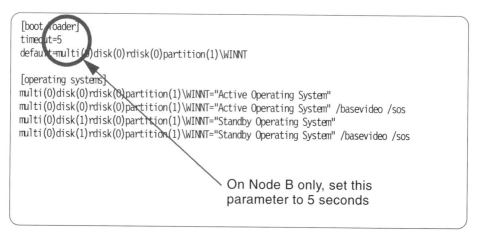

```
[boot loader]
timeout=5
default=multi(0)disk(0)rdisk(0)partition(1)\WINNT

[operating systems]
multi(0)disk(0)rdisk(0)partition(1)\WINNT="Active Operating System"
multi(0)disk(0)rdisk(0)partition(1)\WINNT="Active Operating System" /basevideo /sos
multi(0)disk(1)rdisk(0)partition(1)\WINNT="Standby Operating System"
multi(0)disk(1)rdisk(0)partition(1)\WINNT="Standby Operating System" /basevideo /sos
```

On Node B only, set this parameter to 5 seconds

Figure 35. BOOT.INI file

Step 6: Configure disks

Now you must create your own worksheets describing the disk layout. The distribution of files is DBMS dependent. Examples of how to configure the disks are provided in 4.4, "Disk layouts" on page 84:

- Oracle: Table 10 on page 95
- DB2: Table 11 on page 99
- SQL Server: Table 12 on page 100

Format shared drives and assign meaningful disk labels to the local and shared drives by means of Windows NT Disk administrator on both nodes.

Step 7: SYMplicity Storage Manager configuration

For Netfinity systems, if the cluster exploits FC-AL technology configure the Fibre Channel configuration software, SYMplicity Storage Manager as described in 4.6, "Fibre Channel configurations" on page 104. See also 4.4, "Disk layouts" on page 84 for a detailed description of how to configure the drives.

At the end of the installation you may see the following error message in the Windows NT Event Viewer:

```
Event ID: 8032. Source Browser. Type Error.
The browser service has failed to retrieve the backup list too many times on
transport \Device\NetBT_IBMFEPCI1. The backup browser is stopping.
```

A simple procedure to correct this problem is to disable the browser service on the private and backbone network. The selective disabling of the browser service is described in Knowledge Base article Q158487 "Browsing Across Subnets with a Multihomed PDC in Windows NT 4.0". In our lab configuration, the CI and DB servers had three identical network adapters. Figure 36 shows the registry key, HKey_Local_Machine\System\CurrentControlSet\Services, containing the configuration of network adapters:

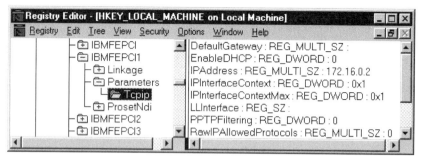

Figure 36. Registry key

Figure 36 shows four subkeys: IBMFEPCI, IBMFEPCI1, IBMFEPCI2, and IBMFEPCI3. The first key contains information about the network driver, while each of the other three corresponds to one particular network adapter. The network adapter can be recognized by looking in the \Parameters\Tcpip subkey. Figure 37 shows how we solved the problem by adding a new value in the subkey HKey_Local_Machine\System\CurrentControlSet\Services \Browser\Parameter:

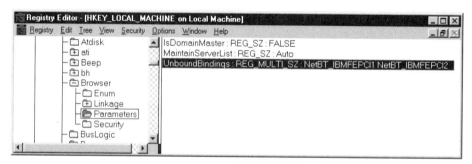

Figure 37. Correcting the entry

5.5 MSCS pre-installation testing

Before beginning the MSCS installation it is useful to verify the hardware and operating system installation. As described in OSS note 0154700 *MSCS Cluster Verification Utility*, the Cluster Verification Utility included in the last release of Windows NT Resource Kit can be useful to test SCSI clusters.

Step 8: MSCS pre-install verification

To use the Cluster Verification Utility it is necessary to install Supplement 3 of the Windows NT Resource Kit. Detailed documentation on how to install this utility is in the Resource Kit Tools Overview Help in the Windows NT Resource Kit Program Group.

Note: The Cluster Verification Utility is really composed of two different programs, the Cluster Verification Utility and the Cluster Diagnostic Utility.

> ┌─ **All data is destroyed** ─────────────────────────────────
> The Cluster Diagnostic Utility will destroy the content of shared disks.

To start the Cluster Verification Utility follow the procedure explained in Help. You need to disconnect one of the nodes from the SCSI channel before beginning the test on the other node.

To use the Cluster Diagnostic Utility follow these instructions:

1. On Node A, execute the command CLUSTSIM /S from the command prompt.

2. Wait until you get the message saying you can start the utility on Node B.

3. On Node B, execute the command CLUSTSIM /N:ServerA from the command prompt, where ServerA is the name of Node A.

4. Examine the log files.

Further information can be found in *Windows NT Microsoft Cluster Server,* by Richard R. Lee.

5.6 Basic Windows NT tuning

Some basic tuning steps are strongly recommended:

- Configure the Windows NT Server service.
- Configure the page file.
- 4 GB tuning.
- Remove unnecessary drivers and protocols.

Each of these is discussed in the following sections.

5.6.1 Server service tuning

Step 9: Configure the Server service

If an application asks the operating system to write data on a disk, this data is only collected in cache memory (write back). When the number of modified pages collected in the cache reaches a predetermined threshold the Cache

Manager starts a thread (the lazy writer) that queues up one quarter of the modified pages and then calls the Virtual Memory Manager. The Virtual Memory Manager then writes the queued pages to disk. This technique allows better use of the I/O system, but to have a real performance improvement it is fundamental to have a correct value of the threshold. As described in Chapter 8 of *Inside Windows NT, Second Edition* by David A. Salomon, the threshold is calculated at the start of the system and depends on the amount of memory and on the value of the registry key Hkey_Local_Machine\System\CurrentControlSet\SessionManager \MemoryManagement\LargeSystemCache.

The default value is 1 and is the same as configuring the Server service (also known as LanmanServer) to the setting **Maximize Throughput for File Sharing**. It is highly recommended by SAP to change the value of this parameter to 0. This is the same as configuring the Server service to **Maximize Throughput for Network Applications** as shown in Figure 38:

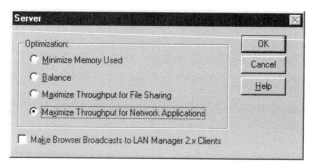

Figure 38. Server service — SAP R/3 recommended value

This parameter can be found also in Windows NT Workstation systems, but it cannot be changed.

For some applications writing directly to disk, bypassing the Windows NT memory cache system is very important. To get this effect, applications use special uncached I/O routines and they manage their memory directly. For these applications the setting of the Server service has no relevance. Microsoft SQL Server is an example of an application doing its own memory management and for which the tuning of this parameter is ignored (see *Optimization and Tuning of Windows NT, Version 1.4,* by Scott B. Suhy).

The effect of the change is to reduce the threshold in systems having large memory. The main reason is that the DBMS and SAP also have their own caches and the use of many levels of caches decreases performance instead of improves it.

5.6.2 Page file tuning

Step 10: Set the page file size

A fundamental SAP memory requirement is to create a very large page file. This is still valid for the zero administration memory management as pointed out in the OSS note 0088416 *Zero administration memory management from 4.0A/NT*. The main recommendation is that the page file size be four times that of physical RAM installed (that is, 4 x RAM). However, while the 4 x RAM recommendation can be considered adequate to face the load when the CI and the DB are on different nodes, it is not adequate when, due to a failure or administrative purposes, both the CI and DB are on the same node. For this reason, SAP recommends the page file be 5xRAM in an MSCS environment.

In reality, the page file size depends on the specific characteristics of the SAP environment such as the modules used and batch activity. As a result, the SAP recommendation can only be considered a suggestion. The page file can be unnecessarily large and also too small.

Because it is not possible to create a page file of more than 4095 MB in a single partition and because it is not recommended for performance reasons to put different page files in different partitions in the same drive, we recommend you put no more than one page file per physical array. This is not a problem for the operating system. Indeed as described in *Inside Windows NT, Second Edition* by David A. Salomon, Windows NT supports up to 16 different page files. See 4.4, "Disk layouts" on page 84 for details on how to configure the page files for systems with large memory. See also *Optimization and Tuning of Windows NT Version 1.4,* by Scott B. Suhy for further information.

Windows NT allows the configuration of a minimum and a maximum size for the page file. The system starts with the minimum size and it expands the page file size when necessary up to the maximum size specified. Because the performance of the system decreases during the expansion of the page file it is recommended to set the minimum dimension equal to the maximum dimension. So the final recommendation is:

Minimum dimension = maximum dimension = 5 x RAM installed

If the page file is exhausted or more precisely if Memory Committed bytes approaches Memory Commit limit (see *Optimization and Tuning of Windows NT Version 1.4,* by Scott B. Suhy for details) you may find three errors in the Event Viewer:

- 2020: The server was unable to allocate from the system paged pool because the pool was empty.

- 2001: The server was unable to perform an operation due to a shortage of available resources.
- 2016: The server was unable to allocate virtual memory.

The exhaustion of the system paged pool can cause blue trap screens. We therefore strongly recommend you respect SAP recommendations on the dimension of the page file. A suggestion we can give to customers who cannot afford having so many disks for the paging activity is to follow these less restrictive rules (Table 18):

Table 18. Page file size recommendations

Memory	Page file
1 GB or less	5 x RAM
From 1 GB to 2 GB	4.5 x RAM
From 2 GB to 4 GB	4 x RAM

5.6.3 4 GB tuning

Step 11: Modify BOOT.INI for 4 GB tuning

Windows NT is a 32-bit operating system using a linear virtual addressing memory system. The virtual addresses are divided into 2 GB sections: user mode and system mode as shown in Figure 39. The user processes can only exploit the 2 GB user mode section:

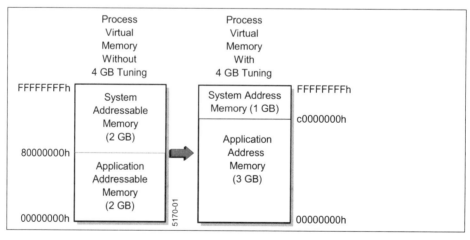

Figure 39. 4 GB tuning

While this is enough for many systems it may not be enough in large SAP and DBMS installations. To resolve these situations Windows NT Enterprise Edition introduced a new feature known as 4 GB tuning. By specifying a /3GB parameter in the BOOT.INI file, as shown in Figure 40, this changes how the operating system manages the virtual addressing: 3 GB for user processes and 1 GB for system processes. Figure 39 shows the result.

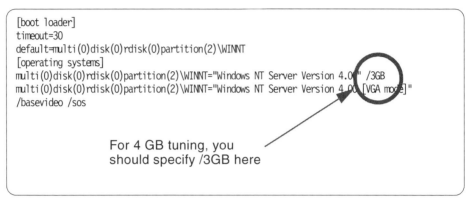

```
[boot loader]
timeout=30
default=multi(0)disk(0)rdisk(0)partition(2)\WINNT
[operating systems]
multi(0)disk(0)rdisk(0)partition(2)\WINNT="Windows NT Server Version 4.0" /3GB
multi(0)disk(0)rdisk(0)partition(2)\WINNT="Windows NT Server Version 4.00 [VGA mode]"
/basevideo /sos
```

For 4 GB tuning, you should specify /3GB here

Figure 40. BOOT.INI contents for 4 GB tuning

No new API is necessary to allow applications to exploit this new feature, but executables need to be modified in order to see this extra space. See the following references for a detailed description of how to configure the SAP system in order to exploit this feature:

- Knowledge Base article Q171793 "Information on Application Use of 4GT RAM tuning"

- OSS note 0110172 *NT: Transactions with large storage requirements*

As described in the Microsoft document *FAQ: All You Ever Wanted To Know about Windows NT Server 4.0 Enterprise Edition*, to be able to exploit this feature the following requirements have to be satisfied:

- The application is memory intensive.
- The application is able to utilize more than 2 GB of memory.
- The server has more than 2 GB of RAM.
- All the other components of the system have enough computing capacity.

5.6.4 Remove unnecessary drivers and protocols

Step 12: Remove drivers and protocols

Do not install unnecessary drivers and protocols. Turn off installed unnecessary services and uninstall unnecessary drivers. The following is a typical list of unnecessary drivers and protocols:

- Because Microsoft Cluster only supports TCP/IP protocol for failover, other network protocols are usually not installed. Not installing IPX/SPX, NetBEUI, or other network protocols reduces the overhead on the server and reduces network traffic. Unused network protocols can still generate network traffic due to various automatic broadcast mechanisms (for instance, the Browser service). If for some reason the server needs more than one protocol, then TCP/IP should be first in the bindings list to reduce connection time.

- If the server is not used for printing, the spooler service should be disabled freeing up memory.

- Typical services that can be disabled to obtain a better performance are:
  - NetDDE
  - Messenger
  - Alerter

However, check to see if your SAP R/3 system needs them first. Specifically for Messenger, this service will be used during SAP R/3 upgrades so it should be re-enabled at that time.

5.7 Microsoft Cluster Server installation

Step 13: Install MSCS on Node A

Before beginning the installation, complete the Microsoft Cluster Server worksheet to collect all the data necessary for the installation:

Table 19. MSCS worksheet

Parameters	Restrictions and recommendations	Lab values	Your values
Cluster name	NetBIOS names rules.	SAPCLUS	
Cluster Service User ID	This account must be created in the SAP domain before beginning the MSCS setup[1].	ClusSvc	
Cluster Service password	Password rules.	ibm	

Parameters	Restrictions and recommendations	Lab values	Your values
Windows NT SAP domain name		SAPDOM	
Shared cluster disks	See disk layout worksheet.	I, J, K, L, etc.	
Quorum drive	See disk layout worksheet.	I:	
Network name for the private network adapter	Select **Enable for cluster use** and **Use for private communications**.	Private	
Network name for the public network adapter	Select **Enable for cluster use** and **Use for all communications.**	Public	
Network name for the backbone network adapter	Select **Enable for cluster use** and **Use for all communications.**	Backbone	
Networks available for internal cluster communication	Arrange in the order public, backbone then public.	Private Backbone Public	
Cluster IP address	In the same subnet of public network adapters.	192.168.0.50[2]	
Cluster Subnet Mask	The same public network adapters.	255.255.255.0	
Network		Public	

Notes:
1 The cluster service account must be a domain user and belong to the local Administrators group in both nodes of the cluster. Moreover, the account must have the following rights: Backup files and directories, increase quotas; increase scheduling priority; load and unload device drivers; lock pages in memory; logon as a service; and restore files and directories.
2 The IP address used in our lab is reserved for private use. However, this is not necessary for your installation except where noted.

Now, start the installation of MSCS on Node A. At the end of the installation reboot Node A. Do not try to open the Cluster Administration utility yet as it is necessary to update the HOSTS file before doing so.

Update the HOSTS file with the following lines:

```
127.0.0.1     localhost
192.168.0.50  sapclus
```

Step 14: Install MSCS on Node B

Install the Microsoft Cluster Service on Node B. Before beginning the installation update the HOSTS file as described in Step 13.

Useful documentation to be used during and after the installation to troubleshoot problems are:

- *MSCS Administrator's Guide* (from Microsoft TechNet)
- *Microsoft Cluster Server Troubleshooting and Maintenance,* by Martin Lucas (from Microsoft TechNet)
- *Deploying Microsoft Cluster Server*, by the Microsoft Enterprise Services Assets Team (from TechNet)
- *Microsoft Cluster Server Release Notes*, (from the Windows NT 4.0 Enterprise Edition CD)
- *Windows NT Microsoft Cluster Server*, by Richard R. Lee

Step 15: Installation of troubleshooting tools

The most important suggestions we can give to the reader to allow in-depth troubleshooting of cluster problems are to:

- Configure the cluster logging feature as described in Knowledge Base article Q168801 "How to Enable Cluster Logging in Microsoft Cluster Server".
- Install a network monitoring tool such as Microsoft Network Monitor to analyze the network traffic between the cluster nodes, other SAP application servers, and clients. Most often cluster problems are actually network problems.

5.8 Service pack and post-SP installation steps

Step 16: Windows NT Service Pack installation

Install Service Pack 4 or later.

Whether you use Windows NT Service Pack 4 or Service Pack 5 the installation has to be done only after the Microsoft Cluster configuration. The main documents to check before beginning the installation are:

- OSS note 0030478 *Service Packs on Windows NT* — this is the first note saying which Service Pack you can install; the answer depends on the DBMS.

- OSS note 0144310 *NT: Installing an NT SP on R/3 MSCS Cluster* — this note describes the Service Pack installation procedure; it also explains that if you are using SP4 you have to install the RNR20.DLL, CLUSRES.DLL postfixes.

- OSS note 0128167 *Service Pack 4 on NT MSCS with Oracle Products* — this note is only relevant for Service Pack 4 and Oracle Fail Safe; it describes how to deal with the incompatibility between these products.

- RELNOTES.TXT file in the Service Pack CD — detailed description of the procedure for a rolling upgrade.

The installation procedure is described in the RELNOTES.TXT file. You should always create the Uninstall directory in case there is any problem with the most recent Service Pack release.

Step 17: DNS or HOSTS file and transport directory configuration

After having completed the SP installation it is necessary to configure either the DNS server, WINS server, or the HOSTS file. If the choice is to use the HOSTS file it is important to remember that the TCP/IP HOSTS file is case sensitive. See Knowledge Base article Q101746 TCP/IP "HosTs File Is Case Sensitive" for details.

You should also reference the following Knowledge Base articles:

- Q195462 "WINS registration and IP address behavior for MSCS" (general information about how to use)

- Q193890 "Recommended WINS configuration for MSCS" (disable WINS client from the private LAN)

- Q217199 "Static WINS entries cause the network name to go offline" (do not use static entries in WINS for clustered computers)

How to configure the HOSTS file during an Oracle installation is shown in Figure 41. The information necessary for the configuration is taken from:

- Table 16 on page 127
- Table 17 on page 129
- Table 35 on page 180
- Table 37 on page 187

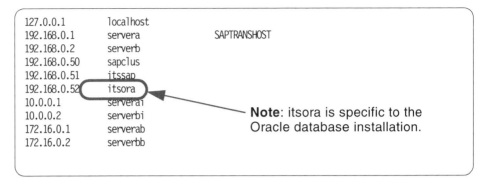

Figure 41. HOSTS file for Oracle

The HOSTS file used in our DB2 installation is shown in Figure 42. The information necessary for the configuration is taken from:

- Table 16 on page 127
- Table 17 on page 129
- Table 47 on page 210
- Table 48 on page 211

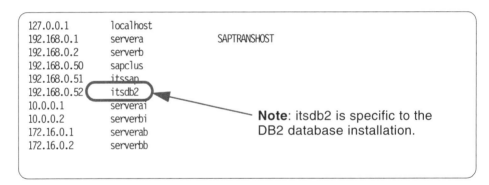

Figure 42. HOSTS file for DB2

The HOSTS file used in our SQL Server installation is shown in Figure 43. The information necessary for the configuration is taken from:

- Table 16 on page 127
- Table 17 on page 129
- Table 56 on page 228
- Table 58 on page 230

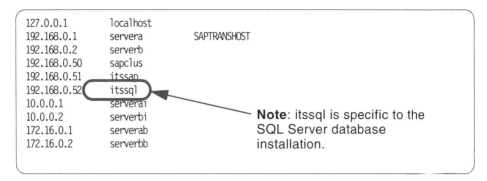

```
127.0.0.1        localhost
192.168.0.1      servera          SAPTRANSHOST
192.168.0.2      serverb
192.168.0.50     sapclus
192.168.0.51     itssap
192.168.0.52     itssql
10.0.0.1         serveral
10.0.0.2         serverbi
172.16.0.1       serverab
172.16.0.2       serverbb
```

Note: itssql is specific to the SQL Server database installation.

Figure 43. HOSTS file for SQL Server

SAPTRANSHOST alias

We raise to your attention the alias SAPTRANSHOST in the three HOSTS files shown above (Figure 41, Figure 42, and Figure 43). This alias allows R3Setup to recognize *servera* as the transport host.

This SAPTRANSHOST line must be changed at the end of the installation. Because the transport directory is on shared drives, the use of the host name is not correct. Instead, the virtual name of the SAP R/3 system (that is, <sid>sap) should be used. We are assuming that you are using the shared drives of the cluster for the transport directory. If the transport directory is on an external system follow these steps:

1. On the transport host create the directory \USR\SAP\TRANS.

2. On this directory grant full control to the global group SAP_<SID>_GlobalAdmin.

3. If no instance will be installed on the transport host share this directory as SAPMNT.

4. Update the HOSTS file (or the DNS server) to make SAPTRANSHOST an alias for the transport host.

Step 18: Installation of IE, ADSI, and MMC

Windows 2000

Per OSS note 0169468 "Windows 2000 support", this step must be skipped if installing on Windows 2000.

Install Microsoft Internet Explorer 4.01 (or later) on both servers by running the IE4SETUP from the \MS_IE4\WIN95_NT\EN subdirectory of the Presentation CD-ROM. Do not install the Active Desktop feature.

Install the Active Directory Service Interfaces (ADSI) component on both nodes by running ADS from the \NT\I386\MMC subdirectory of the SAP Kernel CD-ROM.

Install the Microsoft Management Console (MMC) on both nodes by running IMMC11 from the \NT\I386\MMC subdirectory from the SAP Kernel CD.

Step 19: Install the latest SAP R/3 DLLs

> **Windows 2000**
>
> As per OSS note 0169468 "Windows 2000 support" a R3DLLINS.EXE patch must be downloaded from the sapserv FTP site if installing on Windows 2000.

Install the latest version of the Dynamic Link Libraries on both nodes by running R3DLLINS from the \NT\I386\NTPATCH subdirectory of the SAP Kernel CD-ROM. You should also verify that there is no newer version of R3DLLINS.EXE available on the sapserv FTP server.

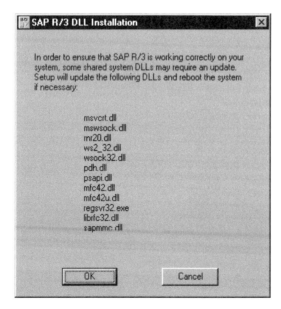

Figure 44. SAP R/3 DLL installation

Step 20: Apply the Post SP4 DLLs

> **Note**
>
> This step only applies if you installed Windows NT Service Pack 4. If you applied later service packs you can skip this step.

Apply the RNR20.DLL and CLUSRES.DLL Post-SP4 hot fixes. The first fix can be downloaded from:

```
ftp.microsoft.com
/bussys/winnt/winnt-public/fixes/usa/nt40/hotfixes-postSP4/Rnr-fix
```

The CLUSRES.DLL can be downloaded directly from the Microsoft site or installed as part of Service Pack 5. See OSS note 0134141 for details.

5.9 MSCS verification

Now the Microsoft cluster should be working without any problem. It is very important to check the cluster configuration to be sure we have made no mistakes during the setup. This is even more important when the team is composed of people responsible for the Microsoft Cluster installation and others responsible for the SAP installation. To make everyone sure that the cluster is working and is correctly configured it is highly recommended to test the cluster configuration in as much detail as possible. The main recommended tests are:

- Check the HOSTS file.
- Test the failover process.

5.9.1 Checking the mapping of host names

Step 21: Correction of network bindings

To be sure that either the HOSTS file or the DNS server is correctly configured, the following simple PING tests should be performed (consider using the -a parameter of the PING command):

Table 20. PING tests

Node	Test
ServerA	PING <NodeA_Name>
ServerA	PING <NodeB_Name>

Node	Test
ServerA	PING <Cluster_Name>
ServerB	PING <NodeA_Name>
ServerB	PING <NodeB_Name>
ServerB	PING <Cluster_Name>

The following condition must always be satisfied:

PING response

The reply to the PING commands must come from the *public* network. Be sure that this is the case.

If this condition is not satisfied when pinging your own host name the SAP installation cannot begin and the following simple procedure should be performed.

Note: Per Microsoft Knowledge Base article Q164023, this procedure only applies to servers having SP4 or later installed:

1. Open the Network applet in the Control Panel.
2. Click **Bindings > Show Bindings for all Protocols**
3. Select the **TCP/IP protocol.**
4. Change the order in which the cards are listed. They should be in the following order:

   a. Public network
   b. Backbone network
   c. Private network

If the above condition is not satisfied while pinging any other host name the correct answer can be obtained by simply correcting the HOSTS file.

5.9.2 Test the failover process

Step 22: MSCS verification

If everything works so far it is possible to continue with the fundamental six-step cluster test. As a preliminary step you should create a Clock group to be used as a test cluster group. The CLOCK.EXE application does not really stress the system but provides enough functionality to test the different failover scenarios.

Table 21. Verification tests

Test	Node A	Node B
Manual failover	Clock	
Manual failover		Clock
Microsoft CASTEST[1]		
Regular shutdown	Clock	
Regular shutdown		Clock
Blue screen[2]	Clock	
Blue screen[2]		Clock
Power off	Clock	
Power off		Clock

Notes:
1 The Microsoft CASTEST is contained in the \MSCS\SUPPORT directory in the second CD-ROM of Windows NT EE. Instructions on how to use the test are contained in the CASREAD.TXT file.
2 The blue screen can be achieved killing the WINLOGON.EXE process by means of the KILL.EXE utility contained in the Windows NT Resource Kit.

If you do not have enough time to complete all the steps at least follow this recommendation:

Basic test

Use the Microsoft CASTEST utility; this should be considered the official MSCS test utility. Carefully examine the log file that is produced — verify what happens when you power off one of the nodes. Specific hardware problems due to the lack of power on one of the I/O adapters are not seen by the Microsoft utility.

5.10 Create the installation user account

Step 23: Create the installation user account

Before beginning the installation process, complete the following steps:

1. Create an account on the primary domain controller (we will use sapinst), and add it to the Domain Admins group. This account will be used during the entire installation process. Once the installation is complete, the account can be removed. During the installation process, R3Setup will assign the following local user policies on Node A and Node B to the installation account:

   - Act as a part of the Operating System
   - Increase Quotas
   - Log on as a Service
   - Replace a Process Level Token

2. Fill out the SAP installation worksheets in this chapter and the database chapters.

We provide, in each of the next sections dedicated to SAP installation, a SAP installation worksheet that has to be completed (see Table 32 on page 177 for an Oracle example). In this worksheet we collect all the information necessary for the local SAP and DBMS installation. These worksheets are DBMS dependent. They must be completed using the recommended disk layouts provided in 4.4, "Disk layouts" on page 84 as reference.

The following Windows NT accounts and groups are created automatically by R3Setup:

- <sid>adm account on the SAPDOM domain controller with the following advanced user rights:

  - Log on as a Service
  - Replace a Process Level Token
  - Increase Quotas
  - Act as a part of the Operating System

- SAPService<SID> account on the SAPDOM domain controller; for DB2 this account is named sapse<sid>

- SAP_<SID>_GlobalAdmin global group on the SAPDOM domain controller

- SAP_<SID>_LocalAdmin local group on each SAP R/3 application server and DB server

- Put the SAP_<SID>_GlobalAdmin global group in the SAP_<SID>_LocalAdmin local group on each SAP R/3 application server and DB server

- Assign the advanced user right Logon as a Service to the user SAPService<SID> (for DB2 user sapse<sid>) on each SAP R/3 application server and DB server

Once installation is complete you should do the following to improve the security of the system:

- Delete the SAP installation account that you created in step 23 (sapinst, in our lab)

5.11 SAP and DBMS installation

Step 24: Installing SAP and the DBMS

To make the installation as clear as possible, Figure 45 shows the major steps for the database and SAP R/3 installation for each DBMS:

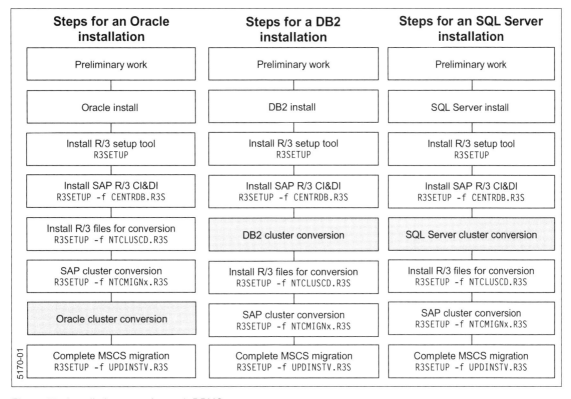

Figure 45. Installation steps for each DBMS

You will note from Figure 45 that the main difference between the installation procedures is the point when the database cluster conversion occurs. These steps are highlighted.

See OSS note 0138765 *Cluster Migration: Terminology and Procedure* for further information.

A detailed description of installation is provided in the next three chapters.

> ### Must always be logged on as the installation user
>
> The whole installation must be done logged on using the same installation user account as described in step 23 on page 149 (the only exception is step 24.15 on page 183). This account must be a member of the Domain Admins group. See OSS note 134135 *4.5B R/3 Installation on Windows NT (General)* for additional information.

Depending on the database you are using, proceed as follows:

- If you are installing SAP with Oracle go to Chapter 6, "Installation using Oracle" on page 171.
- If you are installing SAP with DB2 go to Chapter 7, "Installation using DB2" on page 193.
- If you are installing SAP with SQL Server go to Chapter 8, "Installation using SQL Server" on page 221.

5.12 SAP verification

Now the SAP R/3 and DBMS installation in a cluster environment is complete. The R/3 system should now function correctly in any configuration - DB and R/3 on different nodes or on the same cluster node.

Step 25: SAP tests

This is a very simple list of tests that should be performed on the SAP system:

- Verify the contents of the SapCluster directory
- Connection test
- SAP system check
- System log analysis
- Profile check
- SAPNTCHK

5.12.1 Verify the contents of the SAPCluster directory

The directory <%windir%>\SapCluster (<%windir%> was C:\WINNT in our lab) is created locally on both nodes during the installation of the cluster. It contains all R/3 files that are required on the host on which the database is running. Table 22 lists the files contained in the directory <%windir%>\SapCluster in dependency of the DB used.

Table 22. Required files in local SAPCluster directory

File	Oracle	DB2 UDB	SQL Server
BRARCHIVE.EXE	Exists	Exists	Exists
BRRESTORE.EXE	Exists	Exists	Exists
<SID>ENV.CMD[1]	Exists	Exists	
BRBACKUP.EXE	Exists		Exists
BRCONNECT.EXE	Exists		Exists
BRTOOLS.EXE	Exists		Exists
COMPRESS.EXE			Exists
CPIO.EXE	Exists	Exists	Exists
CPQCCMS.DLL	Exists	Exists	Exists
DD.EXE	Exists	Exists	Exists
DSCDB6UP.EXE [1]		Exists	
MKSZIP.EXE	Exists	Exists	Exists
MT.EXE	Exists	Exists	Exists
PSTAT.EXE	Exists	Exists	Exists
RFCOSCOL.EXE	Exists	Exists	Exists
SAPDBA.EXE	Exists		Exists
SAPNTCHK.EXE	Exists	Exists	Exists
SAPOSCOL.EXE	Exists	Exists	Exists
SAPSTARTSRV.EXE	Exists	Exists	Exists
SAPXPG.EXE	Exists	Exists	Exists
UNCOMPRESS.EXE	Exists	Exists	Exists
1 Created in step 29 on page 165.			

5.12.2 Update SAP R/3 executables

If you have not done so already, you should now download the latest SAP R/3 executables from the SAP FTP server and install them on the two cluster nodes.

The steps are as follows:

1. Download SAP R/3 executables.

   Check Appendix B.5, "SAPSERV FTP site" on page 285 for additional information on how to download files from an SAP FTP server.

   Additional comments:

   - Download the files to a temporary directory.

   - Get the latest database *independent* executables (with the highest number) first, from the FTP directory:
     `/general/R3server/patches/rel45B/NT/I386/`

   - Then get the database *dependent* files from the following directory:

     - Oracle: `/general/R3server/patches/rel45B/NT/I386/ORA`
     - DB2 UDB: `/general/R3server/patches/rel45B/NT/I386/DB6`
     - SQL Server: `/general/R3server/patches/rel45B/NT/I386/MSS`

2. Back up the original files.

   Back up all files from the directory `\usr\sap\<sid>\sys\exe\run` before replacing any of the files. For an easier restore, you should also back up the directory `<%WINDIR%>\SapCluster` on *both* cluster nodes.

3. Stop the R/3 instance.

   Several of the R/3 executables cannot be overwritten as long as the R/3 instance or the database is running. Therefore, you need to stop the R/3 instance, the DBMS, and two SAP services.

   a. Verify that no users are logged in to the R/3 instance with transaction SM50.

   b. Take the cluster resource SAP-R/3 <SID> (*not* the whole group) offline.

   c. Take the database cluster group offline.

   d. Stop the Windows NT services SAP<SID>_<Instance number> and SAPOSCOL using the Services applet from the Control Panel on *both* cluster nodes.

4. Replace the executables.

   a. Log on to Node A as user <sid>adm.

   b. Verify that all cluster resources are owned by Node A.

c. Extract all the executables you downloaded earlier into the directory `\usr\<SID>\sys\exe\run`.

d. Perform any database-specific steps needed. For example, with DB2 UDB you may need to re-execute the following command to install the latest administration utilities:

`sddb6ins -i 45B -s <SID>`

e. Compare the files in the local directory <%WINDIR%>\SapCluster with the files in the directory \usr\sap\<sid>\sys\exe\run and replace any outdated files in the first directory with the corresponding files from the second directory. Use Table 22 on page 153 for a list of files to verify.

f. Log on to Node B.

g. Move the R/3 cluster group to Node B.

h. Compare the files in the local directory <%WINDIR%>\SapCluster with the files in the directory \usr\sap\<sid>\sys\exe\run and replace any outdated files in the first directory with the corresponding files from the second directory. Use Table 22 on page 153 for a list of files to verify.

5. Restart the R/3 instance.

a. Start the services SAP<SID>_<Instance number> and SAPOSCOL using the Services applet from the control panel on *both* cluster nodes

b. Bring the database cluster group online.

c. Bring the cluster resource SAP-R/3 <SID> online.

5.12.3 Connection test

Install the SAP GUI interface and log on as one of the SAP standard users:

Table 23. Client connection tests

Client	User	Default password
000	SAP*	06071992
000	DDIC	19920706
001	SAP*	06071992
001	DDIC	19920706
066	EARLYWATCH	SUPPORT

The purpose of the tests is to confirm that it is possible to connect to the SAP server from a client in which the SAP GUI has been installed and exploit the server's services.

5.12.4 SAP system check

There is a simple tool to check the SAP installation. Log on to the R/3 system using the client 000 and then click **Tools > Administration > Administration > Installation Check** or use transaction code SM28. If everything goes well you should receive the message:

```
SAP System Check. No errors reported
```

5.12.5 System log check

In each application server, a system log is continually updated. The log file is \USR\SAP\<sid>\<instance>\SLOG00.LOG. It is possible to examine this log from a GUI by clicking **Tools > Administration > Monitor > System Log** or by using transaction code SM21. The window asks you to provide the time interval you want to consider. Figure 46 shows a log with many CPIC errors:

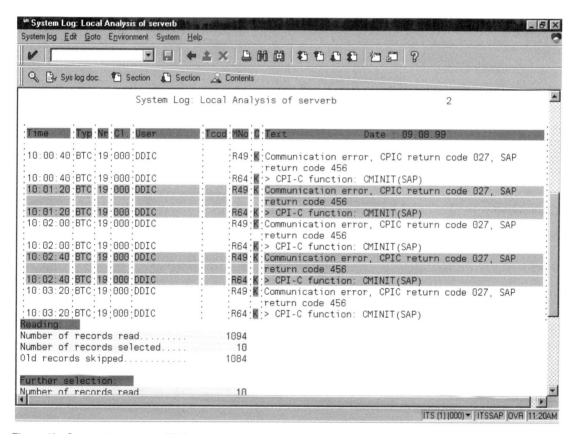

Figure 46. System log showing CPIC errors

These errors can be analyzed by double-clicking them.

5.12.6 Profiles check

R/3 has three profiles stored on the directory \USR\SAP\<sid>\SYS\PROFILE during the installation:

- DEFAULT.PFL

- START_<INSTANCE><INSTANCE_NUMBER>_<virtual R/3 server name> (lab value: START_DVEBMGS00_ITSSAP)

- <SID>_<INSTANCE><INSTANCE_NUMBER>_<virtual R/3 server name> (lab value: ITS_DVEBMGS00_ITSSAP)

The DEFAULT profile contains settings that apply to the entire system, while the START and SID profiles are instance specific. The START profile determines how the individual R/3 services or processes are started. The SID profile determines how many work processes of each type are started.

Profiles can be imported by clicking **Tool > CCMS > Configuration > Profiles Maintenance** (or by using transaction code RZ10) and then choosing **Utilities > Import Profiles > Of Active Servers**. During the import a consistency check is performed. You can then look in the profile log to see if any error message is displayed (Figure 47):

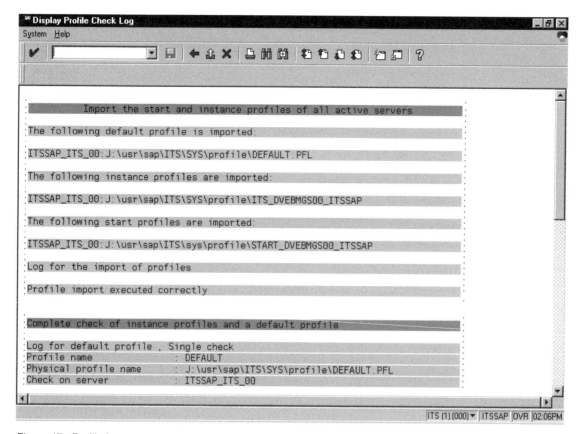

Figure 47. Profile log

5.12.7 Processes check

By selecting transaction SM51 or clicking **Tools > Administration > Monitor > System Monitoring > Process Overview**, a window similar to Figure 48 appears:

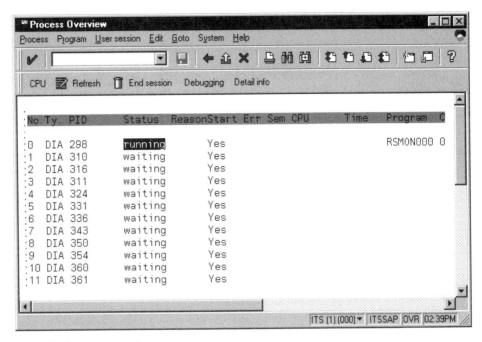

Figure 48. Process overview

A healthy system has all dialog processes but one in waiting status as shown in Figure 48.

5.12.8 SAPWNTCHK

As described in OSS note 0065761 *Determine Configuration Problems under Windows NT,* it is possible to download from Sapserv<x> FTP servers (see B.3, "Related Web sites" on page 282 for details) a couple of utilities, SAPNTCHK and SAPWNTCHK, to test the SAP configuration. The only difference between these utilities is in the graphic interface. Detailed information about the utilities is contained in the readme files enclosed. As an example of the result, Figure 49 shows the output of SAPWNTCHK:

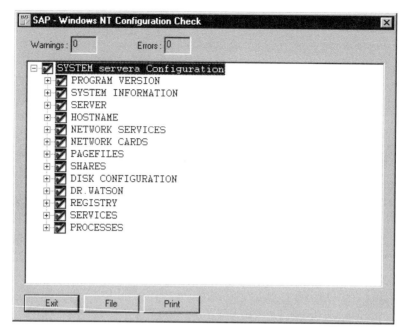

Figure 49. Output from SAPWNTCHK

5.13 DBMS verification

Step 26: DBMS verification

This section describes the tests for each of the three database products. The tests are specific for the DBMS used.

5.13.1 Oracle

Oracle verification: You can log on to the DBMS using Oracle Enterprise Manager. To log on you can use the standard Oracle account:

User ID: system
Password: manager
Service: <SID>.world
Connect as: normal

You are then asked if you want to create the Oracle Repository and you have to answer OK.

Oracle Fail Safe verification: You can log on to the Oracle Fail Safe manager using the following account:

User ID: <sid>adm
Password: ibm
Cluster alias: SAPCLUS
Domain: SAPDOM

Then you can start the Oracle Fail Safe Cluster Verification utility by clicking **Troubleshooting > Verify Cluster**. Look at the log to see if there is any problem.

5.13.2 DB2

You should log on to the databases <SID> and ADM<SID> using a DB2 command window. Please follow the test steps described below:

1. Log on as user <sid>adm to Node A.

2. Move the DB2 cluster group to Node B and bring online.

3. Open a DB2 command window (DB2CMD at a command prompt).

4. Enter the following command after replacing the SID and the Windows NT password for the user sapr3, which should succeed without error:

   db2 connect to <SID> user sapr3 using <sapr3 NT password>

5. Enter the following command after replacing the SID and the Windows NT password for the user sapr3, which should succeed without error:

   db2 connect to ADM<SID> user sapr3 using <sapr3 NT password>

6. Log on as user <sid>adm to Node B.

7. Move the DB2 cluster group to Node A and bring online.

8. Open a DB2 command window (DB2CMD at a command prompt).

9. Enter the following command after replacing the SID and the Windows NT password for the user sapr3, which should succeed without error.

   db2 connect to <SID> user sapr3 using <sapr3 NT password>

10. Enter the following command after replacing the SID and the Windows NT password for the user sapr3, which should succeed without error:

    db2 connect to ADM<SID> user sapr3 using <sapr3 NT password>

5.13.3 SQL Server

You can log on to the DBMS using the SQL Enterprise Manager. This utility runs under the MMC and can be installed only on one of the cluster nodes. The installation routine checks if it is already installed on the other node and stops with an error in that case. To use the SQL Enterprise Manager in any possible cluster configuration it is recommended to install it also on an administrative desktop.

Test the SQL Server installation as follows:

- Register the virtual database by clicking the button **Register Server** in the toolbar, and providing the database virtual name (ITSSQL, in our installation).

- Perform simple queries (from the sample *pubs* database, for example).

5.14 Backbone configuration

Splitting the network in two (a public one used by clients to connect to the application servers, and a backbone one used by application servers to communicate to the DB server) can improve security and performance. Security is improved because you get a better control on the unencrypted traffic between application and DB servers. Performance is improved because the backbone allows you to separate the *dialog traffic* between the SAPGUI and Dialog work processes from the *update traffic* between Update work processes and the DB server (see 9.2, "Benefits of the backbone configuration" on page 245 for details).

As a rule of thumb we can say that each dialog step generates approximately 1.7 KB of data flows between the SAPGUI and the application server and 20 KB of data flows between the database and the application server (see Chapter 11 of *SAP R/3 Implementation with ASAP*, by Hartwig Brand). So while a 100 Mbit Fast Ethernet network could be enough for the public network (dialog traffic), a 1 Gigabit Ethernet network could be necessary for the backbone (update traffic).

Step 27: Additional steps for backbone configuration

Refer to Chapter 9, "Backbone network" on page 233:

- 9.1, "Backbone configuration" on page 233 provides a detailed description of the additional configuration steps necessary for backbone configuration.

- 9.2, "Benefits of the backbone configuration" on page 245 contains a concise description of how the packets flow on the public and backbone network if the backbone configuration described in 9.1, "Backbone configuration" on page 233 is used.

5.15 SAP cluster verification

Now that the installation is complete, it is time to verify that everything is working. We repeat the cluster tests that were done at the end of the cluster installation, although now we have three different cluster groups: Cluster, SAP and DB. These groups can be all in one node or spread between the nodes. All possible configurations should be tested.

Due to installation errors it is possible to have a working system in all the possible configurations but one. As a result, we strongly recommend you test all possible configurations. If time does not allow you to test all configurations we strongly recommend you test at least the more problematic ones as listed in Table 24:

Table 24. Minimum recommended test configurations (bold indicates expected node changes)

#	Test	Action	Status before test	Status after test	X
1	Manual failover using the Cluster Administrator	Move Cluster Group from Node A to Node B	Cluster Group: **Node A** SAP Group: Node A DB Group: Node B	Cluster Group: **Node B** SAP Group: Node A DB group: Node B	
2	Manual failover using the Cluster Administrator	Move SAP Group from Node A to Node B	Cluster Group: Node A SAP Group: **Node A** DB Group: Node B	Cluster Group: Node A SAP Group: **Node B** DB group: Node B	
3	Manual failover using the Cluster Administrator[1]	Move DB Group from Node B to Node A	Cluster Group: Node A SAP Group: Node A DB Group: **Node B**	All groups on Node A	
4	Manual failover using the Cluster Administrator	Move Cluster Group from Node B to Node A	Cluster Group: **Node B** SAP Group: Node B DB Group: Node A	Cluster Group: **Node A** SAP Group: Node B DB group: Node A	
5	Manual failover using the Cluster Administrator	Move SAP Group from Node B to Node A	Cluster Group: Node B SAP Group: **Node B** DB Group: Node A	Cluster Group: Node B SAP Group: **Node A** DB group: Node A	
6	Manual failover using the Cluster Administrator[1]	Move DB Group from Node A to Node B	Cluster Group: Node B SAP Group: Node B DB Group: **Node A**	All groups on Node B	
7	Regular shutdown of Node A	Shut down Node A	Cluster Group: **Node A** SAP Group: **Node A** DB Group: Node B	All groups on Node B	
8	Regular shutdown of Node B	Shut down Node B	Cluster Group: Node A SAP Group: Node A DB Group: **Node B**	All groups on Node A	

#	Test	Action	Status before test	Status after test	X
9	Regular shutdown of Node A	Shut down Node A	Cluster Group: Node B SAP Group: Node B DB Group: **Node A**	All groups on Node B	
10	Regular shutdown of Node B	Shut down Node B	Cluster Group: **Node B** SAP Group: **Node B** DB Group: Node A	All groups on Node A	
11	Blue screen on Node A[2]	Run KILL.EXE on Node A as per Note 2	Cluster Group: **Node A** SAP Group: **Node A** DB Group: Node B	All groups on Node B	
12	Blue screen on Node B[2]	Run KILL.EXE on Node B per Note 2	Cluster Group: Node A SAP Group: Node A DB Group: **Node B**	All groups on Node A	
13	Blue screen on Node A[2]	Run KILL.EXE on Node A per Note 2	Cluster Group: Node B SAP Group: Node B DB Group: **Node A**	All groups on Node B	
14	Blue screen on Node B[2]	Run KILL.EXE on Node B per Note 2	Cluster Group: **Node B** SAP Group: **Node B** DB Group: Node A	All groups on Node A	
15	Power off of Node A	Power off	Cluster Group: **Node A** SAP Group: **Node A** DB Group: Node B	All groups on Node B	
16	Power off of Node B	Power off	Cluster Group: Node A SAP Group: Node A DB Group: **Node B**	All groups on Node A	
17	Power off of Node A	Power off	Cluster Group: Node B SAP Group: Node B DB Group: **Node A**	All groups on Node B	
18	Power off of Node B	Power off	Cluster Group: **Node B** SAP Group: **Node B** DB Group: Node A	All groups on Node A	

Notes:

1 DB2 currently does not support the manual failover of the DB Group using the Cluster Administrator if there are active connections open to the database.

2 The blue screen can be obtained by killing the WINLOGON.EXE process by means of the KILL.EXE utility contained in the Windows NT Resource Kit.

5.16 Tuning

Step 28: Tuning

Basic information about how to tune an SAP system plus bibliographic references can be found in Chapter 10, "Tuning" on page 249.

5.17 Configuring a remote shell

Step 29: Configure a remote shell

Several R/3 transactions, such as DB13, use external programs to perform their tasks. These external programs, such as BRARCHIVE.EXE, must run on the database server. R/3 normally uses an R/3 instance running on the DB server to start the external program via the helper program SAPXPG.EXE. If no R/3 instance is found on the DB server, the program is started via a remote function call (RFC) to rsh (remote shell).

Note

As of SAP Release 4.5, the SAPXPG program can be started via an SAP gateway, which must be set up on the stand-alone database server.

Check OSS note 0108777 *CCMS: Message 'SAPXPG failed for BRTOOLS' for further information.*

In a cluster environment no R/3 instance is running on the DB server in the normal configuration and therefore R/3 tries to start the external program using rsh. A standard Windows NT environment does not provide an rsh and you have to use third party tools to provide this functionality.

One program recommended by SAP is Ataman TCP Remote Logon Services at:

http://www.ataman.com

The rest of this section describes the setup of an rsh using the Ataman product. For the latest information please check the notes listed at the end of this section.

1. Install the Ataman TCP Remote Logon Services on Node A and Node B of your cluster into a directory on a non-shared disk. Carry out the installation in accordance with the description in the document USERMAN.DOC which is part of the Ataman package.

2. Configure the Ataman TCP Remote Logon Service on Node A and Node B as follows:

   a. Via the Windows NT start menu select **Control Panel > Services**.
   b. Select the service **Ataman TCP R.L. Service**.
   c. Set the Startup Type via the Startup button to **Automatic**.

3. Define the environment for the rsh users on Node A:

   With the Ataman software this is possible by specifying an environment file in the user settings. To generate an environment file with the variables required by R/3 follow these steps:

   a. Log on as user <sid>adm to Node A.

   b. Open a command window and change the directory to <%WINDIR%>\SapCluster (in our lab, C:\WINNT\SapCluster).

   c. Run the following command from the prompt:

      ```
      ntreg2cmd <SID>
      ```

      The command ntreg2cmd generates the command file <SID>env.cmd in the directory in which ntreg2cmd was called.

   d. You must make the following changes in this file using an editor:

      • Remove all "@set" at the beginning of each line. **Note**: Do not remove only the "@" but also the "set".

      • Adjust the value of the variable PATH to the current value of PATH in the environment <sid>adm. To get this value enter the following command at the command prompt:

        ```
        PATH > POUT
        ```

        Open the file POUT in an editor and copy the line to the file <SID>END.CMD replacing the original PATH line.

      • Replace further variable specifications with their respective values. Supplement the following parameters:

        ```
        SAPMNT=\\<virt. R3.host\sapmnt
        SAPEXE=<%windir%>\SapCluster
        ```

   e. Verify that the file <SID>ENV.CMD is located in the directory <%windir%>\SapCluster.

4. Copy the environment file <SID>env.cmd from Node A to the directory <%windir%>\SapCLuster on Node B.

5. Configure the rsh users as listed in Table 25:

Table 25. Required rsh users per database

Database	rsh users required
ORACLE	<sid>adm SAPService<SID>
DB2	<sid>adm db2<sid> sapse<sid>
MS SQL	<sid>adm SAPService<SID>

Perform the following steps for *each* required rsh user for your specific DBMS.

a. Select Control Panel and double-click there on the icon **Ataman TCP R.L. Services**.

b. The window Ataman Remote Logon Services appears. Select **user** and click on **Add users**.

c. The Add user window is opened. Fill in the required fields as shown in Table 26 on page 167.

d. Repeat steps a-c for the other required rsh users.

Table 26. Ataman user configuration parameters

Parameters	Restrictions and recommendations	Lab values	Your values
User Name	rsh user name, for example, <sid>adm	itsadm	
NT User Name	rsh user name, for example, <sid>adm	itsadm	
NT User Domain	<domain name>	SAPDOM	
Home Directory	<%windir%>\SapCluster Environment variables cannot be used.	C:\WINNT\SapCluster	
Interactive CMD Processor	not used	<EMPTY>	
Batch CMD Processor	not used	<EMPTY>	

Parameters	Restrictions and recommendations	Lab values	Your values
Environment File	<%windir%>\SapCluster\<SID>env.cmd	C:\WINNT\SapCluster\ITSenv.cmd	
NT password	Windows NT password for user	ibm	
Host Equivalence List (see Note 1)	1	servera, serverb, SAPCLUS, ITSSAP, ITSDB2	

Notes:

1 Enter the addresses of Node A and B and the virtual address of the cluster, the SAP R/3 and the DB group or a wildcard string which includes the hosts above. If you are using host names these must follow the domain name notation. Additional application servers must also be mentioned here.

6. After setting up everything correctly on Node A perform the following steps to copy the configuration to Node B:

   a. Open command prompt on Node A.
   b. Change into the Ataman installation directory.
   c. Execute the following command:
      `auseradm dump >uconfig.cmd`
   d. Open a command prompt on Node B after installing the Ataman software.
   e. Copy the file uconfig.cmd from Node A to Node B into the Ataman directory.
   f. Execute the following command:
      `uconfig.cmd`

7. Check the Ataman configuration:

   a. Log on as <sid>adm to Node A.

   b. Open a command prompt and enter the following command with <hostname> replaced with each of the values in servera, serverb, SAPCLUS, ITSSAP, and ITS<DB>:

      `rsh <hostname> set`

      Verify that the variable values returned are correct.

   c. Log on as <sid>adm to Node B.

   d. Open a command prompt and enter the following command with <hostname> replaced with each of the values in servera, serverb, SAPCLUS, <SID>SAP, and <SID><DB>:

      `rsh <hostname> set`

      Verify that the variable values returned are correct.

> **Note**
>
> For the latest information regarding remote command execution and setup, see the following OSS notes:
>
> 0114287: *SAPDBA in a Microsoft Cluster Server environment (ORACLE, MSCS)*
>
> 0126985: *Configuration of Ataman Remote Shell for DB2CS/NT*

5.18 Configuration of the SAPOSCOL destination

Step 30: Configuration of the SAPOSCOL destination

> **Note**
>
> If you installed the cluster on Windows 2000 you must replace the SAPOSCOL executable with the latest version from the SAP FTP server. Check section 5.12.2 on page 154 for the procedure.
>
> OSS note 0169468: *Windows 2000 support provides additional information*

The SAP operating system collector (SAPOSCOL) is used to gather statistical information from the operating system. The SAPOSCOL destination is the definition of an R/3 application server running an SAPOSCOL service. The definition is internal to the R/3 system.

> **Note**
>
> Check the following OSS note for additional information:
>
> 0114287: *SAPDBA in a Microsoft Cluster Server environment (ORACLE, MSCS)*

In a cluster, two SAPOSCOL destinations must be maintained:

- SAPOSCOL_<virtual_DB_hostname>
- SAPOSCOL_<virtual_R3_hostname>

To maintain the two SAPOSCOL destinations for <virtual_DB_hostname> (lab value: ITS<DB>) and <virtual_R3_hostname> (lab value: ITSSAP) repeat the following steps for each destination:

1. Call Transaction SM59. Select TCP/IP connections and open the available SAPOSCOL destination by double-clicking.

2. Select **Destination > Copy** to copy the destination both to SAPOSCOL_<virtual DB Host> and to SAPOSCOL_<virtual R3 Host>. Adjust the name of the target machine accordingly. The program is called via the default search path as defined in the environment variable PATH. Therefore there are no adjustments necessary here.

3. Test the connection by clicking **Test connection**. If the test fails, check the Ataman configuration.

4. Save the destinations that were created.

5. Call Transaction AL15 and select ADD SAPOSCOl-Dest. Select the SAPOSCOL destination created in step 2 above and enter a suitable description. When you add the SAPOSCOL_<virtual DB Host> destination you need to mark the DB server box before you save the entry.

Chapter 6. Installation using Oracle

In this chapter we describe the installation of SAP R/3 Release 4.5B on Oracle 8.0.5.x. This material forms part of the overall installation as described in Chapter 5, "Installation and verification" on page 119. Specifically, this chapter is referenced in step 24 on page 151.

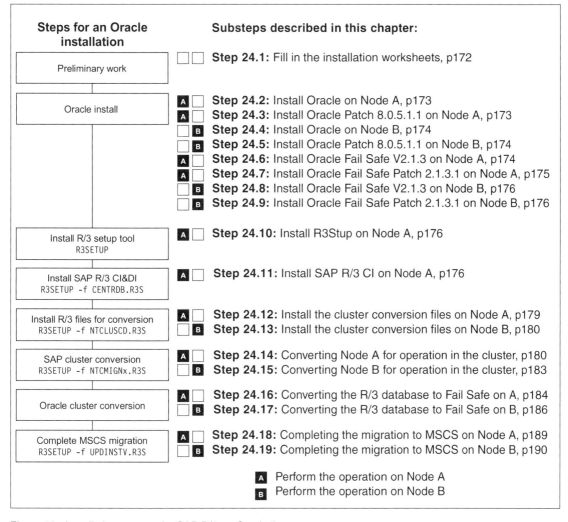

Steps for an Oracle installation

- Preliminary work
- Oracle install
- Install R/3 setup tool
  R3SETUP
- Install SAP R/3 CI&DI
  R3SETUP -f CENTRDB.R3S
- Install R/3 files for conversion
  R3SETUP -f NTCLUSCD.R3S
- SAP cluster conversion
  R3SETUP -f NTCMIGNx.R3S
- Oracle cluster conversion
- Complete MSCS migration
  R3SETUP -f UPDINSTV.R3S

Substeps described in this chapter:

Step 24.1: Fill in the installation worksheets, p172

Step 24.2: Install Oracle on Node A, p173
Step 24.3: Install Oracle Patch 8.0.5.1.1 on Node A, p173
Step 24.4: Install Oracle on Node B, p174
Step 24.5: Install Oracle Patch 8.0.5.1.1 on Node B, p174
Step 24.6: Install Oracle Fail Safe V2.1.3 on Node A, p174
Step 24.7: Install Oracle Fail Safe Patch 2.1.3.1 on Node A, p175
Step 24.8: Install Oracle Fail Safe V2.1.3 on Node B, p176
Step 24.9: Install Oracle Fail Safe Patch 2.1.3.1 on Node B, p176

Step 24.10: Install R3Stup on Node A, p176

Step 24.11: Install SAP R/3 CI on Node A, p176

Step 24.12: Install the cluster conversion files on Node A, p179
Step 24.13: Install the cluster conversion files on Node B, p180

Step 24.14: Converting Node A for operation in the cluster, p180
Step 24.15: Converting Node B for operation in the cluster, p183

Step 24.16: Converting the R/3 database to Fail Safe on A, p184
Step 24.17: Converting the R/3 database to Fail Safe on B, p186

Step 24.18: Completing the migration to MSCS on Node A, p189
Step 24.19: Completing the migration to MSCS on Node B, p190

A Perform the operation on Node A
B Perform the operation on Node B

Figure 50. Installation process for SAP R/3 on Oracle 8

171

An overall description of the installation process is shown in Figure 50. You will note that some steps are to be done on Node A, some on Node B, and some are to be carried out on both nodes.

Before beginning the installation we recommend you read the following documents:

- The continually updated OSS note 0134135 *4.5 B R/3 Installation on Windows NT (general)*.

- OSS note 0114287 *SAPDBA in a Microsoft Cluster Server Environment*.

- The document *Checklist - Installation Requirements: Windows NT*. The main points of the checklist are discussed in 4.1, "Checklist for SAP MSCS installation" on page 70.

- *Oracle: Conversion to Microsoft Cluster Server: Oracle 4.0B 4.5A 4.5B* (document 51005504).

- The continually updated OSS note 0134070 *4.5 B Installation on Windows NT: Oracle* containing a description of known problems.

- The installation guide *Oracle DBMS: R/3 Installation on Windows NT: Oracle Database Release 4.5B* (51004599).

Step 24

The steps in this database chapter are substeps of step 24 on page 151 in Chapter 5.

6.1 Preliminary work

Step 24.1: Fill in the installation worksheets

Before you begin, you should fill in all the SAP installation worksheets in this chapter.

Log on as the installation user

Throughout the entire installation process, make sure you are always logged on as the installation user (in our lab, saplnst). This user must be a domain administrator as described in step 23.

6.2 Oracle installation

Step 24.2: Install Oracle on Node A

To install Oracle on Node A, complete the following:

1. Power on both Node A and Node B.

2. Move all cluster resources to Node A using Microsoft Cluster Administrator.

3. Log on to Node A as the installation user (in our lab, sapinst).

4. Insert the Oracle RDBMS CD-ROM in Node A and start the Oracle Installer by running ORAINST from the \NT\I386\WIN32\INSTALL directory.

5. You are asked to provide several values we have listed in Table 27:

Table 27. Oracle installation

Parameters	Lab values	Your values
Company name	IBM	
Oracle Home: Name	DEFAULT_HOME	
Oracle Home: Location	C:\orant	
Oracle Home: Language	English_SAP	
Path update	Leave path unchanged	
Type of installation	Oracle8 Enterprise Edition	

At the end of the installation reboot the system.

Note: If you realize you have used the Administrator account instead of the sapinst account, you can correct the error by simply logging on as sapinst and repeating all the installation steps in this section.

Step 24.3: Install Oracle Patch 8.0.5.1.1 on Node A

To install the Oracle patch on Node A, complete these steps:

1. Log on to Node A as the installation user (in our lab, sapinst).

2. Move all cluster resources to Node A using Microsoft Cluster Administrator.

3. From the Services applet in the Control Panel, stop all Oracle Services (it should be necessary to stop only the OracleTNSListener80 service).

4. Insert the Oracle RDBMS CD-ROM and start the Oracle Installer program by running SETUP.EXE in the \NT\I386\PATCHES\8.0.5.1.1.\WIN32\INSTALL directory.

5. You are asked to provide several values we have collected in Table 28:

Table 28. Oracle patch installation

Parameters	Lab values	Your values
Company name	IBM	
Oracle Home: Name	DEFAULT_HOME	
Oracle Home: Location	C:\orant	
Oracle Home: Language	English_SAP	
Software Asset Manager	Select only **Oracle8 Server Patch 8.0.5.1.1**	
Oracle 8 Server Patch components	Select all the components	

6. Ignore the request to run the scripts.

7. At the end of the installation reboot the system.

Step 24.4: Install Oracle on Node B

Repeat step 24.2 on page 173 for Node B.

Step 24.5: Install Oracle Patch 8.0.5.1.1 on Node B

Repeat step 24.3 on page 173 for Node B.

Step 24.6: Install Oracle Fail Safe V2.1.3 on Node A

To install OFS on Node A, do the following:

1. Log on to Node A as the installation user (in our lab, sapinst).

2. Move all cluster resources to Node A using Microsoft Cluster Administrator.

3. From the Services applet in the Control Panel, stop all Oracle Services (it should be necessary to stop only the OracleTNSListener80 service).

4. Insert the Oracle Fail Safe CD and start the Oracle installer program by running ORAINST in the \NT\I386\WIN32\INSTALL directory.

5. You are asked to provide several values we have collected in Table 29.

Table 29. Oracle Fail Safe installation

Parameters	Lab values	Your values
Company name	IBM	
Oracle Home: Name	DEFAULT_HOME	
Oracle Home: Location	C:\orant	
Oracle Home: Language	English_SAP	
Path update	Accept path change	
Software Asset Manager	Select only Oracle Fail Safe Manager 2.1.3.0.0 and Oracle Fail Safe Server 2.1.3.0.0 under Available Products	
Oracle Fail Safe docs	Select all	

6. If you are installing on Node B, ignore the Oracle Fail Safe discovery error message.

7. Continue to step 24.7 without rebooting the system.

Step 24.7: Install Oracle Fail Safe Patch 2.1.3.1 on Node A

To install the OFS patch on Node A, do the following:

1. Insert the Oracle Fail Safe CD and start the Oracle installer program by running ORAINST.EXE in the \NT\I386\2131\WIN32\INSTALL directory.

2. You are asked to provide several values we have collected in Table 30.

Table 30. Oracle Fail Safe patch

Parameters	Lab values	Your values
Company name	IBM	
Oracle Home: Name	DEFAULT_HOME	
Oracle Home: Location	C:\orant	
Oracle Home: Language	English_SAP	
Path update	Leave path unchanged	
Software Asset Manager	Select only Oracle Fail Safe Server 2.1.3.1.0 from the list of available products	

3. At the end of the installation exit the Oracle installer and reboot the node.

Step 24.8: Install Oracle Fail Safe V2.1.3 on Node B

Repeat step 24.6 on page 174 for Node B.

Step 24.9: Install Oracle Fail Safe Patch 2.1.3.1 on Node B

Repeat step 24.7 on page 175 for Node B.

6.3 Installation of the R/3 setup tool on Node A

Step 24.10: Install R3Stup on Node A

To install R3Setup, do the following:

1. Log on to Node A as the installation user (in our lab, sapinst).

2. Move all cluster resources to Node A using Microsoft Cluster Administrator.

3. Start the R3Setup program from \NT\COMMON on the SAP Kernel CD-ROM.

4. You are asked to provide several values you can take from Table 31:

Table 31. R3Setup tool installation

Values	Restrictions and recommendations	Lab values	Your values
SAP system name (SAPSYSTEMNAME)	See *R/3 Installation on Windows NT: Oracle Database Release 4.5B*, page 4-5	ITS	
Installation directory path (INSTALLPATH)	Leave default	c:\users\itsadm\install	
Do you want to log off? (EXIT)		Yes	

6.4 Installation of the R/3 Central Instance on Node A

Step 24.11: Install SAP R/3 CI on Node A

To install the Central Instance on Node A, do the following:

1. Log on to Node A as the installation user (in our lab, sapinst).

2. Click **Start > Programs > SAP R/3 > SAP R/3 Setup - Central & Database Instance**. This is equivalent to using the command:

```
R3SETUP.EXE -f CENTRDB.R3S
```

3. You are asked to provide many values that you can take from Table 32. While inserting drive letters you must always use uppercase followed by the colon symbol, for example "J:".

Table 32. R/3 Central Instance installation

Parameters	Restrictions and recommendations	Lab values	Your values
SAP System Name (SAPSYSTEMNAME)	See *R/3 Installation on Windows NT: Oracle Database Release 4.5B,* page 4-5. Use uppercase characters.	ITS	
Number of the central system (SAPSYSNR)	Any two-digit number between 00 and 97	00	
Drive of the \usr\sap directory (SAPLOC)	• On the shared disks • Not on the Quorum disks • Not on Oracle disks	J:	
Windows NT domain name (SAPNTDOMAIN)		SAPDOM	
Central transport host (SAPTRANSHOST)		SAPTRANSHOST	
Character set settings (NLS_CHARACTERSET)		WE8DEC	
Default \Oracle<SID> drive SAPDATA_HOME	Home directory for SAPDATA<x> files	N:	
SAPDATA1	• On the shared disks • Not on the Quorum disks • Not on the SAPLOC disk • Not on the OrigLog disks • Not on the MirrorLog disks • Not on the Archive disks	N:	
SAPDATA2	Same as for SAPDATA1	O:	
SAPDATA3	Same as for SAPDATA1	P:	
SAPDATA4	Same as for SAPDATA1	P:	
SAPDATA5	Same as for SAPDATA1	N:	

Parameters	Restrictions and recommendations	Lab values	Your values
SAPDATA6	Same as for SAPDATA1	O:	
OrigLogA	Same as for SAPDATA1	K:	
OrigLogB	Same as for SAPDATA1	L:	
MirrorLogA	Same as for SAPDATA1	L:	
MirrorLogB	Same as for SAPDATA1	K:	
SapArch	Same as for SAPDATA1	M:	
SapBackup		K:	
SapCheck		K:	
SapReorg		L:	
SapTrace		L:	
sapr3 account password		ibm	
RAM that is reserved to the R/3 system (RAM_INSTANCE)	Change the default only if you install multiple R/3 Systems in a single host	default	
Empty directory to which the Export1-CD is to be copied	Leave default	Leave default	
Empty directory to which the Export2-CD is to be copied	Leave default	Leave default	
Port number of the message server (PORT)	Leave default	3600 (default)	
<sid>adm password		ibm	
SAPService<SID> password		ibm	
Do you want to use the SAP Gateway? (R2_CONNECTION)		NO	
Number of R3load processes (PROCESSES)	For Oracle, set this to 1 regardless of the number of CPUs installed	1	

Parameters	Restrictions and recommendations	Lab values	Your values
Operating system platform for which the report loads will be imported	Must be Windows NT	Windows NT	

4. Continue on to step 24.12 without rebooting the system.

6.5 Install the R3Setup files for cluster conversion

Step 24.12: Install the cluster conversion files on Node A

To install the R3Setup files required for cluster conversion, do the following. When you begin these steps you should still be logged on Node A as sapinst.

1. Start the cluster conversion program by running NTCLUST.BAT in the \NT\COMMON directory on the CD ROM drive. Essentially the batch file executes the following command:

R3SETUP - NTCLUSCD.R3S

2. You are asked to provide many values you can take from Table 33:

Table 33. R3Setup files for the cluster conversion: Node A

Parameters	Restrictions and recommendations	Lab values	Your values
SAP System Name (SAPSYSTEMNAME)	See *R/3 Installation on Windows NT: Oracle Database. Release 4.5B,* page 4-5. Use uppercase characters.	ITS	
Installation directory path (INSTALLPATH)	Leave default	c:\Users\itsadm\install	
Do you want to log off? (EXIT)		Yes	

3. Log on to Node B as the installation user (in our lab, sapinst).

4. Start the cluster conversion program by running NTCLUST.BAT in the \NT\COMMON directory on the CD-ROM.

5. You are asked to provide many values you can take from Table 34:

Table 34. R3Setup files for cluster conversion on Node B

Parameters	Restrictions and recommendations	Lab values	Your values
SAP System Name (SAPSYSTEMNAME)	See *R/3 Installation on Windows NT: Oracle Database Release 4.5B,* page 4-5. Use uppercase characters.	ITS	
Installation directory path (INSTALLPATH)	Leave default	c:\Users\itsadm\install	
Do you want to log off? (EXIT)		Yes	

6. Continue to step 24.13 without rebooting Node A.

Step 24.13: Install the cluster conversion files on Node B

Repeat step 24.12 for Node B.

6.6 SAP cluster conversion

Step 24.14: Converting Node A for operation in the cluster

Do the following on Node A:

1. Log on to Node A as the installation user (in our lab, sapinst).

2. Click **Start > SAP R/3 Setup for ITS > SAP R3 Setup - Configuring Node A for a MSCS.**

   This is the same as the command:

   R3SETUP.EXE -f NTCMIGNA.R3S

3. You are asked to provide many values we have collected in Table 35:

Table 35. Conversion of Node A for cluster operation

Parameters	Restrictions and recommendations	Lab values	Your values
Virtual host name of the R/3 Cluster Group (NETWORKNAME)		ITSSAP	
Virtual IP address of the R/3 Cluster Group (IPADDRESS)	If the HOSTS file has been configured the proposed value is the correct one.	192.168.0.51	

Parameters	Restrictions and recommendations	Lab values	Your values
Subnet mask for the virtual IP address for the R/3 Cluster group (SUBNETMASK)		255.255.255.0	
Name of the public network used for the R/3 Cluster group (NETWORKTOUSE)	Name of the network to which the virtual IP address belongs as defined in MSCS	Public	
SAP System Name (SAPSYSTEMNAME)	See *R/3 Installation on Windows NT: Oracle Database Release 4.5B*, page 4-5. Use uppercase characters.	ITS	
Number of the central system (SAPSYSNR)	See Note 1	00	
Drive of the \usr\sap directory (SAPLOC)	See Note 1	J:	
Windows NT domain name (SAPNTDOMAIN)	See Note 1	SAPDOM	
Virtual host name of the R/3 Oracle Group (DBHOSTNAME)	Attention! Do not use the virtual host name of the Oracle group here. Instead use the local host name of Node A.	servera	
Character set settings (NLS_CHARACTERSET)	See Note 1	WE8DEC	
Default \Oracle<SID> drive SAPDATA_HOME	See Note 1	N:	
SAPDATA1	See Note 1	N:	
SAPDATA2	See Note 1	O:	
SAPDATA3	See Note 1	P:	
SAPDATA4	See Note 1	P:	
SAPDATA5	See Note 1	N:	
SAPDATA6	See Note 1	O:	
OrigLogA	See Note 1	K:	

Parameters	Restrictions and recommendations	Lab values	Your values
OrigLogB	See Note 1	L:	
MirrorLogA	See Note 1	L:	
MirrorLogB	See Note 1	K:	
SapArch	See Note 1	M:	
SapBackup	See Note 1	K:	
SapCheck	See Note 1	K:	
SapReorg	See Note 1	L:	
SapTrace	See Note 1	L:	
sapr3 account password		ibm	
RAM that is reserved to the R/3 system (RAM_INSTANCE)	Change the default only if you install multiple R/3 systems in a single host.	default	
Port number of the message server (PORT)	Leave the default value.	3600 (default)	
<sid>adm password		ibm	
SAPService<sid> password		ibm	
Do you want to use the SAP Gateway? (R2_CONNECTION)		No	
Note 1: Value previously used, see Table 32 on page 177.			

Possible error

The R3Setup program may stop at this point. You may see the error message shown in Figure 83 on page 276. If this happens perform the following steps:

1. Exit from R3Setup.
2. Start R3Setup a second time with the same parameters as before.
3. Provide the password values as required.

Step 24.15: Converting Node B for operation in the cluster

1. When R3Setup has finished, log off and log on again to Node A as user <sid>adm (in our lab itsadm); do not use sapinst here. (**Note**: You are logging on to Node A here, not Node B).

2. Connect to the Oracle Instance Manager by clicking **Start > Oracle Enterprise Manager > Instance Manager**. Use the following information:

   User name: internal
   Password: oracle
   Service: ITS.WORLD
   Connect as: Normal

3. Shut down the instance as shown in Figure 51:

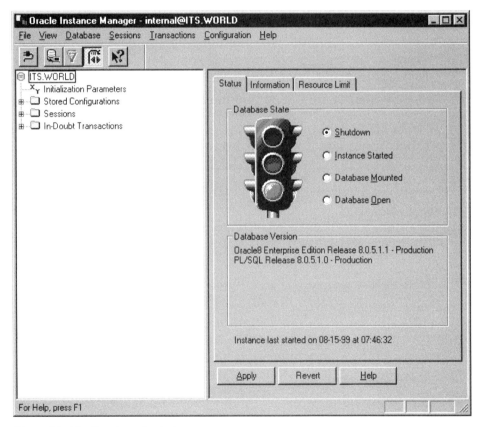

Figure 51. Shutting down the instance

4. At the warning message click **Yes.**

5. Select **Immediate** in the Shutdown Mode window.

6. Move the Cluster Group and the Disk groups to Node B using Microsoft Cluster Administrator.

7. Take the SAP-R/3 ITS group offline and move it to Node B.

8. On Node B bring all the resources in the SAP-R/3 ITS group online except the SAP-R/3 ITS resource. You can do this by starting from the bottom of the dependency tree and following the dependencies up the tree.

9. Log on to Node B as itsadm.

10. Click **Start > SAP R/3 Setup for ITS > SAP R3 Setup - Configuring Node B for a MSCS**, which corresponds to launching the program.

   R3SETUP.EXE -f NTCMIGNB.R3S

11. You are asked to provide many values you must take from Table 35. Do not change any value in the table. We particularly recommend you be careful with the DBHOSTNAME. You must use servera again, not serverb.

6.7 Oracle cluster conversion

Step 24.16: Converting the R/3 database to Fail Safe on A

Do the following to convert the database installed on Node A to a Fail Safe database:

1. Shut down Node A.

2. Shut down Node B.

3. Restart Node A.

4. Restart Node B.

5. Log on to Node A as the installation user (in our lab, sapinst).

6. Restart the Oracle Instance by clicking **Start > Oracle Enterprise Manager > Instance Manager** and connect using these values:

   User name: internal
   Password: oracle
   Service: ITS.WORLD
   Connect as: Normal

7. Select **Database Open** as shown in Figure 52:

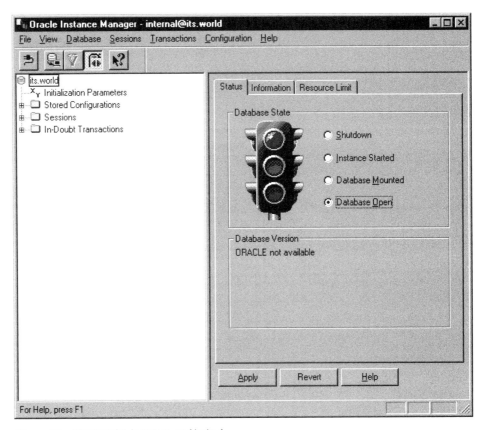

Figure 52. Starting the instance on Node A

8. You are asked to provide the local parameter file as shown in Figure 53. Select **initITS.ora.**

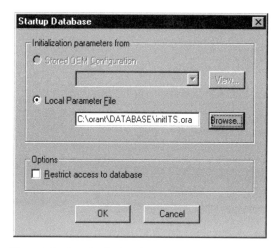

Figure 53. Specify the local parameter file

Step 24.17: Converting the R/3 database to Fail Safe on B

Do the following to convert the database on Node B to a Fail Safe database:

1. Copy the init<SID>.ORA file (in our lab, initITS.ORA) from
   \<Oracle_Home>\Database (in our lab c:\orant\database) on Node A to the
   same directory on Node B.

2. Click on **Start > Programs > Oracle Enterprise Manager > Oracle Fail
   Safe Manager** and connect using the values in Table 36.

Table 36. Connecting to Fail Safe Manager

Parameters	Meanings	Lab values	Your values
User Name	User ID of the account used for the Cluster Server service	ClusSvc	
Password	Password of the account used for the Cluster Server service	ibm	
Cluster Alias	Cluster Group network name	SAPCLUS	
Domain	Windows NT domain	SAPDOM	

3. Create the Fail Safe group ORACLE<SID> (in our lab, ORACLEITS). In
   Oracle Fail Safe Manager, click **Groups > Create**.

Provide information from Table 37:

Table 37. Conversion of Oracle DB to a Fail Safe DB: Table 1

Parameters	Meanings	Lab values	Your values
Group Name	Name of the Oracle Cluster Group	ORACLEITS	
Network	Network used to connect to the Oracle Cluster Group	Public	
Network Name	Oracle Cluster Group: Network Name	ITSORA	
IP Address	Oracle Cluster Group: IP Address	192.168.0.52	
Subnet Mask	Oracle Cluster Group: Subnet Mask	255.255.255.0	
Failover Period	Leave default	6 Hours	
Failover Threshold	Leave default	10 times	
Failback Mode	Prevent failback	Prevent failback	

4. In Oracle Fail Safe Manager click **SAPCLUS > Databases > Standalone Databases**, right-click **ITS.WORLD** and select **Add to Group**.

5. Provide the following values:

Table 38. Conversion of an Oracle DB to a Fail Safe DB: Table 2

Values	Meanings	Lab values	Your values
Group Name		ORACLEITS	
Service Name		ITS.WORLD	
Instance Name		ITS	
Database Name	<SID>	ITS	
Parameter file	\<Oracle_Home>\database\init<SID>.ora where <Oracle_Home> is environment variable	c:\orant\database\initITS.ora	
Account to access the database	Internal	Internal	
Password	oracle	oracle	

Values	Meanings	Lab values	Your values
Oracle Fail Safe Policy: Pending Timeout	Leave default	180 sec	
Oracle Fail Safe Policy: "IsAlive" interval	Leave default	60000 millisecs	
Oracle Fail Safe Policy: The cluster software has to restart the DB in case of failure		Yes	

6. Confirm the operation Add Database to Fail Safe Group and click **Yes.**

7. When the Add Agent to Group OracleITS window appears select **M:** (this is the SAP archive drive in our lab) as the disk for the Oracle Fail Safe repository.

Note

Be careful not to select the quorum disk as the disk for the Oracle Fail Safe repository, because making this error requires a complete reinstallation of the Oracle and R/3 software. The Oracle DBMS cluster group has to be independent from the MSCS cluster group.

---

8. Move the SAP cluster group to Node B using Microsoft Cluster Administrator.

9. Using either SAPPAD.EXE or Notepad, open the file J:\usr\sap\<SID>\sys\profile\DEFAULT.PFL and modify the SAPDBHOST line as shown in Figure 54. Change servera to itsora as shown.

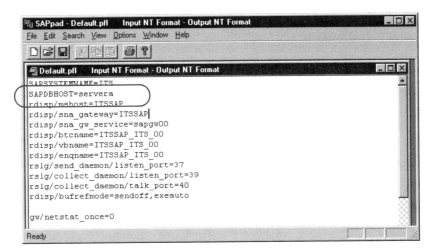

Figure 54. Changing DEFAULT.PFL

For troubleshooting, detailed information can be found in *Oracle Fail Safe Concepts and Administration Release 2.0.5* (document A57521-01). Particularly relevant are:

- The description of the modifications in the TNSNAMES.ORA and LISTENER.ORA files in section 2.5.
- Chapter 6, Troubleshooting.
- Appendix B, containing the list of Oracle Fail Safe Messages.

6.8 Completing the migration to an MSCS

Step 24.18: Completing the migration to MSCS on Node A

Do the following:

1. Log on to Node A as the installation user (in our lab, sapinst).
2. Using Microsoft Cluster Administrator:
   - Move the Quorum Disk resource to the Cluster Group if you have not already done that.
   - Delete the empty Cluster Groups.
   - Move all the Cluster Groups to Node A.
   - Take the SAP-R/3 ITS resource online on Node A.

3. Click **Start > Programs > SAP R/3 Setup for ITS > SAP R/3 Setup - Completing the Migration to an MSCS (Instvers)**, which corresponds to the command:

```
R3SETUP.EXE -f UPDINSTV.R3S
```

4. You are asked to provide values we have collected in Table 39.

Table 39. Completion of the MSCS migration on Node A

Parameters	Meanings	Lab values	Your values
Network Name for Cluster Resource Central Instance (CIHOSTNAME)		ITSSAP	
SAP System Name (SAPSYSTEMNAME)	See *R/3 Installation on Windows NT: Oracle Database Release 4.5B*, page 4-5. Use uppercase characters.	ITS	
Number of the central system (SAPSYSNR)	Any two-digit number between 00 and 97	00	

5. Reboot Node A.

Step 24.19: Completing the migration to MSCS on Node B

Do the following:

6. Log on to Node B as the installation user (in our lab, sapinst).

7. Move all cluster groups from Node A to Node B using Microsoft Cluster Administrator.

8. Click **Start > Programs > SAP R/3 Setup for ITS > SAP R/3 Setup - Completing the Migration to an MSCS (Instvers),** which corresponds to using the command:

```
R3SETUP.EXE -f UPDINSTV.R3S
```

9. You are asked to provide some values we have collected in Table 40.

Table 40. Completion of the MSCS migration on Node B

Parameters	Meanings	Lab values	Your values
Network Name for Cluster Resource Central Instance (CIHOSTNAME)		ITSSAP	
SAP System Name (SAPSYSTEMNAME)	See *R/3 Installation on Windows NT: Oracle Database Release 4.5B*, page 4-5. Use uppercase characters.	ITS	
Number of the central system (SAPSYSNR)	Any two-digit number between 00 and 97.	00	

10. Reboot Node B.

Return to step 25 on page 152 to continue the installation.

Chapter 7. Installation using DB2

In this chapter we describe the installation of SAP R/3 Release 4.5B on DB2 RDBMS 5.2 patch level 7 or later.

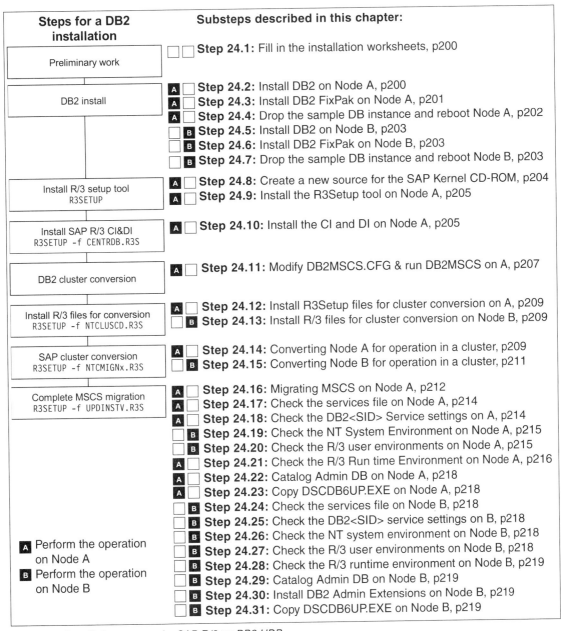

Figure 55. Installation process for SAP R/3 on DB2 UDB

This material forms part of the overall installation as described in Chapter 5, "Installation and verification" on page 119. Specifically, this chapter is referenced in step 24 on page 151.

An overall description of the installation process is shown in Figure 55. You will note that some steps are to be done on Node A, some on Node B, and some are to be carried out on both nodes.

The main references for the installation are:

- *R/3 Installation on Windows NT DB2 Common Server Release 4.5B* (document 5100 5502).

- *Conversion to Microsoft Cluster Server: DB2 Universal Database Server 4.5B* (document 5100 6418).

- The redpaper, *SAP R/3 and DB2 UDB in a Microsoft Cluster Environment*, available from http://www.redbooks.ibm.com.

- The IBM publication *DB2 Universal Database and SAP R/3 Version 4*, SC09-2801.

- The continually updated OSS note 0134135 *4.5 B R/3 Installation on Windows NT (General)*.

- *Checklist - Installation Requirements: Windows NT*. The main points of the checklist are discussed in 4.1, "Checklist for SAP MSCS installation" on page 70.

- The continually updated OSS note 0134159 *4.5 B Installation on Windows NT: DB2/CS*.

- The OSS note 0183184 *MSCS Template Update*.

7.1 The SAP R/3 with DB2 UDB cluster configuration explained

This section explains the "Standard Configuration" and the "Failover Configuration" of the R/3 cluster using DB2 UDB and explains how each configuration provides a running R/3 system.

7.1.4, "DB2 UDB administration extensions in the MSCS environment" on page 199 highlights topics in the contents of the DB2 UDB Administration Extensions for R/3 and MSCS.

7.1.1 The basics of DB2

A database manager instance in DB2 controls one or more databases. To gain access to a database, a user has to have access to a local database instance, before he or she can access a local or remote database. The database instance to use for the connection request is determined by the environment variable DB2INSTANCE and the requested database has to be cataloged in this local database instance.

7.1.2 The "Standard Configuration"

The configuration where the SAP R/3 instance is running on one node and the database is running on the other node is the "Standard Configuration".

In a clustered environment the R/3 database is controlled by the database instance db2<sid>. This database instance is part of the DB2 cluster group and can be started on Node A or Node B.

The work processes of the R/3 instance access the R/3 database through the local database instance db2l<sid>. A database instance with this name is installed locally, which means on a local disk under C:\SQLLIB\db2l<sid>, on both cluster nodes during the R/3 cluster migration steps.

The virtual database server ITSDB2 is the owner of the database instance db2<sid>, which controls the R/3 database <SID>. The virtual database server ITSDB2 and the R/3 database <SID> are cataloged in each local database instance db2l<sid>. The administration database ADM<SID> is also cataloged in each local database instance db2l<sid> but is not shown in the following sections.

Figure 56 shows the path taken by a request from an R/3 work process to the R/3 database <SID> in the standard configuration.

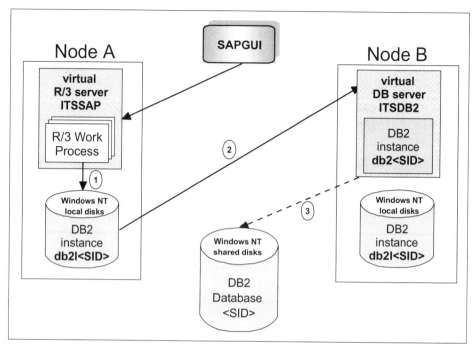

Figure 56. The "Standard Configuration"

1. The R/3 cluster group is running on Node A and the DB2 cluster group is running on Node B. The local database instances db2l<sid> are started on both nodes. The clustered database instance db2<sid> is running on Node B. The value of the environment variable DB2INSTANCE is set to db2l<sid> on both nodes.

2. The R/3 work process issues a CONNECT TO <SID> statement to connect to the database. This request is handled by the local database instance db2l<sid>, as defined in the environment variable DB2INSTANCE.

3. The local database instance checks its database catalog for the database <SID> and finds that this database is remote on server ITSDB2. ITSDB2 is the virtual name of the DB2 database server. So the local database instance routes the request via TCP/IP to the database instance db2<sid> on server ITSDB2. The connection is made via the service port sapdb2<SID>, as defined in the file services. Because the DB2 cluster group is currently running on Node B the request is actually routed to the physical Node B.

4. The clustered database instance db2<sid> checks its database catalog, finds that the database <SID> is a local database - controlled by this database instance - and routes the request to the database itself. The database engine is actually running on Node B, but the configuration information, data, and log files are stored on shared disks.

> **Note**
>
> In an MSCS configuration, the remote SAPGUI always connects to the virtual server ITSSAP, and not to the physical Node A or Node B.

7.1.3 The "Failover Configuration"

The configuration, where only one cluster node is active and runs both the R/3 central instance and the database, is the "Failover Configuration".

Figure 57 shows the path taken by a request from an R/3 work process to the R/3 database <SID> in the "Failover Configuration" - Node A active and Node B inactive.

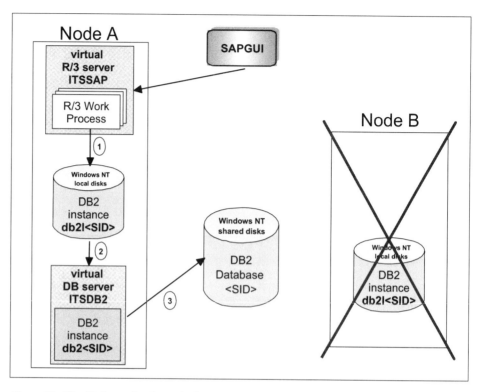

Figure 57. The "Failover Configuration"

1. The R/3 work process issues a CONNECT TO <SID> statement to connect to the database. This request is handled by the local database instance db2l<sid>.

2. The local database instance checks its database catalog for the database <SID> and finds that this database is remote on server ITSDB2. The local instance does not recognize that the database instance db2<sid> is actually running on Node A as well. So the local database instance routes the request via TCP/IP to the database instance db2<sid> on server ITSDB2. Because the DB2 cluster group is currently running on Node A, the request is actually routed to Node A again.

3. The clustered database instance db2<sid> checks its database catalog, finds that the database <SID> is a local database - controlled by this database instance - and routes the request to the database itself. The database engine is actually running on Node A, but the configuration information, database data, and log files are stored on shared disks.

> **Note**
>
> In an MSCS configuration, the remote SAPGUI always connects to the
> virtual server ITSSAP, and not to the physical Node A or Node B.

In a "Failover Configuration" the R/3 work process could actually access the
database instance db2<sid> directly, without going through the database
instance db2l<sid>. But this would mean, that every time you change from a
"Standard Configuration" to a "Failover Configuration" you have to change the
environment variable DB2INSTANCE at several places in the registry and to
restart the R/3 system to activate these changes. Because this would be error
prone and the performance impact of always using a local database instance
is very small, this was not implemented.

7.1.4 DB2 UDB administration extensions in the MSCS environment

During the installation of the R/3 system with R3Setup, a second DB2
database named ADM<SID> is created. It is cataloged in the local database
instance db2l<sid> on Node A and Node B. This database contains
information used for database log file management: backup, restore and tape
management. This database is also controlled by the clustered database
manager instance db2<sid> like the R/3 database <SID>. Its data files are
stored on the shared disks assigned to the DB2 cluster group.

The DB2 UDB Administration Extensions are a plug-in to the DB2 control
center and allow easy handling of database log file management. These
administration extensions rely on information stored in the ADM<SID>
database. The program SDDB6INS.EXE is used to install the server-side
extensions and to create the AMD<SID> database.

> **Note**
>
> In an MSCS environment, this program needs to be executed twice, once
> for Node A and then for Node B.

For further information about the administration extensions and the
installation program SDDB6INS.EXE check the following OSS notes:

- 0144839 — DB2/CS: SAP-DB2admin functions in DB2 Control Center
- 0141619 — DB2/CS: Installation program sddb6ins for SAP DB2admin

7.2 Preliminary work

Step 24.1: Fill in the installation worksheets

Before you begin, you should fill in all the SAP installation worksheets in this chapter.

> **Log on as the installation user**
>
> Throughout the entire installation process, make sure you are always logged on as the installation user (in our lab, sapinst). This user must be a domain administrator as described in step 23.

7.3 DB2 installation

Step 24.2: Install DB2 on Node A

1. Check SAPNET for more DB2 information by viewing OSS Notes 0134135, 0134159 and 0183184.

2. Log on as the installation user (in our lab, sapinst).

3. Insert the DB2 RDBMS CD-ROM and start the DB2 Installer by running SETUP.EXE in the \NT_i386\DBSW directory. Figure 58 appears:

Figure 58. Selection of products

4. Follow the installation process to install DB2 on Node A. Use Table 41 to help you enter all the installation parameters.

Do not reboot

Do not reboot Node A at the end of the installation.

Table 41. DB2 installation values for Node A

Parameters	Lab values	Your values
Select products	DB2 Universal Database Enterprise Edition	DB2 Universal Database Enterprise Edition
Installation type	Typical	
Destination directory	Leave default. Destination drive needs to be a local non-shared drive.	
db2admin and password	Leave default name. Enter password.	
Restart system	No	

Step 24.3: Install DB2 FixPak on Node A

1. Insert the DB2 RDBMS CD and start the DB2 Installer by running SETUP.EXE in the \NT_i386\FIXPAK directory. Figure 59 on page 202 appears.

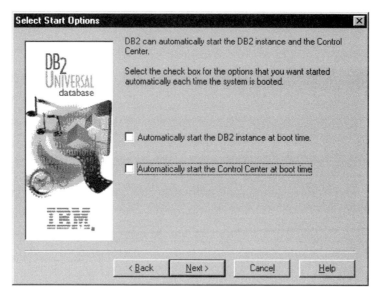

Figure 59. Start options

2. Deselect both check boxes.

3. When prompted, *do not* reboot the server.

Step 24.4: Drop the sample DB instance and reboot Node A

1. Log off and log on as the installation user (in our lab, sapinst) to enable the changes to the environment variables such as the search path.

2. Do not create the sample database as described in DB2 First Steps.

3. Remove the environment variable DB2INSTANCE from the SYSTEM environment.

   a. Open the System applet in the Windows NT Control Panel.
   b. Select the **Environment** tab.
   c. In the System Variables window, select the entry DB2INSTANCE.
   d. Click **Delete**.

4. Open a command prompt.

5. Remove the default database instance of DB2 using the command below:

   ```
   db2idrop DB2
   ```

6. Reboot Node A.

Step 24.5: Install DB2 on Node B

1. Insert the DB2 RDBMS CD and start the DB2 Installer by running SETUP.EXE in the \NT_i386\DBSW directory.

2. Follow the installation process to install DB2 on Node B. Use Table 42 to help you enter all the installation parameters.

> **Do not reboot Node B**
>
> Do not reboot Node B at the end of the installation.

Table 42. DB2 installation values for Node B

Parameter	Lab values	Your values
Select products	DB2 Universal Database Enterprise Edition	DB2 Universal Database Enterprise Edition
Installation type	Typical	
Destination directory	Leave default	
db2admin and password	Leave default name	
Restart system	No	

Step 24.6: Install DB2 FixPak on Node B

1. Insert the DB2 RDBMS CD and start the DB2 Installer program by double clicking SETUP in the \NT_i386\FIXPAK directory. Figure 59 on page 202 appears.

2. Deselect both values.

3. When prompted, *do not* reboot the server.

Step 24.7: Drop the sample DB instance and reboot Node B

1. Log off and log on as the installation user (in our lab, sapinst) to enable the changes to the environment variables such as the search path.

2. Do not create the SAMPLE database as described in DB2 First Steps.

3. Remove the environment variable DB2INSTANCE from the SYSTEM environment.

   a. Open the System applet in the Windows NT Control Panel.
   b. Select the **Environment** tab.
   c. In the System Variables window, select the entry DB2INSTANCE.
   d. Click **Delete**.

4. Open a command prompt.

5. Remove the default database instance of DB2 using the command below.

   ```
   db2idrop DB2
   ```

6. Reboot Node B.

7.4 Install the R3Setup tool on Node A

Step 24.8: Create a new source for the SAP Kernel CD-ROM

> **R3Setup templates**
>
> Check OSS note 183184 for the latest information on new R3Setup templates and procedures.
>
> **Do NOT use the original R3Setup templates from the original 4.5B installation package because they contain severe errors.**

Download the file R3SETUPCOMMON_**X**.CAR, with **X** >= 2, from the following location - replace sapserv3 with the name of your SAP FTP server:

```
ftp://sapserv3/general/R3server/patches/rel45B/NT/I386/DB6
```

See B.5, "SAPSERV FTP site" on page 285 for details on how to access this FTP site. Always obtain the most current version of the package files in case there are bug fixes. Download the file with the highest version number.

1. Create the directory C:\SAPKERNEL.

2. Copy the entire contents of the SAP Kernel CD-ROM into this directory.

3. Create a SAPPATCHES subdirectory.

4. Download the above R3SETUPCOMMON_**X**.CAR file from SAPSERV into the SAPPATCHES directory.

5. Unpack the R3SETUPCOMMON_**X**.CAR file into the SAPPATCHES directory using the command:

   ```
   C:\SAPKERNEL\NT\I386\car -xvf R3SETUPCOMMON_X.car
   ```

6. Copy the content of the SAPPATCHES directory into the directory C:\SAPKERNEL\NT\COMMON.

7. This is now the location of the new Kernel CD when the R3Setup program requests the path for the Kernel CD.

Step 24.9: Install the R3Setup tool on Node A

1. Log on as the installation user (in our lab, sapinst).

2. Move all cluster resources to Node A.

3. Explore the directory C:\SAPKERNEL\NT\COMMON and start the R3Setup program by runing R3SETUP in that directory.

4. Proceed with the installation using Table 43 for the installation parameters.

Table 43. Values for the installation of R3Setup on Node A

Value	Restrictions and recommendations	Lab value	Your values
SAP system name SAPSYSTEMNAME	See *R/3 Installation on Windows NT: DB2 Database. Release 4.5B*, page 4-5	ITS	
Path to installation directory INSTALL PATH	Leave default	Default	
Do you want to log off? CDINSTLOGOFF_NT_IND		Yes	

7.5 Install the Central Instance and Database Instance

Step 24.10: Install the CI and DI on Node A

1. Click **Start > Programs > SAP R3 Setup > SAP R3 Setup - Central & Database Instance**.

2. Proceed with the installation using Table 44 for the installation parameters.

Table 44. Values for the installation of Central Instance and Database Instance

Parameters	Restrictions and recommendations	Lab values	Your values
SAP system name (SAPSYSTEMNAME)	See *R/3 Installation on Windows NT: DB2 Database Release 4.5B*, page 4-5	ITS	
Number of the central system (SAPSYSNR)	Any two digit number between 00 and 97	00	
Drive of the \usr\sap directory SAPLOC	On the shared disks Not on the Quorum disk Not on any DB2 disks	J: (SAP software shared disk)	

Parameters	Restrictions and recommendations	Lab values	Your values
Windows NT domain name (SAPNTDOMAIN)		SAPDOM	
Central transport host SAPTRANSHOST		SAPTRANSHOST	
Encryption Key DB2DB6EKEY	<SID><virt. R/3 server>	ITSitssap	
db2<sid> password		ibm	
<sid>adm password		ibm	
DB2 instance directory DFTDBPATH	LOG_ARCHIVE directory on shared disks	L:	
DIAGPATH_DRIVE	Drive with db2dump directory	L:	
LOGDIR_DRIVE	LOG_DIR directory on shared disks	K:	
LOGARCHIVEDIR_DRIVE	LOG_ARCHIVE directory on shared disks	L:	
SAPREORGDIR_DRIVE	SAPREORG subdirectory on the same drive as the LOG_ARCHIVE directory (shared disks)	L:	
SAPDATA1_DRIVE	• On the shared disks • Not on the Quorum disk • Not on the SAPLOC disk • Not on the LOG_DIR disk • Not on the LOG_ARCHIVE disk	N:	
SAPDATA2_DRIVE	Same as above	O:	
SAPDATA3_DRIVE	Same as above	P:	
SAPDATA4_DRIVE	Same as above	P:	
SAPDATA5_DRIVE	Same as above	N:	
SAPDATA6_DRIVE	Same as above	O:	
sapr3 user password		ibm	

Parameters	Restrictions and recommendations	Lab values	Your values
RAM that is reserved to the R/3 system (RAM_INSTANCE)		default	
Kernel CD location	This is the copy of the CD on the local drive.	C:\SAPKERNEL\	
Port number of the message server (PORT)	Leave the default value	3600 (default)	
Database Services (PORT)	Leave the default value	5912 (default)	
SAPServer<SID> password	The password of the user sapse<sid> has to be entered	ibm	
R2_Connection		No	
SMSTEMP		No	
Number of R3load processes (PROCESSES)	• When RAM is ≤ 512 MB, use the value 2. • When RAM is > 512 MB, use a value equal to the number of CPUs.	4	
SAP gateway		No	
REPORT_NAMES		Windows NT	

7.6 DB2 cluster conversion

Step 24.11: Modify DB2MSCS.CFG & run DB2MSCS on A

On Node A, do the following:

1. Log on as the installation user (in our lab, sapinst).

2. Verify that all MSCS resources are owned by Node A

3. Copy the file DB2MSCS.CFG from the C:\SAPKERNEL\NT\Common directory to the install directory, C:\USERS\<sid>adm\INSTALL.

4. Edit DB2MSCS.CFG using the SAPPAD utility, which is available in the directory C:\USERS\<sid>adm\INSTALL. Figure 60 shows the modifications we did in our lab environment.

DB2MSCS.CFG before modifications	DB2MSCS.CFG with lab modifications
CLUSTER_NAME=<cluster name>	CLUSTER_NAME=SAPCLUS
GROUP_NAME=DB2 <SAPSID> Group	GROUP_NAME=DB2 ITS Group
DB2_INSTANCE=DB2<SAPSID>	DB2_INSTANCE=DB2ITS
IP_NAME=DB2 IP <SAPSID>	IP_NAME=DB2 IP ITS
IP_ADDRESS=<virtual IP address of DB2 group>	IP_ADDRESS=192.168.0.52
IP_SUBNET=<subnet mask of DB2 group>	IP_SUBNET=255.255.255.0
IP_NETWORK=<network named used to communicate>	IP_NETWORK=PUBLIC
NETNAME_NAME=DB2 NetName <SAPSID>	NETNAME_NAME=DB2 NetName ITS
NETNAME_VALUE=<hostname of DB2 group>	NETNAME_VALUE=ITSDB2
DISK_NAME=<resource name of shared disk	DISK_NAME=DISK K:
containing database files>	DISK_NAME=DISK L:
DISK_NAME=<...more shared disks>	DISK_NAME=DISK M:
INSTPROF_DISK=<resource name of the shared disk	DISK_NAME=DISK N:
where DBDFTPath is pointing to>	DISK_NAME=DISK O:
	DISK_NAME=DISK P:
	INSTPROF_DISK=DISK L:

Figure 60. DB2MSCS.CFG modifications

5. Stop the R/3 system.

6. Stop the database manager instance DB2<SID> by issuing db2stop at a command prompt.

   Note: If executing the command db2stop you may get the error: SQL1390C The environment variable DB2INSTANCE is not defined or is invalid. If this happens, check the value of the environment variable DB2INSTANCE. If this value is still DB2 then you must delete the environment variable DB2INSTANCE from the system environment using the System applet in the Control Panel. Then proceed as follows:

   a. Set the value for DB2INSTANCE in your current command prompt session to DB2<SID> using the command:

      set DB2INSTANCE=DB2<SID>
   b. Re-execute the db2stop command.

7. Change to the C:\USERS\<SID>ADM\INSTALL directory.

8. Run DB2MSCS.

Note: The values for the DISK_NAME and INSTPROF_DISK are not only dependent on the drive letter but also the type of disk subsystem used. For our example we used a Fibre Channel controller, thus there was no need for the prefix IPSHA as required for the IBM ServeRAID controller.

7.7 Install R3Setup files for cluster conversion

Step 24.12: Install R3Setup files for cluster conversion on A

- Open the explorer to C:\SAPKERNEL\NT\Common and start the conversion program by running NTCLUST.

Table 45. Values for the cluster conversions on Node A

Parameters	Lab values	Your values
System Name	ITS	
Install Directory	c:\users\itsadm\install	
Logoff	No	

Step 24.13: Install R/3 files for cluster conversion on Node B

- Copy the new SAPKERNEL directory from Node A to Node B.

- Open Explorer to C:\SAPKERNEL\NT\Common and start the conversion program by running NTCLUST.

Table 46. Values for the cluster conversion on Node B

Parameters	Lab values	Your values
System Name	ITS	
Install Directory	c:\users\itsadm\install	
Logoff	Yes	

7.8 SAP cluster conversion

Step 24.14: Converting Node A for operation in a cluster

1. Click **Start > Programs > SAP R/3 Setup > Configuring Node A for MSCS.**

Error message

When you initially launch the Configuring Node A for an MSCS program, you will get the following error message:

```
Error: OSUSERSIDADMRIGHTS_NT_DB6 installationDo
Phase failed
```

You get this because R3Setup does not wait for the MSCS R/3 group to go online. You will need to launch the R3Setup program a second time.

---

2. Proceed with the conversion using Table 47 for the parameters.

Table 47. Values for converting Node A to MSCS

Parameters	Restrictions and recommendations	Lab values	Your values
Virtual host name of the R/3 Cluster Group (NETWORKNAME)		ITSSAP	
Virtual IP address of the R/3 Cluster Group (IPADDRESS)		192.168.0.51	
Subnet mask for the virtual IP address for the R/3 Cluster group (SUBNETMASK)		255.255.255.0	
Name of the public network used for the R/3 Cluster group (NETWORKTOUSE)	Name of the network to which the virtual IP Address belongs as defined in MSCS	Public	
SAP system name (SAPSYSTEMNAME)	See *R/3 Installation on Windows NT: DB2 Database Release 4.5B*, page 4-5	ITS	
Number of the central system (SAPSYSNR)	Any two-digit number between 00 and 97	00	
Drive of the \usr\sap directory SAPLOC	• On the shared disks • Not on the Quorum disk • Not on any DB2 disk	J: (SAP software shared disk)	
Windows NT domain name SAPNTDOMAIN		SAPDOM	
Host name of R/3 Database Server (DBHOSTNAME)	See Figure 60 on page 208	ITSDB2	

Parameters	Restrictions and recommendations	Lab values	Your values
Encryption Key DB2DB6EKEY	<SID><virt. R/3 server>	ITSitssap	
db2<sid> password		ibm	
<sid>adm password		ibm	
RAM that is reserved to the R/3 system (RAM_INSTANCE)		Default	
SAPService<SID> password	The password of the user sapse<sid> has to be entered	ibm	
Gateway R2_Connection		No	

Step 24.15: Converting Node B for operation in a cluster

1. Log on to Node B as the installation user (in our lab, sapinst).

2. Take the SAP-R/3 ITS group offline and move it to Node B. **Note**: Only take this resource offline.

3. On Node B bring all the resources in the SAP-R/3 ITS group online except the SAP-R/3 ITS resource. You can do this by starting from the bottom of the dependency tree and following the dependencies up the tree.

4. Click **Start > Programs > SAP R/3 Setup > Configuring Node B for an MSCS.**

5. Enter the values per Table 48.

Table 48. Values for converting Node B to MSCS

Parameters	Restrictions and recommendations	Lab values	Your values
Virtual host name of the R/3 Cluster Group (NETWORKNAME)		ITSSAP	
Virtual IP address of the R/3 Cluster Group (IPADDRESS)		192.168.0.51	
Subnet mask for the virtual IP address for the R/3 Cluster group (SUBNETMASK)		255.255.255.0	

Parameters	Restrictions and recommendations	Lab values	Your values
Name of the public network used for the R/3 Cluster group (NETWORKTOUSE)	Name of the network to which the virtual IP address belongs as defined in MSCS	Public	
SAP system name (SAPSYSTEMNAME)	See *R/3 Installation on Windows NT: DB2 Database Release 4.5B*, page 4-5	ITS	
Number of the central system (SAPSYSNR)	Any two-digit number between 00 and 97	00	
Drive of the \usr\sap directory (SAPLOC)	• On the shared disks • Not on the Quorum disk • Not on any DB2 disk	J: (SAP software shared disk)	
Windows NT domain name (SAPNTDOMAIN)		SAPDOM	
Host name of R/3 Database Server (DBHOSTNAME)	See Figure 60 on page 208	ITSDB2	
Encryption Key (DB2DB6EKEY)	<SID><virt. R/3 server>	ITSitssap	
db2<SID> password		ibm	
<sid>adm password		ibm	
Port number of the message server (PORT)	Leave the default value	3600	
Database Services port	Leave the default value	5912	
SAPService<SID> password	The password of the user sapse<sid> has to be entered	ibm	
SAPR3 Password	You need to enter the same value three times because of an error in the R3Setup profile	ibm	

7.9 Complete the migration to MSCS

Step 24.16: Migrating MSCS on Node A

Note: This section replaces the section "Completing the Cluster Conversion" in the SAP publication *Conversion to Microsoft Cluster Server: DB2 Universal Database Server*.

The SAP R/3 system contains a table INSTVERS where the R/3 server name and the latest installation status are stored. During each startup SAP R/3 checks if the current R/3 server exists in this table and if the installation status is correct. If the server name is not found or the installation status is invalid, the system shows an error message saying that the installation was not completed successfully.

During the initial installation of the non-clustered R/3 system an entry for server Node A was made with the correct status. After the conversion to a clustered R/3 system, the name of the R/3 server is changed to the virtual name, in our lab, ITSSAP. To avoid the error message, an entry for this virtual server name has to be created in the table INSTVERS. This can be done with the help of R3Setup in the following way:

1. Log on to Node A as the installation user (in our lab, sapinst).

2. Using Microsoft Cluster Administrator:

    a. Move the Quorum Disk resource to the Cluster Group if you have not already done that.

    b. Delete the empty disk Cluster Groups.

    c. Move all the Cluster Groups to Node A.

    d. Take the SAP-R/3 ITS resource online on Node A.

    e. Verify that you can connect to the R/3 instance using SAPGUI.

3. Click **Start > Programs > SAP R/3 Setup for ITS > SAP R/3 Setup - Completing the Migration to an MSCS (Instvers)**, which corresponds to the command:

```
R3SETUP.EXE -f UPDINSTV.R3S
```

Table 49. Values for completing the migration to MSCS

Parameter	Restrictions and recommendations	Lab values	Your values
Virtual host name of the R/3 Cluster Group (RFCUPDATEINST VERS_IND_IND)		ITSSAP	
SAP system name (SAPSYSTEMNAME)	See *R/3 Installation on Windows NT: DB2 Database Release 4.5B*, page 4-5	ITS	
Number of the central system (SAPSYSNR)	Any two-digit number between 00 and 97	00	

Step 24.17: Check the services file on Node A

The file <%WINDIR%>\System32\drivers\etc\services on both nodes needs to contain at least the lines shown below. The port numbers shown are the default values offered by R3Setup during the installation.

```
sapdp00  3200/tcp
sapdp00s 4700/tcp
sapgw00  3300/tcp
sapgw00s 4800/tcp
sapmsITS 3600/tcp
sapdb2ITS 5912/tcp
sapdb2ITSi 5913/tcp
db2cDB2 50000/tcp
db2ciDB2 50001/tcp
```

Step 24.18: Check the DB2<SID> Service settings on A

The startup setting for the service DB2<SID> needs to be set to manual and the service has to be run under the user db2<sid>. This is because the service is controlled by the cluster software and cannot be running on both nodes at the same time in the same cluster.

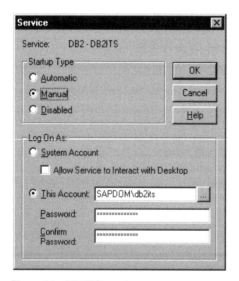

Figure 61. DB2ITS service

Step 24.19: Check the NT System Environment on Node A

Verify and correct the following settings:

- The System variable DB2INSTANCE is either not set or set to the value db2l<sid>. Do not forget the character 'l' (lowercase L) between db2 and the <sid>.
- The System variable TEMP is set to a local directory; for example, C:\TEMP.
- The System variable PATH has to contain the following string in this sequence:

    ...;%WINDIR%\SapCluster;<**X**>:\usr\sap\<SID>\sys\exe\run;...

    Where **X** stands for the drive letter of the shared NT disk containing the SAP binaries (J: in our lab).
- DB2DB6_ADMTRC=OFF — see note
- DB2DB6_TRCLEVEL=5 — see note

Note: The variable DB2DB6_ADMTRC is normally not defined. If it is defined with any value, the DB2 user exit and the SAP R/3-specific DB2 tools generate trace files during their execution. The details shown in these trace files are defined by the environment variable DB2DB6_TRCLEVEL (0 = little, 5 = very detailed).

To activate a new setting of the system variable DB2DB6_ADMTRC or DB2DB6_TRCLEVEL for the DB2 user exit, you need to reboot the Windows NT server.

Step 24.20: Check the R/3 user environments on Node A

This section shows the important environment variables that have to be set for the users <sid>adm and db2<sid>. Environment variables not directly needed by the SAP R/3 environment have been omitted.

Log on to Node A as each user, execute a SET command at a command prompt and verify the values shown in Table 50 on page 216.

> **Note**
>
> The values shown reflect the lab settings. Adjust the <SID> and drive letters according to your environment.

Table 50. Important environment variables for <sid>adm and db2<sid>

Variable Name	Variable value
DB2CODEPAGE	819
DB2DB6EKEY	ITSitssap
DB2DBDFT	ITS
DB2DSCDB6HOME	ITSSAP
DB2INSTANCE	db2lits
DB6EKEY	ITSitssap
DBMS_TYPE	DB6
DIR_LIBRARY	J:\usr\sap\RSD\sys\exe\run
DSCDB6HOME	ITSSAP
PATH	C:\WINNT\system32;C:\WINNT;C:\IMNNQ_NT;C:\ifor\WIN\BIN; C:\ifor\WIN\BIN\EN_US;C:\SQLLIB\BIN;C:\SQLLIB\FUNCTION ;C:\SQLLIB\SAMPLES\REPL; C:\SQLLIB\HELP; **C:\WINNT\SAPCluster;J:\usr\sap\ITS\sys\exe\run**
TEMP	C:\TEMP
TMP	C:\TEMP

Note: The home directory of user <sid>adm and db2<sid> should be set to <%WINDIR%>\SapCluster. (Replace %WINDIR% with the actual value.)

Step 24.21: Check the R/3 Run time Environment on Node A

R/3 4.5B with DB2 UDB uses the old method of a dedicated set of environment variables on each node as defined in the Windows NT registry under the key HKLM\SOFTWARE\SAP\<SID>\Environment. Table 51 on page 217 shows the name of each entry under this key and the correct value. Verify that all entries exist and have the correct value.

> **Note**
>
> The values shown reflect the lab settings. Adjust the <SID> and drive letters according to your environment.

Table 51. R/3 registry settings

Name	Data	Comment
(Default)	(value not set)	Not used
DB2CODEPAGE	819	Code page used by DB2
DB2DB6_ARCHIVE_PATH	L:\db2\its\log_archive	Directory with archived log files
DB2DB6_AUDIT_ERROR_ATTR	a	Append to error logs
DB2DB6_RETREIVE_PATH	L:\db2\its\log_archive	Directory where log files are restored to from backup medium in case of a DB recovery
DB2DB6_TEMP_DIR	C:\temp	Temporary directory used by the DB2 user exit - must exist
DB2DB6EKEY	ITSitssap	En-/Decryption key
DB2DBDFT	ITS	R/3 database name
DB2DSCDB6HOME	ITSSAP	Server, where file dscdb6.conf is stored
DB2INSTANCE	db2lits	DB manager instance to use
DB6EKEY	ITSitsap	En-/Decryption key
DBMS_TYPE	DB6	R/3 database type
DSCDB6HOME	ITSSAP	Server, where file dscdb6.conf is stored
INSTHOME	L:\db2its	Directory with DB manager instance control files
PATH	;C:\WINNT\SAPCluster;J:\usr\sap\ITS\sys\exe\run	WINNT is the standard NT installation directory
SAPEXE	C:\WINNT\SAPCluster	Path to executable's like brarchive, ... You may need to replace "C:\WINNT" with your Windows NT installation directory
SAPLOCALHOST	ITSSAP	

Name	Data	Comment
SAPMNT	\\ITSSAP\sapmnt	Mount point for \usr\sap directory

Step 24.22: Catalog Admin DB on Node A

The R3Setup profiles we used in our lab didn't catalog the R/3 administration database ADM<SID> in the DB manager instance db2l<sid>. Follow the steps to verify/correct this error:

1. Log in as user <sid>adm and open a command prompt.

2. Start a DB2 command window with `db2cmd`.

3. Enter the following command in the db2 command window:

   ```
   db2 list database directory
   ```

   If the database aliases <SID> and ADM<SID> are listed in the command output you are finished with this step.

4. Otherwise enter the following command in the DB2 command window after replacing <sid> and <SID> in the following command with the actual value:

   ```
   db2 catalog db ADM<SID> at node <SID>NODE Authentication Server
   ```

Step 24.23: Copy DSCDB6UP.EXE on Node A

This executable needs to be locally available on each node. Perform the following steps:

1. Move the R/3 cluster group to Node A.

2. Copy the file <X>:\usr\sap\ITS\sys\exe\run\dscdb6up.exe to <%WINDIR%>\SAPCluster. (In our lab, <X> had the value J).

Step 24.24: Check the services file on Node B

Repeat step 24.17 on page 214 for Node B.

Step 24.25: Check the DB2<SID> service settings on B

Repeat step 24.18 on page 214 for Node B.

Step 24.26: Check the NT system environment on Node B

Repeat step 24.19 on page 215 for Node B.

Step 24.27: Check the R/3 user environments on Node B

Repeat step 24.20 on page 215 for Node B.

Step 24.28: Check the R/3 runtime environment on Node B

Repeat step 24.21 on page 216 for Node B.

Step 24.29: Catalog Admin DB on Node B

Repeat step 24.22 on page 218 for Node B.

Step 24.30: Install DB2 Admin Extensions on Node B

During the R/3 installation the administration extensions are only installed on Node A, but they need to be installed on Node B also. Perform the following steps:

1. Log in as user <sid>adm on Node B.

2. Move all cluster resources to Node B and bring them online.

3. Open a command prompt.

4. Set the environment variable DB2INSTANCE with the following command:

   ```
   set DB2INSTANCE=db2<sid>
   ```

5. Run the program SDDB6INS.EXE:

   ```
   sddb6ins.exe -i 45B -s <SID>
   ```

Step 24.31: Copy DSCDB6UP.EXE on Node B

This executable needs to be locally available on each Node. Perform the following steps:

1. Move the R/3 cluster group to Node B.

2. Copy the file <X>:\usr\sap\ITS\sys\exe\run\dscdb6up.exe to <%WINDIR%>\SAPCluster. (In our lab, <X> had the value J).

Return to step 25 on page 152 to continue the installation.

Chapter 8. Installation using SQL Server

In this chapter we describe the installation of SAP R/3 Release 4.5B using Microsoft SQL Server 7.0 as the database. This material forms part of the overall installation as described in Chapter 5, "Installation and verification" on page 119. Specifically, this chapter is referenced in step 24 on page 151.

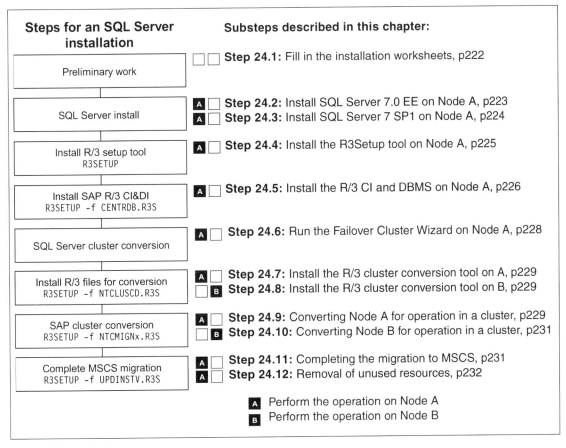

Figure 62. Installation process for SAP R/3 on SQL Server 7.0

An overall description of the installation process is shown in Figure 62. You will note that some steps are to be done on Node A, some on Node B, and some are to be carried out on both nodes.

The main references for the SQL Server installation are:

- *R/3 Installation on Windows NT: Microsoft SQL Server, Release 4.5B* (document number 51005503)

- *Conversion to Microsoft Cluster Server: Microsoft SQL Server, 4.0B 4.5A 4.5B* (document number 51005504)

- *How to Install SQL Server 7.0, Enterprise Edition on Microsoft Cluster Server: Step by Step Instructions* (white paper from http://www.microsoft.com/sql)

From this point, we assume that Windows NT 4.0 Enterprise Edition is installed on both nodes with Service Pack 3, and MSCS is running.

Step 24

These steps are part of installation step 24 as described on page 151 in Chapter 5.

8.1 Preliminary work

Step 24.1: Fill in the installation worksheets

Before beginning, you should fill in all the SAP installation worksheets in this chapter.

Log on as the installation user

Throughout the entire installation process, make sure you are always logged on as the installation user (in our lab, sapinst).

8.2 Install SQL Server and SAP R/3

Step 24.2: Install SQL Server 7.0 EE on Node A

An SAP cluster with MSCS requires you to install SQL Server in the active/passive mode. This means that only one copy of SQL Server has to be installed. This installation procedure is performed *only on one node*, no matter which one. We will install it on Node A.

The target directory must be on a shared disk. Refer to 4.4.2.5, "SQL Server 7.0 files" on page 99 to know which disk to use for the different SQL Server components (software files, temporary files, log files, and data files).

Complete the following steps:

1. Check that all the cluster resources are owned by Node A.

2. Insert the SAP RDBMS CD-ROM for SQL Server Enterprise Edition (not the Standard Edition). Start the program SETUP.BAT from the root directory.

3. The installation program guides you through a series of windows. Use Table 52 as a reference for the most important parameters:

Table 52. Installation of SQL Server 7

Parameters	Restrictions and recommendations	Lab values	Your values
Setup type	Select **Custom**	Custom	
Destination folders	• See 4.4.2.5, "SQL Server 7.0 files" on page 99 to know to which target disk drive to install • Program files: The default location is \MSSQL7 • Database files for the Master, Msdb, and Pubs databases; we recommend you install them in a different directory: \MSSQL7DB	K:\MSSQL7 K:\MSSQL7DB	
Select components	Confirm the default settings	Leave default	
Character set/ sort order	Required values	• Char Set: 850 Multilingual • Sort Order: Binary Order • Unicode Collation: Binary Order	

Parameters	Restrictions and recommendations	Lab values	Your values
Network libraries	The components Named Pipes, TCP/IP sockets, and Multiprotocol must be installed.	Leave default	
Services accounts	Specify the user name of the two service accounts created prior to SQL Server installation. Repeat this step for both SQL Server and SQL Agent. Do not select AutoStart service.	• Customize the settings for each service • SQL Server: sqlsvc / password / SAPDOM • SQL Agent: sqlagent / password / SAPDOM	
Remote information	(For the cluster administrator account) Specify the cluster service account information	clussvc/ password/ SAPDOM	

4. After SQL Server is installed, it is normal for the cluster group to be offline. By default, neither SQL Server nor SQL Server Agent are automatically started when the installation is complete.

5. Reboot the sever and test the SQL Server installation as follows:

   a. Start SQL Server on Node A.
   b. Register Server A.
   c. Perform simple queries.
   d. Set up SQLMail if you intend to use it.
   e. Stop SQL Server.

Step 24.3: Install SQL Server 7 SP1 on Node A

1. Download Service Pack 1 from the Microsoft FTP server at the following address or get it from the Microsoft TechNet CDs:

   ftp://ftp.microsoft.com/bussys/sql/public/fixes/usa/sql70

2. All the cluster resources must be online on Node A.

3. Start the Service Pack installation program, and use the information in Table 53:

Table 53. Service Pack 1 for SQL Server 7

Values	Restrictions and recommendations	Lab values
Connect to Server		Windows NT authentication
Remote information	Specify the SAP cluster administrator account	itsadm/password/SAPDOM

4. Reboot both nodes after completion.

8.3 Install the R/3 Setup tool

Step 24.4: Install the R3Setup tool on Node A

To install R3Setup on Node A, do the following:

1. Log on to the Windows NT system on Node A as the installation user (in our lab, sapinst).

2. Check that the TEMP environment variable has been set, using the System applet in the Windows NT Control Panel. TEMP is normally set to C:\TEMP. Make sure that the specified directory really exists in the file system.

3. From the SAP Kernel CD-ROM, start the program \NT\COMMON\R3SETUP.BAT.

4. You are asked to provide values you can take from the following table:

Table 54. Installation of R/3 Setup tool

Parameters	Restrictions and recommendations	Lab values	Your values
SAP system name SAPSYSTEMNAME	<SID>	ITS	
Path to installation directory INSTALL PATH	Leave default	Leave default	
Do you want to log off? CDINSTLOGOFF_NT_IND		Yes	

5. At the end of this step, you will be logged off from your Windows NT session. For the next step, you must log on with the same Windows NT user account because the installation of the R/3 setup tool assigns the rights necessary for performing an installation to the user who is installing the R/3 setup tool.

8.4 Install the SAP R/3 Central Instance

Step 24.5: Install the R/3 CI and DBMS on Node A

1. On Node A, log on as the installation user (in our lab, sapinst).

2. Check that all the cluster resources are owned by Node A, and move them to Node A if necessary.

3. Click **Start > Programs > SAP R/3 Setup > Central and Database Instance**. This will install a central instance, and build and load the database.

4. You are prompted to enter values for a number of parameters. The following table summarizes these:

Table 55. Installation of the R/3 Central and Database instance

Parameters	Restrictions and recommendations	Lab values	Your values
SAP system name (SAPSYSTEMNAME)	<SID>	ITS	
Number of the central system (SAPCISYSNR)	Any two-digit number between 00 and 97	00	
SAPLOC - Drive of the \usr\sap directory	• On the shared disks • Not on the Quorum disk • Not on the SQL Server disks	J: (SAP software shared disk)	
Windows NT domain name (SAPNTDOMAIN)		SAPDOM	
Central transport host (SAPTRANSHOST)		SAPTRANSHOST	
RAM that is reserved to the R/3 system (RAM_INSTANCE)		Leave the default (2176 MB in our configuration)	
Port number of the message server (PORT)	Leave the default value	3600 (default)	
<sid>adm password		password	
SAPService<SID> password		password	
SAP gateway		No	
TEMPDATAFILESIZE	Leave the default value	300 (default)	

Parameters	Restrictions and recommendations	Lab values	Your values
TEMPDATAFILEDRIVE	See 4.4.2.5, "SQL Server 7.0 files" on page 99	K:	
Type of installation	Choose custom if you intend to optimize the parameters for data and log files. Otherwise, select No.	Automatic installation	
DATAFILEDRIVE1	• On the shared disks • Not on the Quorum disk • Not on the SAPLOC disk • Not on the Log disk • Not on the Archive disk	M:	
DATAFILEDRIVE2	• On the shared disks • Not on the Quorum disk • Not on the SAPLOC disk • Not on the Log disk • Not on the Archive disk	N:	
DATAFILEDRIVE3	• On the shared disks • Not on the Quorum disk • Not on the SAPLOC disk • Not on the Log disk • Not on the Archive disk	O:	
LOGFILEDRIVE	• On the shared disks • Not on the Quorum disk • Not on the SAPLOC disk • Not on SAPDATA disks • Not on the Archive disk	L:	
Number of R3load processes (PROCESSES)	Number of CPUs	4	
REPORT_NAMES		NT	

5. When R3Setup has obtained all the information it needs, it automatically begins with installation processing. This phase can take up to several hours depending on the global configuration and the server performance.

6. Reboot Node A.

8.5 Convert the database to cluster operation

Step 24.6: Run the Failover Cluster Wizard on Node A

The Failover Cluster Wizard is a tool that is part of SQL Server making the database aware of the cluster. To run the wizard do the following:

1. Log on to Node A as the installation user (in our lab, sapinst).
2. Click **Start > Programs > SQL Server > Failover Cluster Wizard**.
3. Enter the information for which you are prompted, using Table 56 as a guide:

Table 56. SQL Failover Cluster Wizard

Parameters	Restrictions and recommendations	Lab values	Your values
SA password	By default there is no password	(empty)	
SQL Server service account	Type the SQL Server service account	password	
IP Address	This is the virtual IP address for accessing the database on the public network, with the correct subnet mask	192.168.0.52 255.255.255.0	
Server Name	Name of the virtual server	ITSSQL	

4. After the installation process, you have to reboot Node B and Node A.
5. When the system is restarted, log on to Node A as the installation user (in our lab, sapinst).
6. Move all resources back to Node A.
7. Redefine the shares on the \USR\SAP directory. You have to manually configure two shares: SAPLOC and SAPMNT (you must respect these names), which points to the same directory: \USR\SAP.
8. Restart the Windows NT services: SAPOSCOL and SAP<SID>.
9. Restart the database service in the Cluster Administrator.
10.All the resources for SQL Server are now displayed in the Cluster Administrator so the database can be moved between nodes.

8.6 Install the cluster conversion tool

Step 24.7: Install the R/3 cluster conversion tool on A

Complete the following steps to install the SAP cluster conversion tool:

1. Make sure that you are logged on to Node A as the installation user (in our lab, sapinst).

2. Insert the SAP Kernel CD-ROM and start the installation of the conversion program by running NTCLUST.BAT from the \NT\COMMON directory.

3. You are asked to provide the installation directory: enter the same directory used during the installation of the R/3 instance.

Table 57. Installation of the cluster conversion tool

Parameter	Restrictions and recommendations	Lab values	Your values
SAPSYSTEMNAME	<SID>	ITS	
\users\<SID>adm\install		C:\users\ITSadm\install	
Do you want to log off? CDINSTLOGOFF_NT_IND		Yes	

4. You are automatically logged off from your Windows NT session.

Step 24.8: Install the R/3 cluster conversion tool on B

Log on to Node B as the installation user (in our lab, sapinst), and run NTCLUST.BAT per step 24.7.

8.7 SAP cluster conversion

Step 24.9: Converting Node A for operation in a cluster

1. Log on to Node A as the installation user (in our lab, sapinst).

2. Make sure that all the cluster resources within MSCS are owned by Node A.

3. Click **Start > Programs > SAP R/3 Setup > Configuring Node A for MSCS**.

4. You are prompted to enter values for a number of parameters described in Table 58:

Table 58. Converting Node A for operation in a cluster

Parameters	Restrictions and recommendations	Lab values	Your values
Network name (NETWORKNAME)	Virtual name for the R/3 system. The name of the SAP cluster group. Do not enter the name of the cluster.	ITSSAP	
IP Address (IPADDRESS)	Virtual IP address for the R/3 system on the public network. The IP address for the SAP cluster group. Do not enter the IP address of the cluster.	192.168.0.51	
Subnet mask		255.255.255.0	
Network to use (NETWORKTOUSE)	Specify the name of the public network.	public	
SAP system name (SAPSYSTEMNAME)	<SID>	ITS	
Number of the central system (SAPCISYSNR)	Any two-digit number between 00 and 97	00	
SAPLOC - drive of the \USR\SAP directory	SAP software shared disk	J:	
Windows NT domain name (SAPNTDOMAIN)		SAPDOM	
Database virtual name DBHOSTNAME		ITSSQL	
RAM that is reserved to R/3 RAM_INSTANCE		Leave the default (2176 MB in our configuration)	
<sid>adm password		password	
SAP gateway (R2_CONNECTION)		NO	

When all entries have been made, the R3Setup tool converts the R/3 instance on Node A for operation in a cluster.

5. When the processing is finished, take the SAP R/3 cluster group offline in the Cluster Administrator, and move it to Node B. On Node B, bring all the resources in that group online, except the R/3 resource.

Step 24.10: Converting Node B for operation in a cluster

1. Log on to Node B as the installation user (in our lab, sapinst).

2. Make sure that the cluster resources for the R/3 system (SAP_R/3<SID>) within MSCS are owned by Node A.

3. Click **Start > Programs > SAP R/3 Setup > Configuring Node B for MSCS**.

4. You are prompted to enter values for a number of parameters. Use Table 58 on page 230 for assistance.

   When all entries have been made, the R3Setup tool converts the R/3 instance on Node B for operation in a cluster.

5. When R3Setup has finished, start the R/3 cluster resource SAP_R/3<SID>. You should now have the SQL Server group online on Node A and the SAP R/3 group online on Node B.

   At this stage, you can swap the two cluster groups between the two nodes manually to make them run where you want them to run.

8.8 Complete the MSCS migration

Step 24.11: Completing the migration to MSCS

To complete the cluster conversion, go to the node where the R/3 system is running. Make sure you are logged on as the installation user (in our lab, sapinst).

1. Click **Start > Programs > SAP R/3 Setup > Completing the Migration to an MSCS**.

2. You are prompted to enter values for a number of parameters described in Table 59:

Table 59. Completing the migration to MSCS

Parameter	Restrictions and recommendations	Lab values	Your values
Central Instance host name CIHOSTNAME	Specify the same SAP server virtual name.	ITSSAP	
SAP system name (SAPSYSTEMNAME)	<SID>	ITS	
Number of the central system (SAPCISYSNR)		00	

3. Restart the server.

Now, the R/3 system has been fully converted and is able to operate in the cluster and make use of the cluster features. Test whether the cluster failover mechanism is working properly by simulating a failover, first on the R/3 group and then on the database group.

8.9 Removal of unused resources

Step 24.12: Removal of unused resources

At the end of the installation the following resources/dependencies are created in the cluster group:

- MSDTC < Cluster Name < Cluster IP Address
- MSDTC < Quorum Disk

The MSDTC resource must be deleted. Before doing that remember to delete the dependencies.

Return to step 25 on page 152 to continue the installation.

Chapter 9. Backbone network

This chapter provides:

- A detailed description of the additional steps necessary to re-route the inter-server traffic on the backbone network in 9.1, "Backbone configuration" on page 233.

- A detailed explanation of the main benefits of the usage of a backbone in 9.2, "Benefits of the backbone configuration" on page 245.

The main bibliographic references for the configuration topics discussed in 9.1, "Backbone configuration" on page 233 are:

- *SAP R/3 in Switchover Environments* (document 50020596) (downloadable from SAPNET)

- *Network Integration of R/3 Servers. Release 4.5B* (downloadable from SAPNET)

Good bibliographic references for the architectural aspects described in 9.2, "Benefits of the backbone configuration" on page 245 are:

- *SAP R/3 System Administration*, by Liane Will, Sybex, ISBN 0782124267l

- *SAP R/3 Implementation with ASAP*, by Hartwig Brand, Sybex, ISBN 0782124725

- *SAP R/3 Performance Optimization*, Sybex, by Thomas Schneider, ISBN 0782125638

9.1 Backbone configuration

During SAP R/3 installation, the existence of the backbone network is ignored. At the end of the installation some further steps are necessary in order to route the inter-server traffic to the backbone network. As shown in Figure 63, our configuration is comprised of five steps:

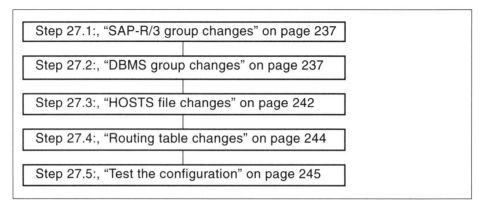

Figure 63. Steps to configure the backbone

To make the following explanation as clear as possible, see Figure 64 on page 235, which shows the network settings of our lab SAP network after the complete installation was finished, but without any changes to the backbone network. The three virtual IP addresses used in this configuration are shown in the shaded boxes.

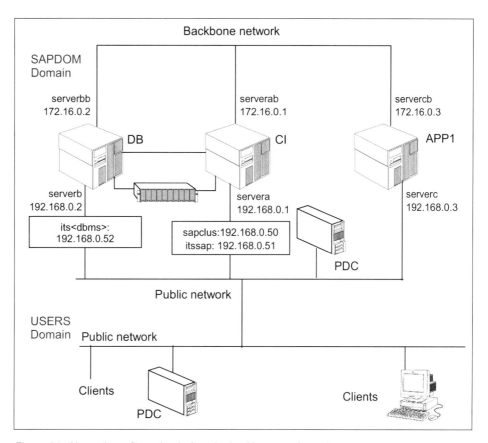

Figure 64. Network configuration before the backbone configuration

The design goals of the backbone configuration are:

- Provide front-end clients unchanged access to the CI and application servers through the public network
- Move the high bandwidth traffic between the DB and the CI and application servers to the backbone network
- Minimal changes to network and/or R/3 configuration files

Figure 65 on page 236 presents the network configuration after applying all required changes for the use of the backbone network. Two new virtual IP addresses were added: one for the DB and one for the CI. These are shown in Figure 65 as highlighted boxes. Additionally, the routing tables were updated on the DB, CI, and the application server(s). The following sections describe the required steps in detail.

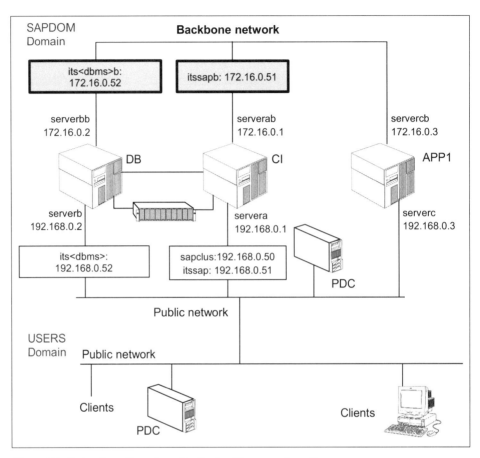

SAPDOM Domain | Backbone network

its<dbms>b: 172.16.0.52 | itssapb: 172.16.0.51

serverbb 172.16.0.2 | serverab 172.16.0.1 | servercb 172.16.0.3

DB | CI | APP1

serverb 192.168.0.2 | servera 192.168.0.1 | serverc 192.168.0.3

its<dbms>: 192.168.0.52 | sapclus:192.168.0.50 itssap: 192.168.0.51 | PDC

Public network

USERS Domain | Public network

Clients | PDC | Clients

Figure 65. Network configuration after the backbone configuration

9.1.1 Creation of new cluster resources

In an MSCS R/3 configuration the DB and CI can run on either cluster node. To access the DB and CI services through the backbone network regardless of which cluster node is currently running which service, we have to use virtual IP addresses for the DB and CI. These new virtual IP addresses need to be defined in the corresponding cluster groups.

9.1.1.1 SAP-R/3 group changes

The following changes must be made in the SAP R/3 group. The new resources have a "-B" attached to their name to distinguish them from the already existing resources:

Step 27.1: SAP-R/3 group changes

Do the following:

1. Create the IP address resource "SAP R/3 IP-B" with a value "172.16.0.51". Ensure to select the correct network to bind this address to when creating the cluster resource.

2. Create the network name resource "SAP R/3 NetName-B" with a value "itssapb".

3. Create a dependency between the resource "SAP R/3 <SID>" and the "SAP R/3 NetName-B". The "SAP R/3 <SID>" resource depends on the "SAP R/3 NetName-B" resource.

4. Create a dependency between the resource "SAP R/3 NetName-B" and the "SAP-R/3 IP-B" resource. The "SAP R/3 NetName-B" resource depends on the SAP-R/3 IPs-B" resource.

Figure 66 shows these additions as highlighted resources and dependencies links:

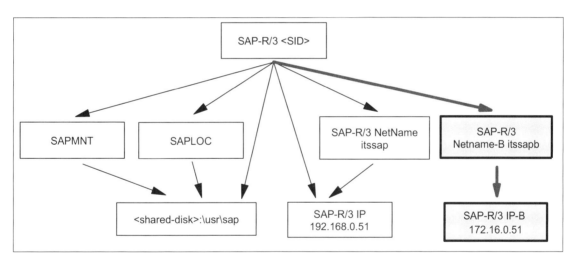

Figure 66. SAP-R/3 resource tree with backbone changes (highlighted)

9.1.1.2 DBMS group changes
This section describes the resource changes required in the DBMS resource group.

Step 27.2: DBMS group changes

The steps you perform depend on which database you are using:

For Oracle:

The Oracle resource tree must be changed in a similar way (see Figure 67) (The new resources have a "-B" attached to their name to distinguish them from the already existing resources):

1. Create the IP address resource "ORACLEITS IP Address-B" with the value "172.16.0.52". Ensure you select the correct network to bind this address to when creating the cluster resource.

2. Create the network name resource "ORACLEITS Network Name-B" with the name "itsorab".

3. Create a dependency between the "OracleAgent80 ITSora" resource and the "ORACLEITS Network Name-B". The OracleAgent80 ITSora" resource depends on the "ORACLEITS Network Name-B".

4. Create a dependency between the "ORACLEITS Network Name-B" resource and the "OracleITS IP Address-B" resource. The "ORACLEITS Network Name-B" resource depends on the "OracleITS IP Address-B" resource.

5. Create a dependency between the OracleTNSListener80Fslitsora resource and the "ORACLEITS Network Name-B" resource. The OracleTNSListener80Fslitsora resource depends on the "ORACLEITS Network Name-B" resource.

Figure 67 shows these additions as highlighted resources and dependencies links:

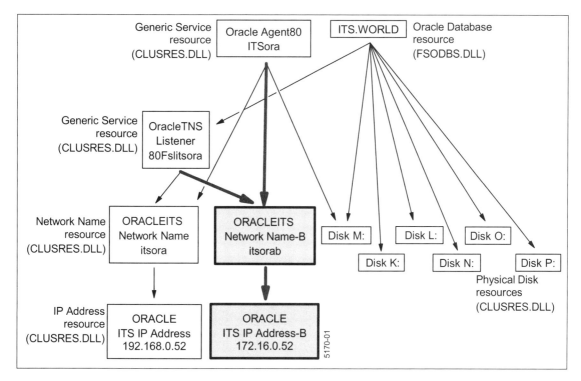

Figure 67. Oracle resource tree with backbone changes

For DB2 UDB:

Similar changes are necessary in the DB2 resource group (see Figure 68). The new resources have a "-B" attached to their name to distinguish them from the already existing resources:

1. Create the IP address resource "DB2 IP ITS-B" with a value of "172.16.0.52". Ensure you select the correct network to bind this address to when creating the cluster resource.

2. Create the network name resource "DB2 NetName ITS-B" with the name "itsdb2b".

3. Create the dependency between the "DB2ITS" resource and the "DB2 NetName ITS-B". The "DB2ITS" resource depends on the "DB2 NetName ITS-B"

4. Create a dependency between the "DB2 NetName ITS-B" resource and the "DB2 IP ITS-B" resource. The "DB2 NetName ITS-B" resource depends on the "DB2 IP ITS-B" resource.

Figure 68 shows these additions as highlighted resources and dependencies links:

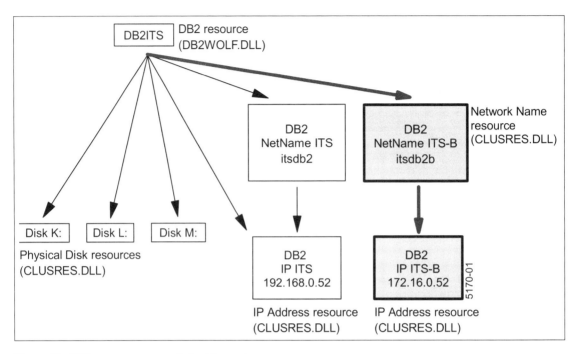

Figure 68. DB2 resource group with backbone changes

For SQL Server:

We close this section with the changes in the SQL Server resource group (see Figure 69). The new resources have a "-B" attached to their name to distinguish them from the already existing resources:

1. Create the IP address resource "ITSSQL IP Address-B" with a value of "172.16.0.52". Ensure you select the correct network to bind this address to when creating the cluster resource.

2. Create the network name resource "ITSSQLNetwork Name-B" with the name "itssqlb".

3. Create a dependency between the "ITSSQL Vserver" resource and the "ITSSQLNetwork Name-B". The "ITSSQL Vserver" resource depends on the "ITSSQLNetwork Name-B".

4. Create a dependency between the "ITSSQLNetwork Name-B" resource and the "ITSSQL IP Address-B" resource. The "ITSSQLNetwork Name-B" resource depends on the "ITSSQL IP Address-B" resource.

Figure 69 shows these additions as highlighted resources and dependencies links:

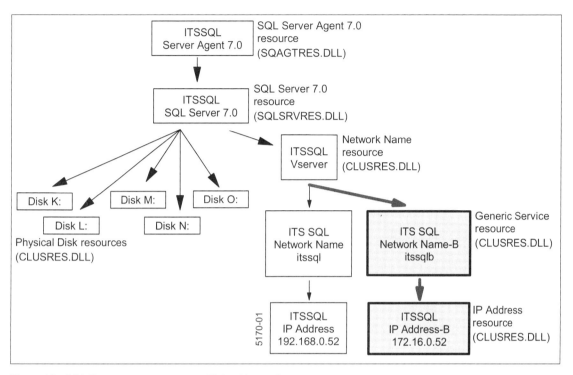

Figure 69. SQL Server resource group with backbone changes

9.1.2 HOSTS file change

The HOSTS file on each R/3 server (DB, CI, application servers) has to be extended with entries for the two new virtual IP addresses created in 9.1.1, "Creation of new cluster resources" on page 236. The HOSTS file is identical for all servers. You can change the HOSTS file on one server and then copy it to all the other servers of the R/3 system. However, don't copy this HOSTS file to any front-end clients.

┌─ **DNS or WINS server** ───┐

We describe the name resolution based on changes in the local HOSTS files on all servers. It is also possible to use a central DNS or WINS server to perform the name resolution, but keep in mind, that this probably adds another point of failure to your configuration.

└──┘

Step 27.3: HOSTS file changes

The following three sections show the changed HOSTS file for each database:

For Oracle:

1. Define the virtual IP address of the CI server. Add the entry:

   172.16.0.51 itssapb

2. Define the virtual IP address of the DB server. Add the entry:

   172.16.0.52 itsorab

3. Move the SAPTRANSHOST alias from the 192.168.0.51 itssap line to the 172.16.0.51 itssapb line.

   This step is necessary if you want to move the transport traffic from the public network to the backbone network. However, there are situations in which the SAPTRANSHOST should not be changed. Examples of such situations include communication with external SAP systems or lack of backbone adapters on the test system.

The changed HOSTS file is shown in Figure 70. The added lines are highlighted:

```
127.0.0.1      localhost              # loopback address
192.168.0.1    servera                # DB static hostname on the public network
192.168.0.2    serverb                # CI static hostname on the public network
192.168.0.3    serverc                # APP1 (static) hostname on the public network
192.168.0.50   sapclus               # Microsoft Cluster network name
192.168.0.51   itssap                # Ci virtual hostname on the public network
192.168.0.52   itsora                # DB virtual hostname on the public network
10.0.0.1       serverai               # CI static hostname on the private network
10.0.0.2       serverbi               # DB static hostname on the private network
172.16.0.1     serverab               # Ci static hostname on the backbone network
172.16.0.2     serverbb               # DB static hostname on the backbone network
172.16.0.3     servercb               # APP1 static hostname on the backbone network
172.16.0.51    itssapb SAPTRANSHOST   # NEW - CI virtual hostname on the backbone network
172.16.0.52    itsorab                # NEW - DB virtual hostname on the backbone network
```

Figure 70. CI, DB, and APP HOSTS file for Oracle

For DB2 UDB:

1. Define the virtual IP address of the CI server. Add the entry:

   172.16.0.51 itssapb

2. Define the virtual IP address of the DB server. Add the entry:

   172.16.0.52 itsdb2b

3. Move the SAPTRANSHOST alias from the 192.168.0.51 itssap line to the 172.16.0.51 itssapb line.

   This step is necessary if you want to move the transport traffic from the public network to the backbone network. However, there are situations in which the SAPTRANSHOST should not be changed. Examples of such situations include communication with external SAP systems or lack of backbone adapters on the test system.

The changed HOSTS file is shown in Figure 71. The added lines are highlighted:

```
127.0.0.1      localhost          # loopback address
192.168.0.1    servera            # DB static hostname on the public network
192.168.0.2    serverb            # CI static hostname on the public network
192.168.0.3    serverc            # APP1 (static) hostname on the public network
192.168.0.50   sapclus            # Microsoft Cluster network name
192.168.0.51   itssap             # Ci virtual hostname on the public network
192.168.0.52   itsdb2             # DB virtual hostname on the public network
10.0.0.1       serverai           # CI static hostname on the private network
10.0.0.2       serverbi           # DB static hostname on the private network
172.16.0.1     serverab           # Ci static hostname on the backbone network
172.16.0.2     serverbb           # DB static hostname on the backbone network
172.16.0.3     servercb           # APP1 static hostname on the backbone network
172.16.0.51    itssapb SAPTRANSHOST # NEW - CI virtual hostname on the backbone network
172.16.0.52    itsdb2b            # NEW - DB virtual hostname on the backbone network
```

Figure 71. CI, DB, and APP HOSTS file for DB2 UDB

For SQL Server:

1. Define the virtual IP address of the CI server. Add the entry:

   172.16.0.51 itssapb

2. Define the virtual IP address of the DB server. Add the entry:

   172.16.0.52 itssqlb

3. Move the SAPTRANSHOST alias from the 192.168.0.51 itssap line to the 172.16.0.51 itssapb line.

   This step is necessary if you want to move the transport traffic from the public network to the backbone network. However, there are situations in which the SAPTRANSHOST should not be changed. Examples of such situations include communication with external SAP systems or lack of backbone adapters on the test system.

The changed HOSTS file is shown in Figure 72. The added lines are highlighted.

```
127.0.0.1      localhost                # loopback address
192.168.0.1    servera                  # DB static hostname on the public network
192.168.0.2    serverb                  # CI static hostname on the public network
192.168.0.3    serverc                  # APP1 (static) hostname on the public network
192.168.0.50   sapclus                  # Microsoft Cluster network name
192.168.0.51   itssap                   # Ci virtual hostname on the public network
192.168.0.52   itssql                   # DB virtual hostname on the public network
10.0.0.1       serverai                 # CI static hostname on the private network
10.0.0.2       serverbi                 # DB static hostname on the private network
172.16.0.1     serverab                 # Ci static hostname on the backbone network
172.16.0.2     serverbb                 # DB static hostname on the backbone network
172.16.0.3     servercb                 # APP1 static hostname on the backbone network
172.16.0.51    itssapb SAPTRANSHOST # NEW - CI virtual hostname on the backbone network
172.16.0.52    itssqlb                  # NEW - DB virtual hostname on the backbone network
```

Figure 72. CI, DB, and APP HOSTS file for SQL Server

9.1.3 Routing table change

To force the usage of the backbone network for inter-server communication the following, new permanent static entries must be added to the routing table of the CI, DB, and APPx servers. The added routes are identical on all servers of the R/3 system.

Step 27.4: Routing table changes

Note: The subnet mask parameter value of 255.255.255.0 used below may need to be changed depending on the subnet you are using in your network configuration.

1. To route each request directed to the DB server with the IP address 192.168.0.52 (name: itsora, itsdb2, itssql) from the public network to the corresponding IP address 172.16.0.52 (name: itsorab, itsdb2b, itssqlb) on the backbone network, execute this route command from a command prompt:

route add -p 192.168.0.52 mask 255.255.255.0 172.16.0.52 metric 1

(The -p switch makes the entry permanent.)

2. To route each request directed to the CI server with the IP address 192.168.0.51 (itssap) from the public network to the corresponding IP address 172.16.0.51 (itssapb) on the backbone network, execute this route command from a command prompt:

```
route add -p 192.168.0.51 mask 255.255.255.0 172.16.0.51 metric 1
```

(The -p switch makes the entry permanent.)

3. To route each request directed to the APP1 server with the IP address 192.168.0.3 (serverc) from the public network to the corresponding IP address 172.16.0.3 (servercb) on the backbone network, execute this route command from a command prompt:

```
route add -p 192.168.0.3 mask 255.255.255.0 172.16.0.3 metric 1
```

(The -p switch makes the entry permanent.)

Note

Step 3 has to be repeated for any additional application server using the corresponding IP address of that server.

9.1.4 Test

Step 27.5: Test the configuration

You should now test the backbone configuration to ensure that your R/3 system is still fully operational.

A thorough description of how to test the installation in order to see if failover works correctly can be found in Appendix A and Appendix B of the SAP document *SAP R/3 in Switchover Environments* (document 50020596).

9.2 Benefits of the backbone configuration

In this section, we describe how various requests are routed in an SAP system exploiting logon load balancing with the backbone configuration implemented as previously described in 9.1, "Backbone configuration" on page 233. We use the simple example of user Mary performing an SAP transaction starting from the SAPLOGON activation until the final transaction commit. The next steps describe the message flows produced by this simple operation. See Figure 73 for a graphical representation.

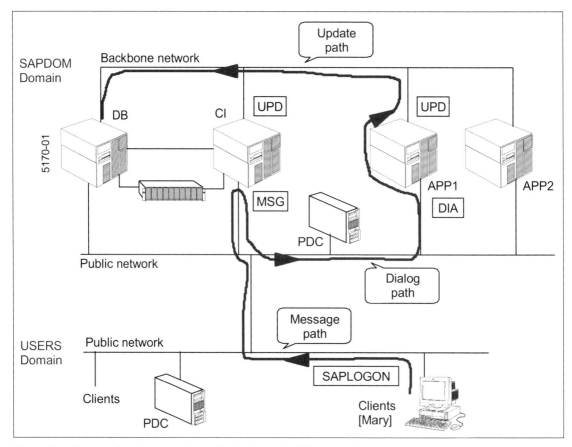

Figure 73. Dialog and update data flows with the simple backbone configuration

1. User Mary opens the connection using either SAPLOGON or SAP Session Manager.

2. The connection request is sent along the public network to the Central Instance (CI) host running the Message service on the TCP port specified in the SERVICES file (line: sapms<SID> <port number>).

3. The Message service on the CI node receives the request and sends the user a list of available logon groups

4. User Mary opens the desired logon group and is connected to the application server having the lightest load.

5. The Dispatcher service of APP1 queues the connection request until one of the Dialog work processes becomes ready to serve a new request.

6. When a Dialog work process becomes available the dispatcher retrieves the request from the queue and assigns the request to it.

7. The Dialog work process rolls in the data and completes the request. To complete the request, the Dialog work process must get access to some temporary tables on the DB (VBMOD and others) exploiting the backbone network. The data is then rolled out.

8. The next user dialog step is still served by APP1 but not necessarily by the same Dialog work process.

9. When the business transaction is complete the dialog service transfers the control of the transaction to the update service by means of the ABAP statement "Commit Work".

10. The Dispatcher selects one Update work process and transfers the update request to it. In Figure 73 on page 246 the dispatcher could have chosen the Update work process on the CI host also.

11. The Update work process, using the backbone network, reads the update tables (for instance, VBMOD) and then updates the affected DB tables.

The backbone plays a critical role starting at step 11. The update work process discovers the name of the DB server using the SAPDBHOST line of the DEFAULT.PFL profile. At the end of the SAP installation the value of SAPDBHOST is itsora for Oracle (itsdb2 for DB2, itssql for MS-SQL). Using the HOSTS file or DNS or WINS the application server hosting the update work process discovers that itsora corresponds to the IP address 192.168.0.52. Checking its routing table, the application server finds a permanent route such that each packet for 192.168.0.52 must be routed to 172.16.0.52. Windows NT 4.0 exploits the following order while checking the routing table:

1. Host route, that is, a single specific IP address

2. Subnet route, that is, a single subnet

3. Network route, that is, an entire network

4. Default route

Given the existence of the host route, any other possible entry of the routing table is ignored and the packets are sent to 172.16.0.52 along the backbone network.

The description above simplified step 7. A more detailed explanation of this step is necessary in order to fully understand the benefits of the backbone network.

If the Dialog work process needs to modify business data a SAP enqueue must be set.

SAP enqueues

A DBMS sets locks on rows or entire tables to avoid inconsistencies in multi-process environments. DB locks are set at the beginning of a DB transaction and released at the end of the DB transaction.

In SAP R/3 a logical unit of work (LUW) usually consists of many DB transactions. This requires some mechanism to lock SAP logical objects during all the SAP transactions of an LUW. This mechanism is provided by enqueues. Enqueues are explicitly set by ABAP programs on SAP logical objects by accessing the enqueue module and explicitly released by ABAP programs accessing the dequeue module.

See Chapter 8 of *SAP R/3 Performance Optimization*, by T. Schneider for further details.

If the Dialog work process is on the CI host it has direct access to the enqueue table and it sets the enqueue on the enqueue table directly. But if the Dialog work process, as shown in Figure 73 on page 246, is on a different server the Dialog work process must get access to the enqueue table as described below:

7.1. The Dialog work process on application server APP1 sends the request to the Message service on the CI host.

7.2. The Message service in turn hands over the request to the Enqueue service on the CI host.

7.3. The Enqueue service directly sets the enqueue on the enqueue table.

The Dialog work process knows where the Message service is because of the rdisp/mshost line of the DEFAULT.PFL profile. At the end of the SAP installation the value of rdisp/mshost is set to itssap. This host name is converted by means of the HOSTS file into the IP address 192.168.0.51. Due to the static host route for this IP address in the routing table, the packets are then addressed to the 172.16.0.51 IP address along the backbone network.

You should now have a functioning backbone network. For more information about backbone configuration, testing, and benefits, see *SAP R/3 in Switchover Environments* (document 50020596), downloadable from SAPNET.

Chapter 10. Tuning

Tuning SAP R/3 on a Microsoft Cluster is a very complex topic. To make the discussion as simple as possible, we will classify the tuning problems in five broad categories:

- **Hardware**

  Tuning the hardware includes having a properly configured disk subsystem and having the latest BIOS, firmware, and drivers. You should carefully design your RAID arrays to ensure maximum performance as described in 4.4, "Disk layouts" on page 84. Also, significant performance increase can be achieved with a better driver design and often, new and useful features are introduced by hardware manufacturers with new driver releases. Hence we strongly recommend you periodically check the hardware manufacturer's Web site in order to see if there is any new driver release.

  Driver upgrades always have the potential to introduce errors into the system and should therefore always be installed on the development and quality assurance systems first. Only after a thorough check, should the upgrades be applied to the production system.

- **Operating system**

  Many books have been written on Windows NT 4.0 tuning. Therefore we will only provide basic recommendations in 10.1, "Advanced Windows NT tuning" on page 250.

- **SAP R/3**

  The most important tuning is done by SAP during the "Going Live" check. Recommendations given by SAP should be carefully examined. To allow the readers to better understand the meaning of these recommendations, 10.2, "General SAP tuning" on page 251 provides general informations about SAP tuning. Moreover, useful bibliographic references are provided.

- **DBMS**

  This is one of the most important and difficult topics. Only an experienced DBA should try to tune the DBMS. Some bibliographic references can be found in 10.3, "Database tuning" on page 259.

- **Network infrastructure**

  Networks are rarely a bottleneck of well-designed SAP systems, but a missing backbone or an undersized public network could cause congestion and reduce the global performance of the system.

10.1 Advanced Windows NT tuning

The most basic steps in operating system tuning have been described in 5.6, "Basic Windows NT tuning" on page 135. More details on how to tune a Windows NT server can be found in:

- *Optimization and Tuning of Windows NT Version 1.4* by Scott B. Suhy
- *Inside Windows NT, Second Edition* by David A. Salomon.

10.1.1 Priority boost for foreground applications

Many Windows NT tuning books recommend that the priority boost for foreground applications be set to **None** as shown in Figure 74. However, this is a typical mistake due to a misunderstanding on how Windows NT works.

This section describes why it is useless to set this parameter on a Windows NT Server system.

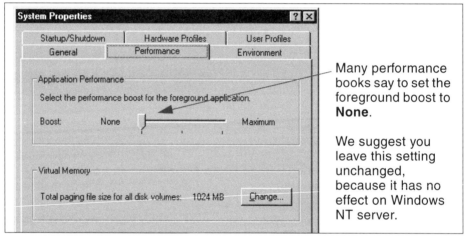

Many performance books say to set the foreground boost to **None**.

We suggest you leave this setting unchanged, because it has no effect on Windows NT server.

Figure 74. Foreground boost set to None

In Windows NT, each thread gets a predefined amount of time for execution called *quantum* before Windows NT checks the threads queue to see if there is any other thread with the same priority waiting for execution. To be precise, the quantum is not a time, but a number of clock interrupts. Each thread starts with a default quantum value (6 on Windows NT Workstation (Boost is set to None), 36 on Windows NT server). Each clock interrupt lowers this value by subtracting 3. When the quantum value is 0 the thread queue is examined to see if there is any thread with the same priority waiting to be executed. Only threads with the same priority are considered because threads with higher priority generate an interrupt which stops the execution of the current thread.

On Windows NT Workstation and Server, the System applet in Control Panel (Performance tab) lets you specify the priority of foreground applications. In Windows NT 3.51 this parameter boosts the thread priority. However, with Windows NT 4.0, this parameter does not alter the priority anymore. Instead it alters the quantum as listed in Table 60 (see Chapter 4 of *Inside Windows NT* by David A. Salomon), and for Windows NT Server, it does nothing at all:

Table 60. How the foreground boost setting affects the quantum value (the base is 36)

Boost	Windows NT Workstation	Windows NT Server
None	6	36
Middle	12	36
Maximum	18	36

As Table 60 shows, the boost setting is only relevant on Windows NT Workstation. That means that on Windows NT Workstation, it can be meaningful to remove the boost of foreground applications if you use the workstation like a server, but it has no effect at all on a Windows NT server.

10.2 General SAP tuning

This section contains basic recommendations on SAP tuning. More details can be found in:

- *SAP R/3 Performance Optimization*, by Thomas Schneider, Sybex, ISBN 0782125638
- *Basis Administration for SAP*, by Robert E. Parkinson et al, Prima Tech, ISBN 0761518878

10.2.1 Distribute work processes

SAP R/3 has six different types of work processes:

- Dialog (DIA)
- Update V1 components (UPD)
- Update V2 components (UP2)
- Background (BTC)
- Enqueue (ENQ)
- Spooler (SPO)

To alter the number of each type of work process follow these steps:

1. Click **Tools > CCMS > Configuration > Profile Maintenance**.

2. Select **Profile > Dynamic Switching > Display parameters**.

3. Select the instance profile (in our lab, ITS_DVEMGS00_ITSSAP).

4. Click **Basic Maintenance > Change**.

See page 380 of *SAP R/3 System Administration* for details. General SAP recommendations on how to distribute work processes and how to alter the number of work processes are contained in sections 10.2.2 to 10.2.4 below.

10.2.2 Run Dialog and Update processes on dedicated servers

To avoid resource contention between Update and Dialog work processes and also to allow specific server tuning, it is recommended to put dialog work processes and update work processes on different servers. In an MSCS cluster environment it is recommended to have an update server running on the cluster node with the central R/3 instance to have at least one update server available at all times.

10.2.3 Run enqueue work processes on a dedicated server

The Central Instance server is the only SAP server in which enqueue and message work processes run. Since this server is a focal point for all the message flow between nodes and also because the overall performance of the system depends on the speed of the locking activity of the enqueue work process, it is recommended to use a dedicated server for enqueue and message work processes. In the MSCS cluster environment, the cluster node running the central R/3 instance is running the enqueue and the message server.

10.2.4 Keep an optimal ratio between work processes

An excessively high or low number of work processes can decrease performance. General recommended ratios between work processes are:

- One update work process of type V1 (UPD) is able to write the data coming from four dialog work processes in the DB.

- One update work process of type V2 (UP2) is able to write statistical data coming from 12 dialog work processes.

- One background work process (BTC) is able to serve four dialog work processes.

10.2.5 Distribute the users between the application servers

Users can be automatically distributed between application servers during the logon phase, achieving a logon load balancing. This dynamic balancing can be obtained by accessing logon groups as described in Chapter 14 of *SAP R/3 System Administration*. Besides this, users should use SAPLOGON or SAP Session Manager. The SAPGUI does not allow you to exploit the logon groups. Here is a short description of how logon load balancing works:

1. The user logs onto the SAP System by SAPLOGON or SAP Session Manager.

2. The user request is directed to the Message Server on the Central Instance node.

3. The Message Server listens on the TCP port defined on the Services file in the line containing the string sapms<SID>.

4. The Message Server logs the user on the SAP application server having the lowest load. To determine the load of the server, the Message Server uses two parameters: the response time and the maximum number of users. These parameters can be configured by the SAP administrator (transaction code SMLG).

If any R/3 instance belonging to the logon group has exceeded the maximum load limits, the limits are simply ignored.

The distribution of users by means of logon groups can improve performance but can also worsen performance if you do not really need this distribution. SAP application servers need to have ABAP preprocessed code in their buffers to avoid the preprocessing being done on a per-user basis. Moving users from one server to another can mean a move from a server with optimal buffers to another having non-optimal buffers. For this reason, it is recommended you create logon groups on a per-module basis. For instance, if you have enough servers you could create one logon group for FI/CO users and a second logon group for SD users.

10.2.6 Operation modes

Often, daily and night activities are different in an SAP system. The first one stresses dialog work processes while the second mainly concerns batch work processes. To optimize the system for these different configurations you should use operation modes. This technique allows you to configure the system in two different ways and schedule the switch between them at predetermined hours. This means you can have two operation modes, one with more dialog processes and the other with more background processes and you can switch from the day mode to night mode at predetermined hours.

A detailed description of how to configure operation modes is contained in Chapter 14 of *SAP R/3 System Administration*.

10.2.7 Page file striping

Improving the page file I/O increases the overall SAP performance, so it is recommended to stripe the page file as much as possible. You can either create up to 16 page files in different disks or use hardware technology such as RAID-1 enhanced and RAID-10 to obtain the striping. It is also important to create large page files because this is the basis of *zero administration memory management* as described in OSS note 0088416.

10.2.8 Memory management

As of Release 4.0, SAP exploits a new technique to manage the memory known as zero administration memory management. This technique aims to make the tuning of memory parameters automatic. If you need to tune these parameters manually see OSS note 0088416.

10.2.9 Performance analysis

SAP R/3 provides many tools allowing you to monitor and tune the SAP system, the most important of which is the Computing Center Control system. This section provides information on how to monitor the system to find out how to improve performance.

10.2.9.1 Workload analysis

Workload analysis can be started from the SAPGUI by clicking **Tools > CCMS > Control/Monitoring > Performance Menu > Workload> Analysis**.

By clicking **Oracle** (or **SQL** or **DB2**, depending on the DBMS used, you can analyze the DBMS. This corresponds to transaction code ST04. Figure 75 appears:

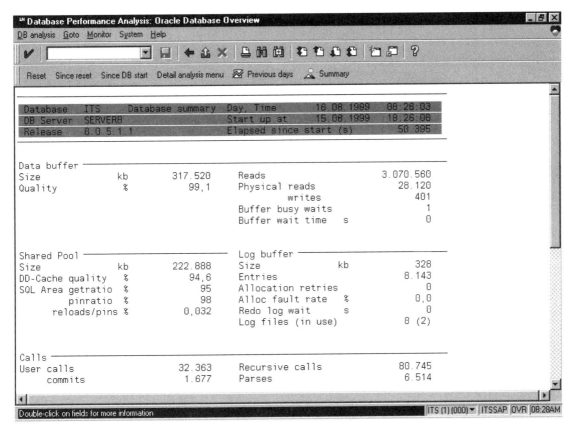

Figure 75. DBMS analysis (Oracle)

Alternatively, you can click **ITSSAP** to analyze the SAP application server. This corresponds to transaction code ST03 as shown in Figure 76:

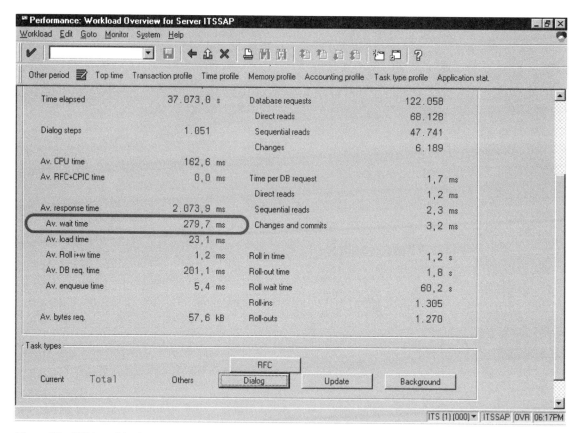

Figure 76. ST03 workload analysis

The Av. wait time parameter has to be no more than 1 percent of the average total response time. If this parameter is higher, either the number of work processes is inadequate or there is something blocking their activity.

10.2.9.2 Buffer Cache quality analysis

Buffer analysis can be started by clicking **Tools > CCMS > Control/Monitoring > Performance Menu > Setup/Buffers > Buffers**. This corresponds to transaction code ST02 (see Figure 77):

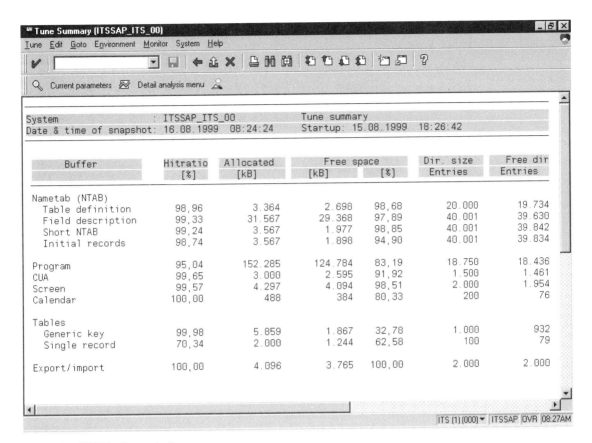

Figure 77. ST02 buffer analysis

10.2.9.3 Database reorganization

Database reorganization can be started by clicking **Tools > CCMS > DB Administration > DBA Planning Calendar** or transaction code DB13. Then it is necessary to double-click the actual day. Figure 78 shows the resulting dialog box for DB2 UDB. If you are using Oracle or SQL Server, the dialog box shown will contain the set of specific functions for the specific DB used.

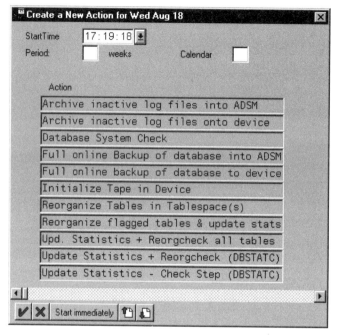

Figure 78. Database reorganization

You must then select the start time, period, calendar, and type of reorganization.

10.2.10 SAP tuning documentation and publications

Primary information sources for SAP tuning in the environment analyzed in this book are:

- OSS note 0103747 *Performance 4.0/4.5: Parameter Recommendations*, a note collecting the recommendations on how to set SAP parameters as of Release 4.0A.

- OSS note 0088416 *Zero Administration Memory Management from 4.0A/N.*

- OSS note 0110172 *NT: Transactions with Large Storage Requirements* describing when and how to exploit the 3 GB feature of Windows NT EE.

For a general description of how SAP manages memory see:

- *Memory Management as of R/3 Release 3.0C* (SAP TechNet Web site). This paper has to be read together with OSS note 0088416.

Useful non-SAP documents about how to tune SAP systems are:

- *Tuning SAP R/3 for Intel Pentium Pro Processor-based Servers Running Windows NT Server 3.51 and Oracle7 Version 7.2.*
- *Netfinity Performance Tuning with Windows NT 4.0*, SG24-5287.

10.3 Database tuning

For detailed information about how to tune the DBMS see:

- *Oracle Architecture,* by S. Bobrowski, Chapter 10
- *Oracle 8 Tuning,* by M. J. Corey et al, Chapter 3
- *DB2 Universal Database and SAP R/3 Version 4,* by Diane Bullock et al, Chapters 8 and 9.
- *SAP R/3 Performance Tuning Guide for Microsoft SQL Server 7.0,* from `http://support.microsoft.com`
- *Inside Microsoft SQL Server 7.0,* by Ron Soukup and Kalen Delaney

Chapter 11. Verifying the installation

This chapter provides detailed information about the SAP configuration, which can be useful while troubleshooting the installation:

- 11.1, "How to troubleshoot the system at the end of the installation" on page 261 provides hints on how to troubleshoot the system.

- 11.2, "Log files" on page 262 contains a list of main logs useful to better understand what is happening. High skills are generally required to understand these logs.

- 11.3, "Services" on page 267 contains a list of services you should expect to see after the installation. This section can to be used as an easy reference to see if everything is installed correctly.

- 11.4, "Accounts and users" on page 270 contains a list of accounts and rights at the end of the installation. This section is a useful reference if you meet permission problems during or after the installation.

- 11.5, "R3Setup" on page 276 contains a description of how to circumvent a typical unpredictable error you might see during R3Setup usage.

11.1 How to troubleshoot the system at the end of the installation

If you encounter any problems at the end of an SAP installation, it can be very difficult to determine the cause of these errors. This section provides hints to face these situations. The main components contributing to the final configuration are:

- Hardware
- Windows NT software
- Microsoft Cluster
- SAP software
- DBMS software
- Network
- Clients

Your first step should be to try to isolate which of these components needs a thorough analysis. The following hints can be useful in this phase:

- If you have connectivity problems from a SAPGUI or you are not able to fail over from one node to the other node, this does not necessarily mean you have a problem with the SAP system. Quite often, network switches or routers are the causes of a non-working SAP system. Also, routing tables on the SAP servers or on the clients must be examined. A network expert able to analyze the network traffic should be called.

- If you need to understand whether you have a cluster or SAP problem, proceed as described here. In both Node A and Node B create a hardware profile (NoSAPNoDB) in which all the SAP and DBMS services are disabled. You can get a list of services you need to disable from 11.3, "Services" on page 267.

  Reboot both nodes and test the cluster using Microsoft CASTEST utility (see 5.9.2, "Test the failover process" on page 148 for more details).

  - If the test is successful you know that your cluster is properly working and so the problem can be looked for in the SAP or DBMS installation.

  - If the test is not successful you can use the CASTEST log and Microsoft Cluster log to understand what is not working.

11.2 Log files

The first place to check when troubleshooting are the various log files.

11.2.1 MSCS log file

The Microsoft Cluster Server log is the most powerful tool to troubleshoot the cluster. To enable logging it is necessary to create a new system variable, ClusterLog, shown in Figure 79.

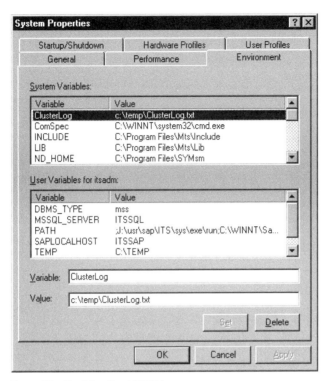

Figure 79. Enabling the MSCS log

To provide you with information about the interpretation of this log, we will show small excerpts of real logs.

This first excerpt, Figure 80, describes the start of the Cluster Service on Node servera.

```
189::19-17:59:33.935 [CPROXY] Service Starting...
189::19-17:59:33.935 [CPROXY] Service Registered
189::19-17:59:33.951 [CPROXY] Process created.
189::19-17:59:33.951 [CPROXY] Service Started.
11f::19-17:59:33.967

11f::19-17:59:33.967 Cluster Service started - Cluster Version 2.224.
11f::19-17:59:33.967    OS Version 4.0.1381 - Service Pack 4.
11f::19-17:59:33.967 We're initing Ep...
11f::19-17:59:33.967 [DM] : Initialization
11f::19-17:59:33.967 [DM] DmpRestartFlusher: Entry
11f::19-17:59:33.967 [DM] DmpStartFlusher: Entry
11f::19-17:59:33.967 [DM] DmpStartFlusher: thread created
11f::19-17:59:33.967 [NM] Initializing...
11f::19-17:59:33.967 [NM] Local node name = servera.
```

Figure 80. MSCS log excerpt — Cluster Service startup

The circled line shows the Cluster Service starting:

11f is the ID of the thread issuing the log
19-17:59:33.967 is the GMT time stamp
Cluster Service started - Cluster Version 2.224 is the event description

The central lines are characterized by the element [DM]. This is an acronym for Database Manager, the cluster component through which the changes in the cluster configuration are done. Table 61 is a list of typical components found in a cluster log:

Table 61. Components listed in the log

Acronym	Component
DM	Database Manager
NM	Node Manager
FM	Failover Manager
API	API support
LM	Log Manager
CS	Cluster Service
INIT	State of a node before joining the cluster
JOIN	State of the node when the node tries to join the cluster

Acronym	Component
EP	Event Processor
RM	Resource Monitor
GUM	Global Update Manager

To understand what the cluster does, it is necessary to understand the internal architecture of MSCS. Good references are:

- *Clustering Architecture* (Microsoft white paper)
- *Windows NT Microsoft Cluster Server* by Richard R. Lee

A fundamental document containing a complete list of Windows NT Event Viewer errors due to cluster problems with descriptions enclosed is:

- *MS Cluster Server Troubleshooting and Maintenance* by Martin Lucas

The next excerpt from the MSCS log, Figure 81, shows the completion of the start process:

```
11f::19-17:59:35.857 [FM] FmJoinPhase2 complete, now online!
11f::19-17:59:35.860 [INIT] Cluster Started! Original Min WS is 204800, Max WS is
                     1413120.
189::19-17:59:35.860 [CPROXY] clussvc initialized
140::19-17:59:42.656 Time Service <Time Service>: Status of Time Service request
                     to sync from node serverb is 0.
```

Figure 81. MSCS log excerpt — cluster started

The next lines in the log, shown in Figure 82, describe the arbitration process to get access to the quorum:

```
16a::19-18:00:07.672 [NM] Checking if we own the quorum resource.
180::19-18:00:07.672 Physical Disk <Disk I:>: SCSI, error reserving disk, error 170.
180::19-18:00:36.860 Physical Disk <Disk I:>: Arbitrate returned status 0.
16a::19-18:00:36.860 [FM] Successfully arbitrated quorum resource
                     9abfb375 -540e- 11d3- bd6a-  00203522d044.
16a::19-18:00:36.860 [FM] FMArbitrateQuoRes: Current State 2 State=2 Owner 2
16a::19-18:00:36.860 [FM] FMArbitrateQuoRes: Group state :Current State 0 State=0
                     Owner 2
16a::19-18:00:36.860 [NM] We own the quorum resource.
```

Figure 82. MSCS log excerpt — quorum arbitration

11.2.2 SAP log files

The most important logs useful in troubleshooting the SAP R/3 installation are:

- \Users\itsadm\Install\CENTRDB.LOG
- \Users\itsadm\Install\NTCMIGNA.LOG
- \Users\itsadm\Install\NTCMIGNB.LOG
- \Users\itsadm\Install\R3CLUS.LOG
- \Users\itsadm\Install\UPDINSTV.LOG
- \Temp\R3Setup\NTCLUSCD.LOG
- \usr\sap\ITS\sys\DVEBMGS00\work\SAPSTART.LOG

The SAP installation procedure was changed with the release of R/3 4.5A. As described in OSS note 0138765 *Cluster Migration: Terminology and Procedure*:

The installation is composed of two main phases:

- The ordinary (non-cluster) installation
- Cluster migration

In the first phase, the CENTRDB.TPL template is used and relevant information is logged in the CENTRDB.LOG file. In the second phase, the NTCMIGNA.TPL (for Node A) and NTCMIGNB.TPL (for Node B) templates are used. In this phase the corresponding logs, NTCMIGNA.LOG and NTCMIGNB.LOG, should be analyzed.

During the creation of the cluster group, three main programs are used:

- INSAPRCT — responsible for registering the SAP Resource Type
- CRCLGRP — responsible for creating the SAP cluster group
- COCLGRP — responsible for creating the R/3 resource

These three programs write errors in the R3CLUS.LOG file. See OSS note 0112266 *R/3 + MSCS Cluster Server: Frequent Questions + Tips* for further information.

As of Release 4.5A, there is a specific R3Setup step dedicated to the correction of the table INSTVERS whose name is "Completing cluster installation (Instvers)" (see OSS note 0112266 *R/3+MSCS Cluster Server: Frequent Questions + Tips*). These steps are logged in the UPDINSTV.LOG file.

If the installation is complete, but the instance does not start, a good source of information can be SAPSTART.LOG where the start of the instance is logged. Further information can be found in OSS note 0002033 S*tartup fails, sapstart.sem, startsap, sapstart.*

11.3 Services

It is possible to take a complete description of the services and their running status using the SCLIST utility from the Windows NT Resource Kit. The following subsections contain a list of services at the end of the installation with a few comments about their meaning.

11.3.1 Oracle

Table 62 contains a complete list of relevant services running on a cluster node just after the completion of the installation.

Table 62. Oracle Services

Service	User account	Startup	Meaning
Cluster Server	ClusSvc	Automatic	Windows NT 4.0 EE Service implementing the cluster features such as resource monitoring, failover, etc.
OracleAgent80	System	Manual	Listens for and responds to job and event requests sent from the OEM console[2].
OracleAgent80<SID>ORA	System	Manual	Listens for and responds to job and event requests sent from the OEM console.
OracleClientCache80	System	Manual	Oracle version 8 provides a client cache service that allows a client on most platforms to store information retrieved from an Oracle Names Server in its local cache
OracleDataGatherer	System	Manual	Gathers performance statistics for the Oracle Performance Manager.
OracleExtprocAgent	System	Manual	Enables information from database queries to be published to a Web page at specified time intervals[2].
OracleFailSafe	System	Manual	Oracle cluster service.
OracleService<SID>[1]	System	Manual	Oracle instance <SID> service.
OracleTNSListener80Fsl<sid>ora	System	Manual	Listens for and accepts incoming connection requests from client applications[2].

Service	User account	Startup	Meaning
SAP<SID>_00	SAPService<SID>	Manual	SAP instance service
SAPOSCOL	SAPService<SID>	Automatic	SAP Operating System Collector service.

Notes:
1 For this service the setting Allow Service to Interact with Desktop must be checked.
2 From the Oracle publication: *Oracle 8 Getting Started*

11.3.2 DB2

Table 63 contains a complete list of relevant DB2 services running on a cluster node just after the completion of the installation:

Table 63. DB2 services

Service	User account	Startup	Meaning
Cluster Server	ClusSvc	Automatic	Windows NT 4.0 EE Service implementing the cluster features such as like resource monitoring, failover, etc.
DB2 - DB2DAS00	db2admin	Automatic	DB2 Administration Server (DAS) instance.[1]
DB2 - DB2L<SID>	System	Automatic	Local database instance used by work processes to access the R/3 database.
DB2 Governor	db2admin	Manual	This service controls application behavior by setting limits and defining actions when the limits are exceeded.
DB2 JDBC Applet Server	SYSTEM	Manual	DB2 Java Applet server - to support Java Applets.
DB2-DB2<SID> (or DB2<SID>)	db2<sid>	Manual	clustered DB2 <SID> instance.
DB2 Security Server	SYSTEM	Automatic	DB2 Security Service.[2]
SAP<SID>_00	sapse<sid>	Manual	SAP instance <SID> .
SAPOSCOL	sapse<sid>	Automatic	SAP Operating System Collector.

Notes:
1 See Chapter 4 of *The Universal Guide to DB2 for Windows NT,* SC09-2800, for details on the meaning of this instance.
2 See Chapter 2 of *The Universal Guide to DB2 for Windows NT,* where the limited usage of this service in the most recent releases of DB2 is explained.

11.3.3 SQL Server

Table 64 contains a complete list of relevant SQL Server services running on a cluster node just after the completion of the installation:

Table 64. SQL Server services

Service	User account	Startup	Meaning
Cluster Server	ClusSvc	Automatic	Windows NT 4.0 EE Service implementing the cluster features such as resource monitoring, failover, etc.
MSSQLServer$<SID>SQL	sqlsvc		MS SQL Server (instance <SID>)[1]
SQLServerAgent$<SID>SQL	sqlsvc		MS SQL Server agent (instance <SID>) allowing the scheduling of periodic activities[1]
VSrvSvc$<SID>SQL	SYSTEM		Virtual Server Service for instance <SID>
SAP<SID>_00	SAPServiceI<SID>	Manual	SAP instance <SID>
SAPOSCOL	SAPService<SID>	Automatic	SAP Operating System Collector
Note: 1 See Chapter 7 of *Microsoft SQL Server Introduction* (Microsoft TechNet) for details			

11.4 Accounts and users

The next step is to look at the accounts and users on your system. .

11.4.1 Oracle

Table 65 shows the accounts stored in the Windows NT account databases on the primary domain controller (PDC) of the SAP domain and in the account database of the cluster nodes:

Table 65. Accounts on the PDC

Account	User rights on the PDC	User rights on the cluster nodes
Cluster Service Account Lab value: ClusSvc Belongs to: Domain users		Back up files and directories, increase quotas, increase scheduling priority, load and unload device drivers, lock pages in memory, log on as a service, restore files and directories
<sid>adm Lab value: itsadm Belongs to: Domain users, Domain Admins, SAP_<SID>_GlobalAdmin	Act as a part of the os, log on as a service, replace a process level token	Act as part of the operating system, increase quotas, replace a process level token
SAPService<SID> Lab value: SAPServiceITS Belongs to: Domain users, SAP_<SID>_GlobalAdmin		Access this computer from the network, log on as a service
Global Group SAP_<SID>_GlobalAdmin Lab value: SAP_ITS_GlobalAdmin Contains:<sid>adm and SAPService<SID>		

Table 66 shows the accounts configured in the Windows NT account database on both nodes of the cluster:

Table 66. Accounts on the cluster nodes

Group	Contains
Local Group ORA_<SID>_DBA (lab value ORA_ITS_DBA)	Contains SAPDOM\ClusSvc and SAPDOM\<sid>adm
Local Group ORA_<SID>_OPER (lab value ORA_ITS_OPER)	Contains SAPDOM\<sid>adm and SAPDOM\SAPService<SID>
Local Group SAP_<SID>_Local Admin (lab value SAP_ITS_Local Admin)	Contains SAPDOM\SAP_<SID>_Global Admin

Table 67 shows the users configured in Oracle tables:

Table 67. Users in the Oracle tables

User	Granted roles	System privileges
DBSNMP	Connect, resource, SNMPagent	Create public synonym, unlimited tablespace
OPS$<SID>ADM Lab value: OPS$ITSADM	Connect, resource, SAPDBA	Unlimited tablespace
OPS$SAPSERVICE<SID> Lab value: OPS$SAPSERVICEITS	Connect, resource	Unlimited tablespace
SAPR3	Connect, DBA, resource	Unlimited tablespace
SYS	All roles	All system privileges
SYSTEM	DBA	Unlimited tablespace

11.4.2 DB2 users

Table 68 shows the accounts stored in Windows NT database on the PDC:

Table 68. Accounts stored in Windows NT database on the PDC

Account/Group	User rights on PDC	User cluster nodes
Cluster Service Account (lab value: ClusSvc) Belongs to: Administrators, Domain users	Back up files and directories, increase quotas, increase scheduling priority, load and unload device drivers, lock pages in memory, log on as a service, restore files and directories	Back up files and directories, increase quotas, increase scheduling priority, load and unload device drivers, lock pages in memory, log on as a service, restore files and directories
db2<sid> (lab value: db2its) Belongs to: Domain users, SYSADM	Not applicable	Access this computer from the network, act as part of the operating system, log on as a service, replace a process-level token
<sid>adm (lab value: itsadm) Belongs to: Domain Admins, Domain users, SAP_<SID>_GlobalAdmin, SYSCTRL	Act as a part of the operating system, increase quotas, log on as a service, replace a process level token	Access this computer from the network, act as part of the operating system, increase quotas, log on as a service, replace a process- level token
sapse<sid> (lab value: sapseits) Belongs to: Domain users, SAP_<SID>_GlobalAdmin, SYSCTRL	Not applicable	Access this computer from the network, log on as a service
Global Group SAP_<SID>_GlobalAdmin (lab value SAP_ITS_GlobalAdmin) Contains: <sid>adm	Not applicable	Not applicable
Global Group SYSADM Contains: db2<sid>	Not applicable	Not applicable
Global Group SYSCTRL Contains: <sid>adm, sapse<sid>	Not applicable	Not applicable

Table 69 shows the accounts stored in Windows NT databases in Server A and Server B:

Table 69. Accounts stored in Windows NT databases in servera and serverb

Accounts	User rights
db2admin Belongs to: Administrators	Act as part of the operating system, create a token object, debug programs, increase quotas, log on as a service, replace a process level token
sapr3 Belongs to: Users	None
Local group: SAP_<SID>LocalAdmin Contains the global group SAPDOM\SAP_<SID>_GlobalAdmin	None

Table 70 shows the database access rights granted to users:

Table 70. Database access rights granted to users

Users/Groups	Authorities
User: db2<sid>	All
User: <sid>adm	All
User: sapr3	Connect database, create tables, create packages, create schemas implicitly
User: sapse<sid>	All
Group: PUBLIC	Create schemas implicitly

11.4.3 SQL Server

Table 71 shows the accounts stored in the Windows NT account databases on the primary domain controller (PDC) of the SAP domain and in the account database of the cluster nodes:

Table 71. Accounts on the PDC

Account	User rights on the PDC	User rights on the cluster nodes
Cluster Service Account Lab value: ClusSvc Belongs to: Domain users	None	Back up files and directories, increase quotas, increase scheduling priority, load and unload device drivers, lock pages in memory, log on as a service, restore files and directories
<sid>adm Lab value: itsadm Belongs to: Domain users, Domain Admins, SAP_<SID>_GlobalAdmin	Act as a part of the OS, Log on as a service, replace a process level token	Act as part of the operating system, increase quotas, replace a process-level token
SAPService<SID> Lab value: SAPServiceITS Belongs to: Domain users, SAP_<SID>_GlobalAdmin	None	Access this computer from the network, log on as a service
Global Group SAP_<SID>_GlobalAdmin Lab value: SAP_ITS_GlobalAdmin Contains:<sid>adm and SAPService<SID>	None	

Table 72 shows the accounts configured in the Windows NT account database on both nodes of the cluster:

Table 72. Accounts on the cluster nodes

Group	Contains
Local Group SAP_<SID>_Local Admin (lab value SAP_ITS_Local Admin)	Contains SAPDOM\SAP_<SID>_Global Admin

Table 73 shows the accounts specific for an SQL Server installation:

Table 73. SQL Server-specific accounts

Account description	Where defined	Account	Lab value
SQL Server Service account	Domain controller of the SAPDOM domain	[not pre-defined]	sqlsvc
Standard SQL Server login with administrator privileges		sa (systems administrator)	sa
Account previously used to connect the work processes to the DBMS	Login stored in the SQL Server DB	sapr3[1]	sapr3
	Local account on SQL Server	SQLAgentCMDExec[2]	SQLAgentCMDExec
	Local account on SQL Server	MTSImpersonators	MTSImpersonators

Notes:
1 The account sapr3 still exists in SAP R/3 Release 4.5x but is no longer used as described in OSS note 0157372
2 See *MS SQL Server Transact-SQL and Utilities Reference, Volume 2* in Microsoft TechNet for a description of this account

11.5 R3Setup

If an error occurs the SAP installation program R3Setup stops and displays an error message. Errors like the one in Figure 83 can appear:

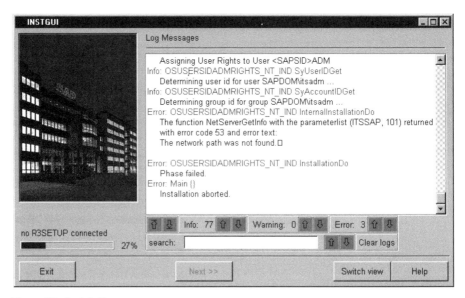

Figure 83. Installation error

The general strategy to face an error during the R3Setup run is to exit from the R3Setup program and to restart R3Setup with the same parameters again. Do not restore the original R3Setup profiles, because R3Setup updates them during its run and stores status information in them. If the problem persists an error analysis will be necessary.

Appendix A. Special notices

This publication is intended to help the Windows NT/Windows 2000 and SAP R/3 consultant install SAP R/3 4.5B in a Microsoft Cluster Server configuration using either Oracle, DB2, or SQL Server as the database. The information in this publication is not intended as the specification of any programming interfaces that are provided by SAP and Microsoft for SAP R/3 and Windows NT. See the PUBLICATIONS section of the IBM Programming Announcement for for more information about what publications are considered to be Netfinity product documentation.

References in this publication to IBM products, programs or services do not imply that IBM intends to make these available in all countries in which IBM operates. Any reference to an IBM product, program, or service is not intended to state or imply that only IBM's product, program, or service may be used. Any functionally equivalent program that does not infringe any of IBM's intellectual property rights may be used instead of the IBM product, program or service.

Information in this book was developed in conjunction with use of the equipment specified, and is limited in application to those specific hardware and software products and levels.

IBM may have patents or pending patent applications covering subject matter in this document. The furnishing of this document does not give you any license to these patents. You can send license inquiries, in writing, to the IBM Director of Licensing, IBM Corporation, North Castle Drive, Armonk, NY 10504-1785.

Licensees of this program who wish to have information about it for the purpose of enabling: (i) the exchange of information between independently created programs and other programs (including this one) and (ii) the mutual use of the information which has been exchanged, should contact IBM Corporation, Dept. 600A, Mail Drop 1329, Somers, NY 10589 USA.

Such information may be available, subject to appropriate terms and conditions, including in some cases, payment of a fee.

The information contained in this document has not been submitted to any formal IBM test and is distributed AS IS. The use of this information or the implementation of any of these techniques is a customer responsibility and depends on the customer's ability to evaluate and integrate them into the customer's operational environment. While each item may have been reviewed by IBM for accuracy in a specific situation, there is no guarantee that the same or similar results will be obtained elsewhere. Customers attempting to adapt these techniques to their own environments do so at their own risk.

Any pointers in this publication to external Web sites are provided for convenience only and do not in any manner serve as an endorsement of these Web sites.

The following terms are trademarks of the International Business Machines Corporation in the United States and/or other countries:

AIX	AS/400
DB2	ESCON
IBM	MQ
MQSeries	Netfinity
Netfinity Manager	OS/390
Parallel Sysplex	RS/6000
S/390	ServeRAID
ServerProven	TrackPoint

The following terms are trademarks of other companies:

Tivoli, Manage. Anything. Anywhere.,The Power To Manage., Anything. Anywhere.,TME, NetView, Cross-Site, Tivoli Ready, Tivoli Certified, Planet Tivoli, and Tivoli Enterprise are trademarks or registered trademarks of Tivoli Systems Inc., an IBM company, in the United States, other countries, or both. In Denmark, Tivoli is a trademark licensed from Kjøbenhavns Sommer - Tivoli A/S.

C-bus is a trademark of Corollary, Inc. in the United States and/or other countries.

Java and all Java-based trademarks and logos are trademarks or registered trademarks of Sun Microsystems, Inc. in the United States and/or other countries.

Microsoft, Windows, Windows NT, and the Windows logo are trademarks of Microsoft Corporation in the United States and/or other countries.

PC Direct is a trademark of Ziff Communications Company in the United States and/or other countries and is used by IBM Corporation under license.

ActionMedia, LANDesk, MMX, Pentium and ProShare are trademarks of Intel Corporation in the United States and/or other countries.

UNIX is a registered trademark in the United States and other countries licensed exclusively through The Open Group.

SET and the SET logo are trademarks owned by SET Secure Electronic Transaction LLC.

Other company, product, and service names may be trademarks or service marks of others.

Appendix B. Related publications

The publications listed in this section are considered particularly suitable for a more detailed discussion of the topics covered in this redbook.

B.1 IBM Redbooks

For information on ordering these ITSO publications see "How to get IBM Redbooks" on page 293.

- *Optimizing IBM Netfinity Servers for SAP R/3 and Windows NT*, SG24-5219
- *Netfinity Performance Tuning with Windows NT 4.0*, SG24-5287
- *Implementing Netfinity Disk Subsystems: ServeRAID SCSI, Fibre Channel and SSA*, SG24-2098
- *Windows NT Backup and Recovery with ADSM*, SG24-2231
- *Disaster Recovery with HAGEO: An Installer's Companion*, SG24-2018
- *Bullet-Proofing Your Oracle Database with HACMP: A Guide to Implementing AIX Databases with HACMP*, SG24-4788
- *Oracle Cluster POWERsolution Guide*, SG24-2019
- *High Availability Considerations: SAP R/3 on DB2 for OS/390*, SG24-2003
- *Using Tivoli Storage Management in a Clustered NT Environment*, SG24-5742
- *TCP/IP Tutorial and Technical Overview*, GG24-3376

B.2 IBM Redbooks collections

Redbooks are also available on the following CD-ROMs. Click the CD-ROMs button at http://www.redbooks.ibm.com/ for information about all the CD-ROMs offered, updates and formats.

CD-ROM Title	Collection Kit Number
System/390 Redbooks Collection	SK2T-2177
Networking and Systems Management Redbooks Collection	SK2T-6022
Transaction Processing and Data Management Redbooks Collection	SK2T-8038
Lotus Redbooks Collection	SK2T-8039
Tivoli Redbooks Collection	SK2T-8044
AS/400 Redbooks Collection	SK2T-2849

CD-ROM Title	Collection Kit Number
Netfinity Hardware and Software Redbooks Collection	SK2T-8046
RS/6000 Redbooks Collection (BkMgr)	SK2T-8040
RS/6000 Redbooks Collection (PDF Format)	SK2T-8043
Application Development Redbooks Collection	SK2T-8037
IBM Enterprise Storage and Systems Management Solutions	SK3T-3694

B.3 Related Web sites

This appendix lists the Web sites that are relevant to the topics discussed in this redbook.

B.3.1 Netfinity technology

Internet sites:

- http://www.pc.ibm.com/netfinity

- http://www.pc.ibm.com/support

IBM intranet sites (available within IBM only):

- http://performance.raleigh.ibm.com/ — Netfinity performance Web site

- http://netfinity.sl.dfw.ibm.com/ — IBM ATS Web site

- http://argus.raleigh.ibm.com/ — Netfinity hardware development

- http://devtlab.greenock.uk.ibm.com/ — Greenock development

B.3.2 Windows NT

- http://www.microsoft.com/security

- http://NTSecurity.ntadvice.com

- http://www.trustedsystems.com

- http://www.microsoft.com/hcl — Microsoft Hardware Compatibility List (select **Cluster**)

B.3.3 Microsoft Cluster Server

- http://www.microsoft.com/ntserver/ntserverenterprise/

B.3.4 SAP

Internet sites:

- http://www.sap.com — Main SAP AG Web site

- http://www.sapnet.sap.com — Technical Web site; to access this site it is necessary to have an account
  - http://www.sapnet.sap.com/r3docu — Documentation
  - http://www.sapnet.sap.com/technet — TechNet
  - http://www.sapnet.sap.com/securityguide — Security
  - http://www.sapnet.sap.com/notes — OSS notes

- http://www.r3onnt.com/ — IXOS Web site containing certified platforms

- http://www.ibm.com/erp/sap — IBM-SAP alliance page

- http://www.microsoft.com/industry/erp/sap/ — Microsoft-SAP alliance

- http://www.microsoft.com/germany/sap/ — Microsoft-SAP Germany

- http://www.sapfaq.com/ — Frequently asked questions Web site

- http://www.sap-professional.org/ — SAP professional organization

- http://www.saptechjournal.com/ — SAP Technical Journal online

IBM intranet sites (accessible to IBM employees only):

- http://w3.isicc.de.ibm.com/ — ISICC Web page (Germany)

- http://w3.isicc.ibm.com/ — ISICC Web page

B.3.5 Oracle

- http://www.oracle.com/ — Oracle Web site

- http://technet.oracle.com/ — Oracle TechNet

B.3.6 DB2

- http://www.software.ibm.com/data/db2/udb/udb-nt/ — IBM DB2 on Windows NT

- http://www.software.ibm.com/data/partners/aelpartners/ — IBM DB2 partners

B.3.7 SQL Server

- http://www.microsoft.com/sql/ — Microsoft SQL Server Web site

B.4 Downloadable documents

These documents are referenced in this redbook.

B.4.1 Microsoft Windows NT

- *Windows NT Security Guidelines,* by Steve Sutton, available from
  `http://www.trustedsystems.com/NSAGuide.htm`

B.4.2 Windows 2000

- *Windows 2000 Reliability and Availability Improvements*, from
  `http://www.microsoft.com/technet/`

B.4.3 Microsoft Cluster Server

- *IBM Netfinity High-Availability Cluster Solutions Using the IBM ServeRAID -3H and IBM ServeRAID-3HB Ultra2 SCSI Controllers Installation and User's Guide*, available from `http://www.pc.ibm.com/netfinity/clustering`

- *IBM Shared Disk Clustering Hardware Reference,* available from
  `http://www.pc.ibm.com/netfinity/clustering`

- *FAQ: All You Ever Wanted to Know about Windows NT Server 4.0 Enterprise Edition*

- *Windows NT Server, Enterprise Edition Administrator's Guide and Release Notes* from `http://www.microsoft.com/technet/`

- *MS Cluster Server Troubleshooting and Maintenance* by Martin Lucas from `http://www.microsoft.com/technet/`

- *Deploying Microsoft Cluster Server* from `http://www.microsoft.com/technet/`

- MSCS Administrator's Guide, from `http://www.microsoft.com/technet/`

- *Microsoft Cluster Server Release Notes*, from the Windows NT 4.0 Enterprise Edition CD

- *IBM Cluster Checklist,* available from
  `http://www.pc.ibm.com/us/searchfiles.html`

B.4.4 SAP R/3

Installation

- *R/3 Installation on Windows NT Oracle Database, Release 4.5B,* 51004599 (May 1999)

- *R/3 Installation on Windows NT DB2 Common Server, Release 3.5B*, 51005502

- *R/3 Installation on Windows NT MS SQL Server, Release 3.5B*, 51005503

- *Conversion to Microsoft Cluster Server: IBM DB2 for NT, Release 3.5B*, 51006418

- *Conversion to Microsoft Cluster Server: Oracle 4.0B 4.5A 4.5B*, 51005504

- *Conversion to Microsoft Cluster Server: MS SQL Server, Release 4.0B, 4.5A, 4.5B*, 51005948

Security

- *R/3 Security Guide: Volume I. An Overview of R/3 Security Services*

- *R/3 Security Guide: Volume II. R/3 Security Services in Detail*

- *R/3 Security Guide: Volume III. Checklist*

Networks

- *Network Integration of R/3 Frontends*, 51006473

- *Network Integration of R/3 Servers*, 51006371

- *SAP R/3 in Switchover Environments*, 50020596

Tuning

- *Tuning SAP R/3 for Intel Pentium Pro Processor-based Servers Running Windows NT Server 3.51 and Oracle 7 Version 7.2* from `http://www.intel.com/procs/servers/technical/SAP/281860.pdf`

- *SAP/Oracle/AIX. Performance Tuning Tips,* by John Oustalet and Walter Orb from `http://www.developer.ibm.com/library/aix4.3/ora_tune.html` (you will need to request a developer ID)

- *SAP R/3 Performance Tuning Guide for Microsoft SQL Server 7.0* from `http://www.microsoft.com/SQL/productinfo/sapp.htm`

B.5 SAPSERV FTP site

You SAPSERV access is provided by SAP as part of your SAP R/3 license. Contact SAP if you need to get access to the server. Here we describe how to connect to SAP's SAPSERVx system by way of an MPN/SOCKSified browser to download patches.

Note: These steps are related to access through the IBM intranet only. More information regarding access to SAPSERVx can be found in the following OSS notes:

- Note Number: 0063786 — FAQ on SAPSERVx.
- Note Number: 0019466 — Downloading a Patch from SAPSERVx.

For IBM intranet access by way of SOCKSified FTP, do the following:

1. Update your SOCKS.CNF file with the following detail:

```
This is screen.# IBM internal Network - without socks-server
#-------------------------------------------------
direct 9.0.0.0 255.0.0.0
# SAP's DMZ - socks-server siccfwl.isicc.ibm.com
#-------------------------------------------------
sockd @=9.165.214.110 147.204.0.0 255.255.0.0
# Internet - socks-server socks.de.ibm.com
#-------------------------------------------------
sockd @=9.165.255.62 0.0.0.0 0.0.0.0
```

Updates to the SOCKS.CNF file are maintained by the ISICC team in Walldorf, Germany. The information above is current as of August 19, 1999. Send an e-mail to infoserv@de.ibm.com if you have questions. The current ISICC SOCKS.CNF information can be found at either of the following URLs:

- ftp://sicc980.isicc.de.ibm.com/perm/socks/os2/socks.conf
- ftp://9.165.228.33/perm/socks/os2/socks.conf

2. Configure your browser for a manual proxy configuration with SOCKS server 9.165.214.110 and port:1080.

3. Make sure you do not have an FTP proxy server identified.

4. Use ftp://147.204.2.5 as the address to access SAPSERVx.

Note: You should reset your browser's proxy configuration to its original settings when you are finished with access to SAPSERVx.

B.6 OSS notes

0008523   DB Backups Using Ccms Do Not Work
0030478   Service Packs on Windows NT (current support status)
0068544   Memory Management under Windows NT

0088416	Zero Administration Memory Management from 4.0A/NT
0098385	R/3 MSCS Installation With Multiple NICs
0098717	4.0B R/3 Installation on Windows NT: DB2/CS
0100163	External Command for Windows NT Not Found
0101412	DBCC Checks with sap_mon_dbcheck
0101896	General problems for Microsoft cluster installation
0103747	Performance 4.0/4.5: Parameter Recommendations
0106275	Availability of R/3 on Microsoft Cluster Server (support status)
0107534	Migration on Microsoft Cluster Server
0107591	INFORMIX: migration stand-alone R/3 system to MSCS (3.1I)
0110172	NT: Transactions with Large Storage Requirements
0110507	Problems with PREPARE/STARTUP in Cluster Environment
0112266	R/3 + MS cluster server: frequent questions + tips
0114287	SAPDBA in a Microsoft Cluster Server environment
0117294	4.5A R/3 Installation on Windows NT: MS SQL Server
0117295	4.5A R/3 Installation on Windows NT: Oracle
0117296	Inst.: Rel. 4.5A R/3 Installation on Windows NT: DB2/CS
0117305	ORACLE: Migration to a Microsoft cluster server 4.5A
0120211	INFORMIX: Migrating to a Microsoft cluster server 4.5A
0124141	Hot Package 40B08 (IPA-TEM)
0126985	Configuration of Ataman Remote Shell for DB2CS/NT
0128167	Service Pack 4 on NT MSCS with Oracle products
0132738	INFORMIX: Using SAPDBA in MSCS or distributed environment
0134073	4.5B R/3 Installation on Windows NT: MS SQL Server
0134135	4.5B R/3 Installation on Windows NT (General)
0134141	Conversion to a Microsoft Cluster Server 4.5B
0134159	4.5B R/3 Installation on Windows NT: DB2/CS
0138765	Migration to a Microsoft Cluster Server 4.5A
0140960	MSCS Installation R/3 3.x on MS SQL Server 7.0
0140990	NT MSCS: How to backup/recover the CLUSDB
0141619	DB2/CS: Install. prog. sddb6ins for SAP DB2admin
0142731	DBCC Checks for SQL Server 7.0
0144310	Installing the NT SP4 on R/3 MSCS clusters
0144839	DB2/CS: SAP-DB2admin functions in DB2 Control Center
0146751	Converting MS SQL Server 6.5 to 7.0 in cluster
0151508	Resource Requirements for Release 4.6A
0154700	MSCS Cluster Verification Utility
0156363	MSCS: NET8 Configuration for Oracle
0166966	Printing in Microsoft Cluster Environment
0169468	Windows 2000 support
0183184	MSCS Template Update

B.7 Knowledge Base articles

The following Microsoft Knowledge Base articles are relevant to this redbook. They can be found at:

http://support.microsoft.com/search/

Hardware installation

Q169414   Cluster Service may stop after failover
Q171793   Information on application use of 4 GB RAM tuning

MSCS software installation

Q185752   MSCS doesn't run with NT Workstation
Q175779   MSCS requires SP3 or later
Q174617   Chkdsk runs while running MSCS setup
Q171883   Visual C++ runtime error when installing MSCS
Q174332   How to install additional cluster administrators
Q171265   Unable to uninstall ClusterAdmin
Q190354   Unattended MSCS setup with -JOIN requires user input (fixed with SP4)
Q214680   Cluster setup does not recognize disk with more than three logical drives (fixed with SP5)
Q232910   Error 1044 when attempting to create a new cluster

MSCS upgrades and hotfixes

Q178924   How to upgrade an evaluation version of MSCS
Q179776   Availability of hotfixes for MSCS
Q174799   How to install service packs in a cluster

Groups, resources, and dependencies

Q169017   Groups and resources in MSCS
Q197047   Failover/failback policies on MSCS
Q171791   Creating dependencies in MSCS
Q178276   Dependencies unavailable in Properties tab
Q174928   Dependencies page empty when running Resource Wizard
Q182193   Error: Cluster resource dependency cannot be found
Q174641   Resource Parameters tab is missing
Q172507   Resources go offline and online repeatedly
Q171277   Resource failover time
Q168948   Information about the cluster group
Q225329   Access violation in resource monitor (fixed with SP5)

Time service resource

Q174331   Error when adding second time service
Q174398   How to force time synchronization between MSCS nodes

Quorum resource

Q175664   Error creating dependency for quorum resource
Q172944   How to change quorum disk designation
Q172951   How to recover from a corrupted quorum log
Q225081   Cluster resources quorum size defaults to 64 KB
Q238173   Quorum checkpoint file may be corrupted at shutdown

Cluster disks

Q171052   Software FT sets are not supported in MSCS
Q175278   How to install additional drives on shared SCSI bus
Q175275   How to replace shared SCSI controller with MSCS
Q176970   Chkdsk /f does not run on the shared cluster disk
Q174797   How to run Chkdsk on a shared drive
Q196655   How to set up file auditing on cluster disk
Q189149   Disk counters on clustered disk record zero values
Q172968   Disk subsystem recovery documentation error
Q195636   Fibre Channel system loses SCSI reservation after multiple restarts (fixed with SP4)
Q193779   MSCS drive letters do not update using DiskAdmin (fixed with SP4)
Q215347   Cluster disk with more than 15 logical drives fails to go online (fixed with SP5)

Cluster networks — general, IP protocols

Q101746   TCP/IP Hosts file is case sensitive
Q158487   Browsing across subnets with a multihomed PDC in Windows NT 4.0
Q171390   Cluster service doesn't start when no domain controller available
Q171450   Possible RPC errors on cluster startup
Q168567   Clustering information on IP address failover
Q170771   Cluster may fail if IP address used from DHCP server
Q178273   MSCS documentation error: no DHCP server failover support
Q174956   WINS, DHCP, and DNS not supported for failover

Cluster networks — name resolution

Q195462   WINS registration and IP address behavior for MSCS
Q193890   Recommend WINS configuration for MSCS
Q217199   Static WINS entries cause the network name to go offline

Q183832   GetHostName() must support alternate computer names (fixed with SP4)
Q171320   How to change the IP address list order returned
Q164023   Applications calling GetHostByName() for the local host name may see the list of IP addresses in an order that does not match the binding order (fixed with SP4)

Cluster networks — network interfaces

Q174812   Effects of using autodetect setting on cluster NIC
Q201616   Network card detection in MSCS
Q175767   Behavior of multiple adapters on same network
Q176320   Impact of network adapter failure in a cluster
Q175141   Cluster service ignores network cards
Q174945   How to prevent MSCS from using specific networks
Q174794   How to change network priority in a cluster

Applications and services — general

Q171452   Using MSCS to create a virtual server
Q175276   Licensing policy implementation with MSCS
Q174837   Microsoft BackOffice applications supported by MSCS
Q188984   Office 97 not supported in a clustered environment
Q198893   Generic application: Effects of checking "Use Network Name for Computer Name" in MSCS
Q174070   Registry replication in MSCS
Q181491   MS Foundation Class GenericApp resources fail
Q224595   DCOM client cannot establish CIS session using TCP/IP address (fixed with SP5)
Q188652   Error replicating registry keys (fixed with SP4)
Q184008   SQL Server cluster setup may fail on third-party disk drives
Q176522   IIS Server instance error message with MSCS

Applications and services — Microsoft SQL Server

Q192708   Installation order for MSCS support for SQL Server V6.5 or MS Message Queue Server
Q187708   Cannot connect to SQL Virtual Server via sockets (fixed with SP4)
Q185806   SQL Server service stopped when IsAlive fails to connect (fixed with SQL Server SP5a (U.S.) for V6.5)
Q216674   Automatic SQL cluster failover does not work with WNT 4.0 SP4
Q195761   SQL Server 7.0 frequently asked questions: failover
Q219264   Order of installation for SQL Server 7.0 clustering setup
Q223258   How to install the WinNT Option Pack on MSCS with SQL Server 6.5 or 7.0

Q183672   How to upgrade a clustered MS MessageQueue SQL to SQL
          Enterprise Edition

Applications and services — Oracle Fail Safe

Q219303   Oracle Fail Safe does not function after SP4 installed (fixed with
          SP5)

Troubleshooting and debugging

Q168801   How to enable cluster logging in MSCS
Q216237   Cluster server will not start if cluster log directory is not created
          (fixed with SP5)
Q216240   Cluster log is overwritten when cluster server starts
Q216329   Cluster log filling with erroneous security descriptor information
          (fixed with SP5)
Q174944   How to use the -debug option for cluster service
Q189469   ClusterAdmin can connect to all NetBIOS names
Q197382   How to keep ClusterAdmin from reconnecting to a cluster
Q171451   Cluster node may fail to join cluster
Q185051   Restarting cluster service crashes services.exe (fixed with SP4)
Q193654   Services continue to run after shutdown initiated (fixed with SP4)
Q216064   Cluster server has Clusdb corruption after power outage (fixed
          with SP5)
Q219309   Disk error pop-up causes cluster service to stop (fixed with SP5)
Q233349   Cluster service issues event 1015 every four hours after applying
          SP5

B.8 Other publications

These publications are also relevant as further information sources:

Computer architecture

- Andrew S. Tanenbaum, *Structured Computer Organization*, Fourth Edition,
  Prentice Hall, ISBN 0130204358

Clustering

- Gregory F. Pfister, *In Search of Clusters*, Second Edition, Prentice Hall
  PTR, ISBN 0138997098

- Mark Sportack, *Windows NT Clustering Blueprints*, SAMS Publishing,
  ISBN 0672311356

- Kai Hwang, Zhiwei Xu, *Scalable Parallel Computing*, McGraw Hill, ISBN
  0070317984

Windows NT

- David A. Salomon, *Inside Windows NT, Second Edition*, Microsoft Press, ISBN 1572316772
- Richard R. Lee, *Windows NT Microsoft Cluster Server*, Osborne McGraw-Hill, ISBN 0078825008
- Presentation: *Beyond 4GB: Extended Server Memory Architecture* (available from http://www.intel.com)

SAP R/3

- Liane Will, *SAP R/3 System Administration*, Sybex, ISBN 0782124267l
- Hartwig Brand, *SAP R/3 Implementation with ASAP*, Sybex, ISBN 0782124725
- Thomas Schneider, *SAP R/3 Performance Optimization*, Sybex, ISBN 0782 125638
- Diane Bullock et al, *DB2 Universal Database and SAP R/3 Version 4*, IBM, SC09-2801
- Robert E. Parkinson et al, *Basis Administration for SAP*, Prima Tech, ISBN 0761518878
- Greg Spence, *SAP R/3 & Oracle. Backup and Recovery*, Addison-Wesley, ISBN 0201 596229
- The redpaper, *SAP R/3 and DB2 UDB in a Microsoft Cluster Environment*, available from http://www.redbooks.ibm.com

Oracle

- Liane Hobbs, *Oracle 8 on Windows NT*, Digital Press, ISBN 1555581900
- Steve Bobrowski, *Oracle Architecture*, Osborne McGraw-Hill, ISBN 0078822742
- Michael J. Corey et al, *Oracle 8 Tuning*, Osborne McGraw-Hill, ISBN 0078823900

DB2

- Jonathan Cook et al, *The Universal Guide to DB2 for Windows NT*, IBM, SC09-2800

SQL Server

- Ron Soukup and Kalen Delaney, *Inside Microsoft SQL Server 7.0*. Microsoft Press. ISBN: 0735605173.

How to get IBM Redbooks

This section explains how both customers and IBM employees can find out about IBM Redbooks, redpieces, and CD-ROMs. A form for ordering books and CD-ROMs by fax or e-mail is also provided.

- **Redbooks Web Site** http://www.redbooks.ibm.com/

  Search for, view, download, or order hardcopy/CD-ROM Redbooks from the Redbooks Web site. Also read redpieces and download additional materials (code samples or diskette/CD-ROM images) from this Redbooks site.

  Redpieces are Redbooks in progress; not all Redbooks become redpieces and sometimes just a few chapters will be published this way. The intent is to get the information out much quicker than the formal publishing process allows.

- **E-mail Orders**

  Send orders by e-mail including information from the IBM Redbooks fax order form to:

	e-mail address
In United States	usib6fpl@ibmmail.com
Outside North America	Contact information is in the "How to Order" section at this site: http://www.elink.ibmlink.ibm.com/pbl/pbl

- **Telephone Orders**

United States (toll free)	1-800-879-2755
Canada (toll free)	1-800-IBM-4YOU
Outside North America	Country coordinator phone number is in the "How to Order" section at this site: http://www.elink.ibmlink.ibm.com/pbl/pbl

- **Fax Orders**

United States (toll free)	1-800-445-9269
Canada	1-403-267-4455
Outside North America	Fax phone number is in the "How to Order" section at this site: http://www.elink.ibmlink.ibm.com/pbl/pbl

This information was current at the time of publication, but is continually subject to change. The latest information may be found at the Redbooks Web site.

IBM Intranet for Employees

IBM employees may register for information on workshops, residencies, and Redbooks by accessing the IBM Intranet Web site at http://w3.itso.ibm.com/ and clicking the ITSO Mailing List button. Look in the Materials repository for workshops, presentations, papers, and Web pages developed and written by the ITSO technical professionals; click the Additional Materials button. Employees may access MyNews at http://w3.ibm.com/ for redbook, residency, and workshop announcements.

IBM Redbooks fax order form

Please send me the following:

Title	Order Number	Quantity

First name _____ Last name _____

Company _____

Address _____

City _____ Postal code _____ Country _____

Telephone number _____ Telefax number _____ VAT number _____

☐ Invoice to customer number _____

☐ Credit card number _____

Credit card expiration date _____ Card issued to _____ Signature _____

We accept American Express, Diners, Eurocard, Master Card, and Visa. Payment by credit card not available in all countries. Signature mandatory for credit card payment.

List of abbreviations

ABAP	Advanced Business Application Programming
ADSI	Active Directory Service Interfaces
ADSM	ADSTAR Distributed Storage Manager
AFT	automatic fault tolerance
ALB	automatic load balancing
API	application programming interface
ARCH	archiver
ASCII	American National Standard Code for Information Interchange
ATM	asynchronous transfer mode
ATP	available to promise
ATS	Advanced Technical Support
BIOS	basic input/output system
BLOB	binary large objects
BTC	batch
CCMS	SAP Computer Center Management System
CD-ROM	compact disk-read only memory
CI	central instance
CMT	IBM Center for Microsoft Technologies
CPIC	common programming interface for communications
CPU	central processing unit
DAS	DB2 Administration Server
DAT	digital audio tape
DB	database
DBA	database administrator
DBMS	database management system
DBWR	database writer
DHCP	Dynamic Host Configuration Protocol
DI	database instance
DIA	dialog
DIMM	dual inline memory module
DLL	dynamic linked library
DLT	digital linear tape
DNS	domain name server
DTC	Distributed Transaction Coordinator
ECC	error checking and correcting
EDI	electronic data interchange
EE	Enterprise Edition
ENQ	enqueue
ERP	Enterprise Resource Planning
ESCON	enterprise systems connection
ESM	Environmental Services Monitor
ESS	Enterprise Storage Server
FAQ	frequently asked questions
FC	Fibre Channel
FCAL	Fibre Channel Arbitrated Loop
FCS	Fibre Channel standard
FDDI	fiber distributed data interface
FEC	Fast EtherChannel
FI	financial accounting
FLA	Fabric Loop Attach
FTP	file transfer protocol
GB	Gigabyte
GBIC	Gigabit Interface Converter
GEC	Gigabit EtherChannel
GL	general ledger
GMT	Greenwich mean time
GUI	graphical user interface
HACMP	high availability cluster multiprocessing

HAGEO	High Availability Geographic Cluster		ODBC	open database connectivity
HCL	hardware compatibility list		OEM	original equipment manufacturer
HCT	hardware compatibility test		OFS	Oracle Fail Safe
HDR	High-availability Data Replication		OLAP	Online Analytical Processing
HTML	Hypertext Markup Language		OLTP	online transaction processing
IANA	Internet Assigned Number Authority		OPS	Oracle Parallel Server
IBM	International Business Machines Corporation		OS	operating system
			OSS	online service system
ICMP	Internet control message protocol		PA	Personnel Administration
ICSM	IBM Cluster Systems Management		PAE	Physical Address Extension
IE	Internet Explorer		PCI	Peripheral Component Interconnect
IIS	Internet Information Server		PDC	primary domain controller
IPX	Internetwork Packet eXchange		PFA	predictive failure analysis
ISBN	international standard book number		PRD	production
ISICC	IBM/SAP International Competency Center		PSW	program status word
			QAS	quality assurance system
JDBC	Java database connectivity		PLDA	Private Loop Direct Attach
LAN	local area network		PSE	Page Size Extension
LED	light emitting diode		RAID	redundant array of independent disks
LGWR	log writer			
LUN	logical unit number		RAM	random access memory
LVDS	low voltage differential signaling		RAS	remote access server
MMC	Microsoft Management Console		RDAC	redundant disk array controller
MPP	massively parallel processor		RDBMS	relational database management system
MS	Microsoft			
MSCS	Microsoft Cluster Server		RFC	remote function call
MSDTC	Microsoft Distributed Transaction Coordinator		RISC	reduced instruction set computer
			RPM	revolutions per minute
MSMQ	Microsoft Message Queue Server		SAPS	SAP Application Performance Standard
MSSQL	Microsoft SQL Server			
MTBF	mean time between failures		SCSI	small computer system interface
MTTR	mean time to repair		SD	sales and distribution
NNTP	NetNews transfer protocol		SDK	software development kit
NDIS	network driver interface specification		SGA	system global area
NTC	NT Competency Center		SID	system identification

SMS	Systems Management Server
SMTP	simple mail transfer protocol
SMP	symmetric multiprocessing
SNA	systems network architecture
SNMP	simple network management protocol
SP	service pack
SPO	spooler
SQL	structured query language
SSA	serial storage architecture
SSI	single system image
TCP/IP	Transmission Control Protocol/Internet Protocol
UDB	Universal Database
UPD	update
UPS	uninterruptible power supply
VHDCI	very high density connector interface
WHQL	Windows Hardware Quality Labs
VRM	voltage regulator module
WINS	Windows Internet Name Service

Index

Numerics

4 GB tuning 89, 138

A

accounts 124
    <sid>adm 150
    DB2 272
    Oracle 270, 274
    SAPService<SID> 150
    SQL Server 275
Active Directory Services Interface 146
AIX and Windows NT solutions 55
architecture 37
asynchronous replication 49
Ataman 165
ATP server 41
auto-sensing network adapters 117

B

backbone 111, 162, 233
    benefits 245
    configuration 233
    database group changes 237
    DB2 239
    design goals 235
    DNS 241
    enqueues 248
    HOSTS file 241
    locks 248
    Oracle 238
    routing tables 235, 244
    SAP-R/3 group changes 236
    SQL Server 240
    table locks 248
    testing 245
    virtual IP addresses 234
    WINS server 241
backup and recovery 62
    alias definitions 65
    CLUSDB files 67
    complete backups 63
    dedicated backup server 64
    issues 63
    MSCS unique files 67
    offline backups 67

backup and recovery, continued
    shared disks 66
    summary 68
    tape drives, local 64
    virtual names for clients 66
backup copy of Windows NT 127
batch work processes 253
binding order 115, 140
BLOBs 49
block size 103
boot partition 87
BOOT.INI 132, 139
browser service error 133
buffer analysis 256

C

CASTEST 149
CDINSTLOGOFF_NT_IND
    DB2 205
    SQL Server 225, 229
CENTRDB.R3S 177
certification 73
    categories 74
    hardware components 75
    IBM 73
    iXOS 73
    Microsoft 45, **76**
    SAP 45
CIHOSTNAME
    Oracle 190, 191
    SQL Server 232
CLNETRES.DLL 22
CLUSRES.DLL 147
cluster 14
    cluster conversion files, Oracle 179
    logging tool 142
Cluster Diagnostic Utility 135
Cluster Verification Utility 135
clustering 1
    cold standby 47
    configurations 4
    Fibre Channel 106
    replicated database 48
    replicated DBMS server 53
    ServeRAID 102
    shared disk 4, 15
    shared nothing 15, 84

IBM Redbooks evaluation

Implementing SAP R/3 Using Microsoft Cluster Server
SG24-5170-01

Your feedback is very important to help us maintain the quality of IBM Redbooks. **Please complete this questionnaire and return it using one of the following methods:**

- Use the online evaluation form found at http://www.redbooks.ibm.com/
- Fax this form to: USA International Access Code + 1 914 432 8264
- Send your comments in an Internet note to redbook@us.ibm.com

Which of the following best describes you?
_ **Customer**   _ **Business Partner**   _ **Solution Developer**   _ **IBM employee**
_ **None of the above**

Please rate your overall satisfaction with this book using the scale:
(1 = very good, 2 = good, 3 = average, 4 = poor, 5 = very poor)

Overall Satisfaction   _____

Please answer the following questions:

Was this redbook published in time for your needs?   Yes____ No____

If no, please explain:

_____

_____

_____

_____

What other Redbooks would you like to see published?

_____

_____

_____

Comments/Suggestions: **(THANK YOU FOR YOUR FEEDBACK!)**

_____

_____

_____

_____